Wealth 101

WEALTH
101

WADE B. COOK

Lighthouse Publishing Group, Inc.
Seattle, Washington

Lighthouse Publishing Group, Inc.
Copyright © 1998 by Wade B. Cook

Library of Congress Cataloging-in-Publication Data
Cook, Wade B.
Wealth 101/Wade B. Cook
p. cm.
1. Finance, Personal.   2. Investments.   3. Real estate investment.
4. Income tax.   5. Securities.   6. Cash management.
HG179.C6663   1997
332.024--dc21   97-37898
ISBN (cloth) 0-910019-83-5

Book Design by Judy Burkhalter
Dust Jacket by Angela D. Wilson

Published by Lighthouse Publishing Group, Inc.
14675 Interurban Avenue South
Seattle, WA 98168-4664
1-800-706-8657
206-901-3100 (fax)

Printed in the United States of America
Second Edition
10 9 8 7 6 5 4 3 2 1

Dedication

To our founding Fathers
    who acted to give us our freedoms.

To the men and women in our military
    who have kept our freedoms safe.

To today's patriots
    who fight to conserve our freedom
    from excessive taxation from an
    obtrusive government and from
    creeping socialism.

CONTENTS

SECTION OUTLINES

SECTION ONE
General Information

SECTION TWO
Cash Flowing Real Estate

SECTION THREE
Stock Market Strategies—Part One

SECTION FOUR
Stock Market Strategies—Part Two

SECTION FIVE
Business Strategies

SECTION SIX
Legal Structures

SECTION SEVEN
Tax Strategies

SECTION EIGHT
You, Inc.

Acknowledgments

This book is the culmination of a decade and a half of experience. There are many people, including my students, who have helped me gain this knowledge along the way. I am truly grateful for all they have taught me and for their continual support. I would like to acknowledge Eric Marler and Tim Berry, as well as Dave Hebert, Sr., Catherine Coval, Tina Wilcoxson, David McKinlay, Kim Brydson, and Larry Keim, who together with all of their dedicated and loyal staff deserve accolades for the important role they have played. Heartfelt thanks goes to Patsy Sanders, Lisa Michaels, and Dick Molter for the tireless job they do for me on a daily basis. A special thank you goes to Lighthouse Publishing Group, Inc., Cheryle Hamilton, Jerry Miller and Alison Curtis, who publish my books together with our Art Department, Mark Engelbrecht, Angela Wilson, Connie Suehiro, Brent Magarrell, Judy Burkhalter, Vicki Van Hise, and Bethany McVannel who carefully edit, proof and create them. Additional thanks goes to Karen Larsen and Allison Elliott for their help in the editing and proofreading of this book. And last, but not least, thanks goes to my wife, Laura, for her never-ending support and encouragement as I tested and perfected all 101 of these financial strategies for getting rich and staying rich.

PREFACE

I started out as a cab driver in Tacoma, Washington—cab #22. I've had a lot of great experiences in my life, things that taught me a lot. But the single most important thing I learned about creating wealth, I learned as a cab driver. It's important that you know this story so that you understand where I'm coming from.

My very first day driving a taxi was spent with a guy named Bill. Bill was a taxi driver trainer and the rule was you had to spend the whole day with him. After about 45 minutes of watching what he did, I thought I had it figured out.

"Bill is there anyway you could just take me back to the lobby and I'll take out my own taxi?" I asked.

"No," he said, "you have to spend the whole day with me."

And I said, "Please just take me back."

I went back and talked to the owner of the company and said, "You don't know me. I'm a brand new driver here. Would it be possible for me to just take out a taxi?"

"Oh, no," the owner answered, "You have to spend the day with Bill first."

"I know that," I said. "I've heard that, but I think I've got this figured out. I know the city really well. I'll tell you what. If you don't like what I do by five or six o'clock tonight you'll never see me again."

"Well, okay," the owner said.

She let me take the taxi out for the day. I made about $110 or $120 dollars for the day. The next day I took it out and I made $90. The third day I made about $140. I was off and running.

I had figured out the absolute best way to make lots of money driving a taxi. To this day after all the financial programs that I've been on, the TV and radio talk shows, of all the people who have attended my seminars, and of all the business ideas I've heard, I have never learned anything that has made me more money than this one concept I learned driving taxi. The number one financial lesson I've learned in my life is this: *the money is in the meter drop.*

As soon as you get in a taxi, what do they do? They push a button now, but when I did it they had the old handles and you had to pull the handle down. It costs you $1.50 to $2 just to get in the taxi. That's called the meter drop.

A lot of taxi drivers would only take a run if it was going to make them $30 or $40. Not me. I took the $3 runs, the $6 runs, the $8 runs. I beat that cab to death. I'd pull up to somebody's house, run up to the door, get them out to the taxi, drive them to their destination, run around and help them out of the cab, take their money, and get on to the next run. Knowing this, the dispatchers would give me all the little runs.

Don't get me wrong, I got my share of big runs too, but at the end of the day I'd have 40, 50, 60 runs whereas a lot of the other drivers would have 8, 10, or 12 runs. Who made more money just off the meter drops?

You see, I quit trying to make a killing on one deal and made a killing on a bunch of small deals. I learned to think big in a whole bunch of bite size pieces. Let me tell you what happened next.

I'd been driving a cab about nine months. I'd purchased about five or six rental properties by that time with taxi money, and I think my lowest month at that time was $3,200 because I took a week off. I was making $3,600 to $3,800 per month.

While waiting for the owner to arrive at a meeting of taxi drivers, everyone was bragging about how much money they were making. One guy said his biggest month was $600, another guy bragged about making $750.

Finally Bill, the taxi driver trainer, said, "Well, I've made more money here in any one month than anybody."

Somebody asked, "Well, how much have you made?"

"One month I made $900," he said.

All the other drivers were impressed and asked how on earth did he make that much money?

I was just kind of sitting off to the side thinking, "What is going on here? What are these guys talking about? My lowest month in nine months was $3,200 and these guys are bragging about $800 and $900 per month!" You see, they had not learned the lesson. They were just dead-broke cab drivers. Instead I was out making all this money, living fairly nicely, paying the bills, and buying all these properties with taxi money—*the money is in the meter drop.*

At that time, I was really excited about getting wealthy. I got involved in real estate because I went to one of those real estate seminars, and I was really excited about becoming a real estate investor.

When I first got started as a cab driver, I was dead broke. I couldn't get a loan on a house. But the seminar said I could become a real estate investor without a lot of money. So I went out and tried it.

I had to borrow money from my father to get the first little house. I thought I was going to build up this perpetual monthly income with rentals. But I ended up doing something totally different.

I purchased many rental properties with my taxi money over about a year's period of time. I had built up $120,000 in equity, but then a $65 electric bill came due and I didn't have the cash to pay it. "This is crazy. I've got all these invest-ments and equities, but I still can't pay my bills," I thought. I decided I'd have to sell one of my properties and get some cash to pay the bills. I discovered something that has since made me a lot of money.

I feel a little like Thomas Edison—in 3,960 tries to find the filament for a light bulb he finally stumbled across tung-sten. After he finally was successful somebody said, "How did you make it? How did you do it?"

He said, "I failed my way to success." I feel the same way—I failed my way to success. I guess I didn't learn my meter drop lesson fast enough, because when I started do-ing real estate I went back to the old way—let's make a killing on each deal. This house is going to go up in value, inflation's going to take this thing up, and there are all these tax write offs. I went for the long term approach.

I tried what all the guys in the seminars talked about. They had books about real estate telling me how easy it was going to be to be a landlord and handle rental proper-ties, but it was not that easy at all. I had equities, but I didn't have the positive cash flow I needed.

I decided to sell a property to get the cash, so I took back a mortgage on the property. I got the down payment from the buyer and carried back a mortgage myself with little monthly checks coming in for the next 28 years. I didn't own the property anymore. I had a note, a deed of trust against the property, making me more money each month than I was making off that same property as a rental unit *and* I got all my cash back.

After I sold that first house and got all my cash back, I said, "Wow, why don't I just go do this again?" So I took a little bit of money, went out, bought and immediately sold little bit of money, went out, bought and immediately sold another house. I then sold a couple more of my rentals and I was off and running. I'd turned real estate into a meter drop.

Do this fifteen or twenty times and you'll end up with two or three hundred thousand dollars on your financial statement and it's not going to cost you anything. You are going to have a note or a group of notes that are going to provide you with monthly checks for the next twenty-five or thirty years and you have no cash tied up. You have no money involved at all.

That was the Money Machine. I wrote a book called **Real Estate Money Machine** and people nicknamed the system the Money Machine because of the book.

I'm flattered by all the attention my strategy has received. There are Wade Cook Seminar Groups that meet around the country and they use my name as a verb. They call this Wade Cooking a property, or Cooking a property, where you buy a house for $110,000, quickly fix it up, and sell it for $130,000. I'm going to tell you more about the Money Machine later on when we get to the real estate section.

Because of my real estate deals, I was able to retire at an early age. I made a lot of money. We're going to talk about that whole process in detail later, but I want you to understand what that allowed me to do. I was 29 years old. I was able to quit my job, quit doing the real estate deals, and retire.

I retired for about seven months. I was out playing golf all the time and it was boring. I don't know if you have been retired before, but it was no fun. There is a lot more fun in the chase than in the catch. I asked myself, "What do I really want to do with my life?" And what I really wanted to do was be a teacher.

I didn't know I was going to be a seminar teacher at that time. I thought I was going to teach college. I went back to college to get a degree so I could teach at the college level.

While I was there, I was buying a new house and the guy at the title company said, "Wade, you ought to write a book about this. I mean, I don't know very many 29 year olds who are retired."

So, I wrote a book. I didn't know I could write a book, I just did it. I sat in my friend's photograph shop on the floor in a sleeping bag and wrote for three weeks. I took the book to New York. I went to Simon & Schuster, McGraw-Hill, Doubleday, a number of publishers, and they all said it was a cute title, however, thanks, but no thanks, we have enough books on real estate. Nobody would publish my book. So I went home and started a publishing company.

I was retired once, but now I have employees, rent, payroll, and everything else associated with being in business, just like everybody else who is in business.

What I teach in the books and in my seminars is a system called Cash-to-Asset-to-Cash. Let me tell you where I learned that. It was taught to me by some really sharp businessmen who were trying to buy my publishing company.

When we finished negotiating (by the way, we ended up not selling) I asked, "How did all of you make your money?"

These guys, ten or twelve of them, were worth about two or three million dollars each. "Wade, you know how to make money. You wrote about it in your book," they said.

"I know how I made money," I replied, "but how did you make your money?"

"Wade, you figured it out," they said. "We know you've got 23 books under copyright. We're trying to buy your publishing company to buy this book, **Real Estate Money Machine**, because it is the only book in the whole country that seriously teaches people how to make money in real estate."

And I said, "Well, thank you, that's really nice. But, again, how did you guys all make your money?"

One of them went to a little white board on the side wall and picked up a marker. "If people want to make big time money in this country, not this mediocre hundreds of thousands of dollars, but really serious money," (he wrote on the board this little word: "cash"), "they need to take cash, whatever little bit of cash they can scrape together, they need to put that cash into an asset and then get that money back to cash as fast as they can."

This is totally different than what most of you have heard. You go to a mutual fund seminar or a brokerage seminar and they tell you to take your money and put it into mutual funds or stocks. If you go to a real estate seminar, they tell you to put it into a duplex or a house and leave your money there. You can't get rich that way very quickly.

Most of you reading this right now are not yet ready to be an investor. You're not there. An investor is someone who can give their money to someone else and let that person or company control their investment. When you invest, you're literally giving up ownership for awhile. You cannot get rich by being out of control of your money.

Instead, you need to build something. You need to make something. You need to manufacture something. You need to take milk and sugar and mix it together and make an ice cream cone. You need to build up a net worth. You need to create an asset base. Then later on after you've done that, after you have become wealthy, if you choose investments wisely, you may be able to *stay* rich being out of control of your money. You cannot *get* rich being out of control of your money.

This cash-to-asset-to-cash idea these men shared with me came back to a concept that I've learned myself. Let me tell you about that concept. It is going to be very important as I go through several of the money making features and strategies that I use on a day-to-day basis for creating cash flow and wealth.

There are three benefits of owning anything. One of those benefits is cash flow or the income that an investment can produce. Another benefit to look for is the tax write offs. The third benefit of ownership is the growth, wealth or equity, something down the road.

Now, real estate as a form of investment has been very, very powerful because you get cash flow, tax write offs, and growth all at the same time. You don't need a lot of money to get started. You can get started with leverage. You can borrow your way in.

You can buy a $100,000 house with $5,000 to $10,000 down. Even if you paid $20,000 down, you sure don't have to pay $100,000 down. You can finance the property. If you keep it as a rental, you can get cash flow, tax write offs, and growth all at the same time with a small amount of money.

Another way to get cash flow, tax write offs, and growth at the same time and with small amounts of money is … well, hold it, let's see if you can guess what it is. No, it's not the lottery. (If you win the lottery you get cash flow, but you get no tax write offs.) It's not commodities or anything like that; it's not municipal bonds—it is owning your own business. The only other thing that you can do with your money to get cash flow, tax write offs and growth is to own your own business *and/or* do real estate.

Now, what I came across at the very beginning was a way of marrying those two things together. Hey, if you could just take real estate and treat it like a business then you could get a double whammy. You could make a lot of money. That's what I set out to design to do and I learned to make a lot of money that way.

By the way, now when I do stock market type investments, I get a few stocks that I like and hold on to them because they are my pet stocks, like AT&T, Microsoft, IBM, and Toys R Us. But I use the same cash-to-asset-to-cash concept in my stock market investing. I use different strategies to turn quick profits in bite sized chunks. You are going to hear about these later on.

My purpose in this book is primarily to show you how to make a lot of money. Later on I'm also going to show you how to preserve and protect that money. I'm going to show you how to make a lot of money in different legal entities so you can minimize your taxes and exposure to risk.

Cash-to-asset-to-cash—the meter drop—is kind of the theme of this whole process; however, this book is much more than that. Throughout these 101 points, I will make references from time to time to the Wealth Institute and the Financial Fortress. This book is really an introduction to a lot of great ideas and money making strategies. If you want to get better at these, you're going to need a lot of information. For more information about these products, please see the Bonus Section in the back of the book or call 1-800-872-7411.

I want to be the most knowledgeable person in this country about Living Trusts and Pension Plans and corporations. I don't think anybody has read or studied as much as I have, and I don't teach anything here, in my financial seminars, or in any of my home study courses unless I've done it myself. So I want to bring you a flavor of all these different things, and then if you need more detailed information, I'll point you in the right direction.

Now, not everything I'm going to share with you here is going to be earth shattering or make you big time money. There are going to be a lot of little savings and a lot of big savings, but as you come through these points I think that you'll see that, all in all, you're going to get a well rounded education.

You may like point number 44 or 68, and you could go out and become an expert in one. Some of you will not want to have anything to do with any angles relating to real estate. Some of you are scared to death of the stock market, yet you don't mind buying duplexes and fixing them up. Everybody reading this right now has their own agenda, and I'm just going to try to give you enough information to help you make better decisions.

No matter what you decide to do, even if you decide to keep making more money with the company you're with right now, I want to help you keep more of what you're making.

But for now let's get on with it.

SECTION ONE

Section One provides general information about a lot of things. I may seem a little disjointed; point 11 does not have anything to do with point 12. These are just some general things I'd like to get out of the way first so that you have a basic knowledge of some things I know can help you make a lot of money.

I really have a hard time with the idea of goal setting. I know that we can be just a little bit picky here with our words. Whether you have priorities or goals, I really believe goals set people up for failure. They limit people. What I'm really into is *doing,* or the phrase "to be." I see people setting goals and then they don't achieve them and they get blown away.

For example, people can make really good money with my Money Machine style of real estate. A young man from Medford, Oregon came up to Portland where I was doing a seminar a few years ago. He was so excited. He bought my set of books in the back of the room and he told me was going to go home and do 75 deals in one year.

I was there again about four months later and he came back to my seminar. He hadn't done even one deal yet. We got to talking and I said, "Why did you set a goal to do 75 and go out and do none?"

"I don't know, but I'm still really excited about it," he says.

"Will you do me a favor?" I said. "Would you go out this week, listen to this tape set, and then follow the advice and buy one property? Just go make one offer on one property by Thursday. I have to leave on Friday, you call me Thursday by 5:00PM."

Well, Thursday about 3:00PM, he calls and tells me, "Okay, I did it. I went out and found one property and I'll probably make about $15,000 to $20,000, maybe $12,000."

I said, "Now here's what you do: run the ad to get that one sold and start running an ad to find another one. By next Thursday try to get the next one sold." He did this, too.

In the next year, because he was working a full time job, he only bought and sold 13 properties. But he made about $150,000 in one year buying and selling those 13 properties. Now, do you see what happened there? He had this incredible goal of doing 75 properties and he did nothing. But when he took it one property at a time, he did it. I call that having a target or priorities. I'm not big into goal setting. I am into goal getting. I just finished writing a whole book on this very thing. ***Don't Set Goals*** shows you how to be a goal getter, not just a goal setter.

You know, a few years back H. L. Hunt, the multimillionaire, died. And, by the way, his principles of wealth were really quite simple. He was being interviewed on a TV show shortly before he died and was asked, "H. L., how did you make all your money? How did you get your wealth?"

He responded, "There are four things that people need to do to obtain success. Number one, they need to decide exactly what it is they want. Number two, they need to decide what it is they are willing to give up for it, what price they are willing to pay, what sacrifices they are willing to make. Number three, they need to set their priorities." (Boy, am I glad he did not say set goals.) And then number four he said, "And then just be about it. Get on with it."

I love the phrase "to be." If you want to be thin, do what thin people do. If you want to be wealthy, do what wealthy people do. Don't set a goal to be wealthy, just do what wealthy people do and you will get wealthy. Everybody is into setting goals. Forget that. Just BE that kind of person. The very essence of living is *to be*. I think this comes down to the real integrity of being who you really are.

My idea of integrity is when what you say, what you do, what you think, and what you are are all the same. For example, I had a friend who really wanted to be a singer, to travel the world and sing. But she was a secretary and she hated her job. She'd sit there and sing songs. What she was doing all day long and who she really was were different.

When she finally got up enough nerve to become a singer, at first she didn't make very much, but then she started making pretty good money. She has traveled the world now. What she says, what she does, what she thinks and what she is are now all the same. And it's that way with all of us. And that, to me, is the true test of integrity. It is also where we find true happiness and peace.

In real estate there is a concept called the "highest and best use." States like to tax a certain property on its highest and best use. Someone may take farm land that is not worth very much but has good road frontage, and turn it into a commercial property. Just putting a building on it could change the use to its highest and best use.

I personally believe that a lot of us need to learn from that. We are not doing anything close to our highest and best use. We have not set our priorities. We don't really know what it is that we are all about and what we can do. For example, in targeting your priorities you need to ask the questions, "What else could I be doing with my time?" and "What else could I be doing with my money?"

Now I'm going to cover this in a little bit more detail from another angle when we get to point number nine, called Effective Decision Making. Right now, just remember that you need to be up to your highest and best use. Ask yourself during the day, "What is the most important thing that I can be doing right now?"

I want to try to use that to jump into another category. The rockets that take off from Cape Canaveral have a huge tank of fuel. What you see there, about 80 percent of the rocket, is a tank full of fuel. That tank of fuel is designed to just get the rocket a few thousand feet off the ground. Once it is up there the fuel tank drops off into the ocean and the rocket can literally maneuver around the world with very little energy at all.

Well, that's the way it is with many of us and our personalities and businesses. We need to get our rockets off the ground, but it takes so much energy. It's worth the effort, though. It doesn't matter when you get there, direction is more important than speed.

If you're having trouble finding direction, I suggest a technique I called Projected Hindsight. Everybody talks about hindsight being 20/20. What I'd like you to do is to think into the future. Project out five or ten years from right now and say to yourself, "What is it that I want to have accomplished in the past five years," and then set about doing those things. Now let me tell you where this became very real to me.

When I married my wife, she had two daughters at the time who were seven and four years old. I was able to adopt them. My wife and I have had three kids since that time, so we have five children. I love those two girls I adopted, but something happened. I don't know if you've ever had teenagers, but when my sweet, innocent daughter turned thirteen years old, she came home one day and said, "Dad, they're having a teen dance on Friday afternoon after school and I really want to go. Can I go?"

"I'm sorry," I said. "You cannot go."

She wanted to go to this dance, but I could not see any good coming from it. Remember Bill Cosby in his book *Fatherhood?* He said, "Knowing what I know now about fourteen year-old boys they should all be arrested and put into

jail." Well, I felt the same way about my sweet, little, innocent daughter dancing with those boys and I just said, "No."
Whoa, suddenly there was weeping and wailing and gnash-
ing of teeth. She wouldn't even talk to me for a couple of
days.

About three days later I went into her bedroom after
school. "Brenda, we've got to talk," I said. "You know,
you're thirteen years old and I'd like you to think about
something with me. About ten years from right now you're
going to come home one day and you're going to have a
little baby in your arms. You'll be twenty-three years old
and you'll be wondering what kind of a mother you're going to be.

"You're going to be thinking about all kinds of things
about raising your own child. You're going to be holding
that little baby in your arms, and you're going to look at me
and you may say, 'Dad, back when I was a teenager I'm
really glad that you didn't care about the friends that I ran
around with. I'm really glad you didn't care about the grades
I got in school.'

"Or, hopefully, you will say, 'Dad, I'm really glad that
you were strict, you had rules and you enforced them. And
I'm glad that you were willing to let me hate you for a little
bit so that I could grow up and learn those kind of things—
I'm glad that you were there.'" Now, hopefully she'll be
saying the latter.

I was asking my daughter to use projected hindsight.
You go out to a point in time and you look back and say,
"What is it that I will want to have had happen during that
period of time?" Now lets get more specific: whatever time
of year you're in, look at December 31st. As you look down
to the end of the year ask yourself, "What is it that I want to
have accomplished this year?" Pretend you are asking the
questions retroactively. If you're in your fifties, shouldn't
your fifties be a real powerful time of your life? Well, if

you're fifty right now, look forward to the time when you're sixty and say, "What is it that I wanted to have accomplished by this time?" and then do it. Set about and accomplish it, but do it from the past tense point of view projected out into the future.

I'll just say one last thing on this. This is not meant to be a time management book, but I talk about this all the time: wealth comes from chaos. You see all these guys carrying day planners trying to get their lives organized, and they are dead broke. You'll seldom see a rich guy carrying a day planner. It does not go hand in hand. I see people trying to get their lives in order, thinking they can buy some book or some thing that is going to make them successful. It really doesn't happen that way.

Whether you use a day planner or a calendar, you can never rise above your calendar. You show me your calendar and what you did yesterday, and I will tell you how much money you made. You cannot rise above your calendar. If you want to make more money, you need to be using your time more wisely.

2

Avoid Costly Entanglements

Avoid costly entanglements. This comment, by the way, came from George Washington. When he left office, somebody asked him how the United States would be successful in dealing with foreign countries and he said, "We will be successful when we avoid costly entanglements."

Look at the history of the United States. When we've gotten into wishy-washy confrontations, when we haven't known where we are as a country politically and we've gotten involved in other countries' affairs, we've always gotten hurt. It's always been detrimental to the psyche of the whole country. When we know exactly what our responsibilities are and what they are not, where to get involved and where not to get involved; then when we do get involved we know how we are going to end the conflict and what it is that constitutes victory.

Now what about you personally? When you form a general partnership with a friend you say, "Let's buy this house together, or let's open this business together." You have a detrimental and potentially costly entanglement. You've entered into an area where there are two or more agendas and no clear guidelines and goals.

I believe general partnerships should be outlawed in this country. They are that dangerous. We'll show you ways to structure entities later on, but that's the main point here. You need to know what you want out of your investments. You need to know what you want out of your business. Let me tell you a quick story about a country-western singer.

I don't remember his name and if I did I probably wouldn't say it anyway. But there was a country-western singer who was very, very successful and was worth millions of dollars. Well, you probably know that when somebody has that high a profile and gets wealthy, there are people that start coming out of the woodwork asking for favors. CPAs and other investment counselors start offering all kinds of ways to save money on taxes, to get tax write offs, and this, that and the other thing.

Pretty soon this man (and many others who have gotten wealthy) ended up with a mishmash of investments that he really didn't understand. When somebody asked him about his money and all of his investments he said, "My one hope right now is to get my whole financial statement, and everything I own, so I can read it on one piece of paper."

Now, I personally think that is wonderful advice. Why own investments and things you can't understand? You need to be able to read and understand all your investments, and have them all listed on one piece of paper.

Partnerships are sinking ships. I'm talking about general partnerships. If you need to get involved in business affairs with other people, do so as a corporation or a limited partnership, where you clearly understand your ownership, your responsibilities, and what each participant is going to get out of it. You need to have investments in businesses that can be monitored.

I am so into avoiding entanglements that when I walk into a movie theater, the first thing I do is to look for the exits. If something goes wrong, I want to know how I'm going to get out. Well, it's the same thing with my investments. I want to know how I'm going to get out of them. I want to know how I'm going to make money and how I define victory.

One last comment on something I learned from a friend of mine back in North Carolina. You've heard the expression, "You get what you expect." Well that may be true, but he changed it a little bit. He said, "You get what you inspect." Whether in business or with your investments it's really true. If you monitor and watch your investments then you can make a lot of money.

One of the fallacies of wealth is that you can become very, very wealthy, and then you can sit back and not have to do anything. People that are wealthy realize how untrue that is.

For example, my wife and I love to go to Hawaii. We always plan a trip for fourteen or fifteen days and then we book the hotel room for twelve days. We call and get the airplane tickets for nine or ten days. We go over there for seven or eight days and end up coming home after five days. Usually our business has already mutated into something we can hardly recognize. If you have a lot of wealth, if you have a lot of business enterprises, then you need to be there to monitor them, to take care of them.

I mentioned before about having perpetual monthly income. I don't want to get into too many of these acronyms, but you've all heard of PMA: Positive Mental Attitude. I firmly believe that a positive mental attitude can come from a lot of income. If you want to test me on that, just take $1,000, maybe 10 one hundred dollar bills, and stick them in your pocket. Just fold them in half, stick them in your pocket, hold them in your hand and rub them and tell me how bad you feel. I mean I know that sounds really cliché, but this is what I call a PFA: Positive Financial Attitude.

3

PFA

My idea about being wealthy is simply this: if you have a lot of income, it will speed you along the road that you're already traveling. If you're a good person, it will make you a better person. If you're a bad person, it will make you a worse person. So my only hope is that when we all get done climbing our ladder of success that it's leaning against the right wall.

So, let's talk about replacement income. Let me tell you what I mean by that. We need to have income that really works for us. We do many active things in our lives, but we take our income and we turn passive and say here, go earn interest. Here money, go earn tax write offs. Here money, go grow for the future. We need to get our money working harder than we do.

We're out there working really hard. We're out producing cash flow, tax write offs, and growth, and then we turn right around with our money and want it to do just one thing. Well, that shouldn't be. If you want to get very, very wealthy you need your money to have more personality.

For example, you need income that you don't have to claim as income, such as municipal bonds or borrowed money. Possibly income that has immediate losses to offset it. You've got income but you've got paper or other types of losses to offset it. Possibly you need to have income that will provide other write offs so you don't have to claim all of it as income.

There are all kinds of income. My job is to show you how to produce income while avoiding high taxes. These offsets could be for the current year or future years.

So the key to wealth is getting your money to work harder. Right now, most of you are too busy to get wealthy. You're so busy doing mundane tasks, trying to get the bills paid, that you don't take the time to go out and get really wealthy. I hope you can take the time.

For example, one of the things I'm really proud of that we've been doing for years is our Cook University. This is a series of events designed to help you make more money, then keep more of what you're making by protecting your income from taxes, and your assets from lawsuits. Thousands of people have attended these courses, and they loved them and my instructors love teaching them.

The success stories I hear from Cook University alumni are phenomenal, and they stretch across every age bracket and every income level you can imagine. Some people come to learn how to make money, some people come to learn how to save money. Some people come to learn how to protect the money that they have already made. No matter what their reason for coming, everybody wants more income. What I try to do is to show people how they can take the time to build up their recurring cash flow.

A lot of you reading this, if you hear about the Cook University, may say, "I'm too busy for that." Well, if that's what you are saying, then you are the one who specifically needs to attend. If you can't take the time off, a few days or a week off, to come be with my staff, then you're the person that *really should* be there. Think this one through.

If the owner doesn't show up, the average small business will last only two and one-half weeks. If you work for someone else your income will stop if you stop going to work. You (that is most of you) are your only "income producing asset." If your asset doesn't show up to work, the income stops. What I've tried to accomplish by writing books and teaching seminars is to help people build up a different grouping of assets that will spin off the income they need, by getting their money to work harder than they do. You can have assets without income, but you can't have income without assets: somebody, something has to produce the income.

This is about those of you who really want to take control of your investments or take control of your business. You are "sine qua non" to your success. Let me tell you what that means. That's a Latin expression meaning "that which without." For example, you could say a football coach is sine qua non to the success of the team. If the team did not have that coach they wouldn't be successful. Or if a team did not have a particular player they would not be so successful. That player is sine qua non to winning.

4

——————————

Sine Qua Non

——————————

You truly are sine qua non to the success of your company or to your investments. You are the quarterback *and* the coach. That's a tough role because in a football game you have the quarterback out on the field, the coach on the sideline, and, usually in football today, you have a coach up in the box. You need to be out there on the field, on the sideline and up in the box all at the same time. Why?

The quarterback is down there in the game, getting his hands dirty and calling the plays. The sideline coach is there to watch out and make sure the quarterback is getting the support he needs from the other players. The coach up in the box is the big picture guy, watching over everything. If you own a business, you need to be all three. You need to be down there communicating with your employees. You need to be watching over your stockbroker, or CPA, or attorney, or whomever and make sure they're giving you good advice. And you need to be the big picture person using your projected hindsight.

In my real estate seminars, as I go through the buying and selling of properties, I make a comment that one of the neatest things about real estate, is that you can be totally ignorant and get filthy rich.

Don't get me wrong, I love knowledge and I love education. But once you understand the basic premise, you still may not understand how to type up the legal documents for a property. You may not understand the exact value of a property in any particular neighborhood. After you lease a property, you may not know how to collect the rents and how to post the payments. You want the $200 a month, but you don't need to learn how to figure out principle and interest, and how to amortize a loan and all that.

Fortunately, you can hire professionals to do that for you. There's a whole team of people waiting for someone to say, "Hike." And that's you. You're the quarterback and coach. You are sine qua non to your success.

Let me tell you what that means to me, and I hope for you, too. One of the biggest thrills of my life was running an ice cream parlor. I ran an ice cream parlor as a manager and, because the owner hadn't paid the bills, he came in and asked, "Do you want it? You can buy it from us." I didn't have much money, but I bought it anyway.

All of a sudden, I was the proud owner of an ice cream parlor. I was trying to train a new manager because I couldn't be there all the time to oversee the day to day flow of the whole business.

I chose a girl who had become one of my best waitresses, to train as my manager. However, when she walked behind the cash register, she'd start cashiering. When she was behind the counter, she'd start scooping ice cream for people. She was great at taking orders and spending time with the customers, but she neglected everything else. I'm sure you know people like this—focused on one thing at a time.

She improved as a manager, but I needed somebody who would float and see everything. That's what you need to be. You can get good at running the cash register, or taking the orders, but you or somebody in your life needs to be good at seeing the whole picture. Somebody needs to sit back and see (and feel) the ebb and flow—the process. You see, everything in life is a trade off.

You need to understand that you are the quarterback on the field making everything happen, the one that's saying, "Hike." You are the coach on the sideline running in different plays, and you are the coach in the box. As soon as you understand that and understand how *important your time is*, then you can really get on the road to making a lot of money.

Now I'd like to give just a brief introduction to estate planning. I'll discuss this at length later on. Let's discuss taxes for a quick second because this will be a fun way to get into this.

5

Estate Planning

By the way, in setting up your tax programs or your accounting programs, one of the best things to do is to set up your accounting program to fit the IRS form which you will have to fill out at the end of the year. Then, just work it backwards. If you make the program fit easily into the form to begin with, April 15 isn't such a struggle.

Estate planning means that you're trying to limit the taxes you pay, limit your exposure to debts due upon death, and make sure that your family gets everything that you've worked so hard for. The point is, where do you want to end up? Now, whether you're single, or whether you're married, somebody or something is going to get your investments, your assets, after you're gone.

In my seminars I usually address people as if they are married. However, there are a lot of single people, and they say, "What if I'm single? What if I don't have any kids?" Well, then the question is, "Who do you want to get your investments upon your death?" If you are single, maybe it's your church, maybe it's a charity. To whom are you going to leave everything? Well, that's the question you need to ask. So let's talk about the three reasons for an estate plan.

The number one reason for creating an estate plan is to avoid probate. Probate is a horrible, ugly process. It sometimes takes between five and twelve months to solve the probate process for an estate. Let me tell you what that means.

When one of your loved ones dies, it could be months before you get access to the estate. The cost to you is horrible. The attorneys and the government get paid very well. Why will an attorney do a will for you? All wills have to go through probate.

One of the biggest fallacies is that people think because they have a will that everything is going to be taken care of. "Oh, no, no, no my family won't have to do that because I have a will and I'm giving the kids all the stuff." A will has to go through probate because upon your death the only person that can transfer anything of yours from one person to another is a court, a judge. That's the probate process. It costs a lot. It opens up your whole estate to all kinds of exposure, to creditors and the like. So, you want to avoid probate. That is number one.

Number two is to reduce and, hopefully, avoid estate taxes. The estate taxes in this country are horrible. I'm shocked that we as a country even have estate taxes. The government doesn't take in that much money from estate taxes because most wealthy people have learned how to get around estate taxes.

If you plan on being wealthy, and if you don't take precautions early, your family could be financially strapped by the estate taxes upon your death. So, to avoid or reduce estate taxes is our second reason for estate planning.

The third reason for an estate plan is to provide, in a tender, loving, caring way, for the continuity of your assets. To make sure that all the businesses, investments, and other assets that you've built up will provide for your children to go to college, get married, to take care of any medical problems, to raise your children or grandchildren, and to make sure that their guardian is appointed. In short, to make sure your assets stay intact and do for your family what you want them to.

The way to accomplish this is to have different entities available. Learn what a Living Trust really does. Learn the power of Nevada Corporations and how the Nevada Corporation, as an estate planning tool, is light years ahead of a Living Trust from several different angles. Also learn about a Family Limited Partnership, especially those of you who have existing assets.

Learn about the incredible Charitable Remainder Trust and how to put aside huge amounts of money, get deductions, lower your taxable estate, control all the investments, live off the income from those investments, and let the charity get the money upon your death. What a phenomenal thing!

Learn about a pension account, and how to put aside considerable amounts of money into a retirement account. These are the five entities that we're going to explore and explain. Living Trusts, Corporations, Family Limited Partnerships, Charitable Remainder Trusts, and Pension Plans are powerful money protecting tools. These entities are needed in your estate planning toolbox.

Build up a fort. Literally build up a financial fortress that cannot be penetrated even if you control millions of dollars. If anybody sues you, the most they could ever get would be $50 or $100 because you don't have anything in your personal name. We're going to talk about this later, but from an estate planning point of view it's simple: avoid probate, reduce taxes, and provide for the continuity of your assets. That's what estate planning is all about.

I alluded to this in the preface—it's about knowing your exit before you ever go in the entrance. I learned this from my attorney many years ago.

6

Know Your Exit

I cannot reinforce point #6 enough. You need to know your exit. Let me tell you what this means.

In setting up an entity to put your business in, you need to know exactly what you want that entity to do, and what you want the results to be. For example, if you have a business, whether the business is a corporation, a partnership, or a sole proprietorship, you are going to do one of three things with that business. One possibility is to shut it down. Just close the doors. Now, that might be voluntary or involuntary but it is one thing that might happen.

The second thing is to sell the business. If you decide to sell the business you have a couple of choices. You can sell it for cash. You can sell it for paper and take back a contract on the business. You could sell it for a combination of those two, some paper, some cash. You could possibly merge with another company and get stock for your company.

The third thing you could do is keep your business. Keep it forever. Keep it for your children. Now, if you decide to keep the business, you are either going to keep it and have a manager run it for you, or you're going to run it yourself.

Whatever you do, whether you shut down the business, whether you sell it, whether you keep it, you're going to want to prepare the accounting system a certain way. For example, if you're going to sell the business you want it to look a certain way and you would prepare a certain set of books. I'm not talking about rigging your records, I'm talking about having your books kept properly so that you can sell the business for its maximum value and have someone really understand what the business is all about.

If you're going to manage the business yourself then you'll run it a different way. Decide what it is that you want out of a business. And, by the way, you may change your mind. You may say, "I love this business and I'm going to run it forever," but after five or six years you may say, "I've got to sell this. I'm so tired of doing this." Things change.

With your investments it is the same thing. You're either going to sell your investments, you're going to keep your investments, or you may even buy more of that particular investment. Now, whatever your investments may be, you should understand the exit before you get involved. That's the point, when you walk in the door you've got to know where the exit is. It's the same in business. You buy a certain stock, you've got to know where you're going to get out. Now, I do that constantly.

I have a few stocks that I just hold onto because I like owning them. I hope they'll go up, but whether they do or not is not really important. I've got a few stocks I hold for dividends, but most of the stocks that I own I'm buying and selling, and I know exactly what price I'm going to sell them for. (I'll cover that more in the Rolling Stock section.) Regardless of what I do with my investments, I always know when I'll be done with that investment before I get it.

7

Tax Free Entities

You're probably going to wonder why I interject this one here, but it is important to understand the power of these tax-free entities.

You've all heard of tax-free investments, like municipal bonds. How would you like to have an entity that turns everything it invests in into a tax free investment? Whether you have your own business or not, one of the simplest things you could do, if you are working, is to have an IRA—an Individual Retirement Account.

I'm really big into IRAs. Even though you are limited on what you can do with the money in them, you should have a self directed IRA. Within this structure, you can have a brokerage account, you can buy and sell stock, you can buy mutual funds, you can buy REITs—Real Estate Investment Trusts, you can buy limited partnerships. There are a number of things you can do. You need to get your IRA into a grouping of investments that you not only control, but that can make you a really good return on your money.

Think about that: if your business is really aggressive and you have to take a lot of time running your business, you may want to put your money into an IRA and let the money passively sit there. Buy some mutual funds without worrying about the rate of return. But later on, as your life changes and you wind down your business, or you sell your business, you may want to be more aggressive with the tax-free entity that you created, and really start working that money. You'll go for the higher returns, buy and sell things, and really make a lot of money.

In an IRA you are allowed to deduct the money from your taxes at certain income levels. If you have a Keogh plan or a corporate pension fund where you can't deduct contributions into an IRA, (you need to check with your CPA to see if the money that you are contributing is deductible), you can still put aside the basic amount.

Here's a quick point: I know a lot of you put aside your money each year, some even wait until April 15th of the next year. My recommendation is when it turns to 1999 put your money in on January 2nd. By getting your money into the IRA the first business day after the first of the year, you get the tax free growth on that money for a whole year. If it is 1998, why would you wait until April 15th of 1999 to put aside the money? You see the point? Get your money put aside so you can have it growing tax free for a longer period of time.

Even if you have a Pension Plan at work, go ahead and put in your $2,000 in an IRA. You may not be able to deduct it, but you still have that money growing tax free for your retirement.

Another point if you have children: any child that is working with your company, especially over the age of 14, could receive $2,000 in wages for coming in and sweeping the floors and cleaning the place. Pay them $2,000, $3,000 or $4,000, whatever, but at least pay them $2,000 and put that $2,000 into an IRA for them.

Let me pose a scenario to you. Say you were 25 years old, you set up an IRA and put aside $2,000 every year for the next ten years until you're 35. Then you stop (I'm not telling you to stop. I just want you to follow this example). At the age of 35, don't put any more money into the IRA and let that money, that $20,000, sit there and grow and accumulate until you're 65 years old. Let's call this amount of money at age 65 Plan A.

In Plan B, you don't even start putting aside money until you're 35, and at the age of 35 you put aside $2,000 faithfully every year. Now, whether the money is earning four, five, or six percent interest, it doesn't matter. You continue to put aside $2,000 every year from age 35 until you're 65. For 30 years you put that money aside, and at age 65 we will call this amount of money Plan B. Which one do you think will be larger?

The answer is Plan A. You should put aside more for yourself and your children as early and as fast as you can.

You see, I think we've got this retirement philosophy wrong. I think that all of a sudden we get to be 40 or 50 years old and we start worrying about our retirement. Doesn't it seem to you that as soon as you get out of college, you ought to go get the best job you can, and put away huge amounts of money into your retirement accounts? Then you can mess around when you're 40 and 50, instead of messing around when you're 20 and 30. We all need to get our money put into a tax free entity and an entity where it is relatively painless to get the money out.

Now think about what I just did in terms of the 14 year old teenager you have. If you could start putting aside $2,000 at the age of 14 and $2,000 more when they're 15, think about the head start they'll have. If you want, when they turn 19 or 20, you could take the penalty and use the money for college. Go ahead and pay the penalty and reclaim it as income if you need to, but you could have huge amounts of money waiting for a great retirement if you get started earlier.

8

Memorialize Everything

This is going to be about using the proper forms and memorializing everything that you do. To say it another way, get it in writing. You need to memorialize everything you're doing with your companies. Learn how to document everything when you set up your corporations: how to take corporate minutes, how to conduct an annual meeting, and how to prepare corporate resolutions. These are not complicated, and a lot of my home study courses and books have the forms to help you. For corporations you can call 1-800-872-7411 and get the Incorporation Handbook.

One of the things that I advocate is Nevada Corporations. I have an entire company that establishes and sets up Nevada Corporations, Living Trusts, Pension Plans and Charitable Remainder Trusts. We actually do all the process work and all the structuring to get these ready to go. One of the programs we offer, (you may want to come to this, by the way) is an Executive Retreat.

Here's another quick point: do you know that purchasing or going to seminars for investment purposes is no longer tax deductible, but seminars for business purposes are tax deductible? All the expenses that you pay for books and similar items for business are tax deductible. Now, what is your intent in purchasing this book or any of the other courses? If it is to run a business, then it could be and probably is a tax deductible expense. If it is for investment purposes, it's not tax deductible.

Let's go back to the Executive Retreat. We sponsor this incredible two day event. We get down to business, and have a giant board of directors meeting for you and your company. We help you prepare corporate resolutions. We actually help you lay the framework for implementing the various corporate strategies you've learned previously, right there at the meeting.

The program is not designed to be a seminar, it's designed to be a workshop. Think about that, because a lot of you will set up your Nevada Corporation, but then you may not type up the certificates, and you may not type up the ledgers in the back of the manual to make sure that the certificates are issued properly. That's why we have a workshop.

We bring our CPAs, we bring our attorneys, and we let you work through all these things, so that you can have a lot of fun with it, and still make sure that your entities are run properly. I bring this up here because I want you to know that you need to make sure that everything is done right with all your entities. All the books need to be filled out and filled out properly and all the paperwork must be done correctly.

The irony is that those characteristics in somebody's personality which causes them to be entrepreneurial and very aggressive are usually the same thing that makes that person not very good at keeping track of receipts and posting information in books. You're great at making money, but you're not good at keeping track of it. So, let's take time out once in awhile and get everything locked down and make sure that everything is in writing.

For example, let's say you have employees or you hire independent contractors to work for you. (By the way, one of your corporations may hire another one of your corporations to provide certain services. Make sure that all those agreements are in writing.) Let me tell you about one of those all important pieces of paper.

It is called a Dispute Resolution Agreement. If you're going to go into business with someone, if you're going to hire an employee, why not sign a piece of paper that says you will not take each other to court? In some states this is called an arbitration agreement. These are legal. You can sign away your rights to take someone to court.

Let's say Joe and Bob go into business together. They can sign an agreement that says they'll never sue each other. Don't get me wrong, they could have cause for grievance against each other, they could have a bad business deal and Joe may hate Bob. He may want to sue him, but they've signed an agreement saying that they will not do that, that they'll work it out. They'll try to solve their grievances.

If that doesn't work they'll go to informal mediation, then to formal mediation. And if that doesn't work, they'll go to binding arbitration. But they will not use the court system. What I'm showing you can literally save you tens of thousands of dollars in grief, anxiety, and actual cash from fighting out battles in court.

Think about having a business relationship with several different people where there is no threat of ever going to court with each other.

I've got to tell you something. My wife and I heard about this when we first got married many years ago. Within five minutes of hearing about this Dispute Resolution Agreement (DRA is what we call it) we looked at each other, nodded our heads and said, "Let's sign it." We loved each other so much that we said, "We don't care what happens in the future, we don't want a court to solve the problems between us." I'll tell you what, when you ask your spouse to sign this agreement you'll find out what true love is really fast.

All of this is just to show you how important memorializing everything is. Verbal agreements don't mean much to the law—whether the agreement is about not suing each other, how profits will be split, or what your corporation is or is not. There is absolutely no better way to run your business than to write everything down where you'll be able to find it when you need it.

This will be a quick point but it is very important. Look at the following diagram. Reading from top to bottom, you'll see "Gather Information," then "Think, Ponder, Meditate," and finally "Implement." Off to the side of the diagram, you'll see the words "Stop" and "Make a Decision."

9

Effective Decision Making

In making effective decisions, we go through a process. First, we gather up information and ask questions. At some point in time that stops. Then we think about it. We ponder it. We meditate upon it.

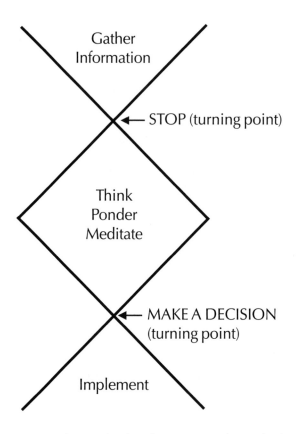

Gather
Information

← STOP (turning point)

Think
Ponder
Meditate

← MAKE A DECISION
(turning point)

Implement

Then the next turning point is where we make a deci-sion. Are we going to do it or are we not going to do it? Are we going to buy this property or are we not going to buy this property? Am I going to buy this stock? Am I not going to buy this stock?

Then we go into the implementation phase. We actu-ally do it. Buy or don't buy. The point that I'm trying to make here is that the better you are at gathering information, the better you're going to be at thinking about it and imple-menting it. Conversely, the worse you are at gathering in-formation, the worse the implementation is going to be.

See, the question again is, what else? What else could you be doing with your time? What else could you be doing with your money?

Someone came up to me in one of my real estate seminars and said, "Wade, should I buy this duplex?" And I said, "I don't know. Tell me about it."

"Well, I just found it yesterday and it is going to be about $15,000 down. It is going to take about $10,000 to fix it up, and even after it's rented I will lose $400 a month on it."

See the point? I mean, they have answered their own question. When I asked them what else could they be doing with their time and money, they look at their $15,000 or $25,000 and say, "I could be doing a lot of other things with this money."

Then somebody else may come up to me and ask, "Wade, should I buy this fourplex?"

My response is, "I don't know. What else could you be doing with your time and money?"

"Well, heavens, I don't know. I've been looking for four months. This is the best deal I've been able to find. It is almost all rented right now. There is one vacancy and that can be rented right away. It is going to require very little money down. When it's all rented, it's going to make me $800 a month."

You see the point? The question is not "Is this a good deal," or "Is this a good investment?" The question is, "What else could you be doing with your time? What else could you be doing with your money?" You see, everything in life is a trade-off. If you take your $5,000 or $10,000 and purchase a property, you can't put it into another property. So the question is, what else? And you need to make sure, again, that you are doing the very best with your money and your time that you can possibly be doing.

10

Answer Questions One Time

This is kind of a fun one. I don't know if it is going to be earth shattering to you, but it was to me. I had gotten tired of people constantly asking me questions, especially when I was fixing up houses. So, in this decision making process I came up with the idea that if I could just learn how to answer questions one time and stick with that answer for as long as possible, it would really help.

For example, I made the decision that I was going to paint all my houses light brown with a dark brown trim. All the outsides of my houses were going to be painted the same color. Why did I come up with that? Because I would show up and have the contractor there, one of my employees, waiting to paint the house and asking, "What color do you want to paint this?" and, "What do you want to do with that?"

I got so tired of them asking what I was going to do and sitting around waiting for me that I just came up with the decision one day, "From now on every house we paint we're going to paint light brown with dark brown trim, and all of the insides will be painted with an off-white. So we never, ever have to make that decision again."

Now let me tell you what happened; some of the things I didn't realize. All of a sudden I could start buying five gallon cans of paint instead of the one gallon cans. I started saving a lot of money. I could go back from one house to another and touch up after somebody moved in because we had the same kind of paint. We could buy huge quantities, touch up, do everything—it was just great. It all worked because we made the decision one time.

What I do right now with my company is make decisions. We put them in a manual. Then there is a set format that my employees and my staff can follow. I make the decisions one time and we live with the process as long as we can. I'm not a creature enamored with change. I like things to run along smoothly so I can focus on the more important questions. When we do have to make a change, we do it. We make the decision again and then we live with that decision as long as we can.

Several years ago *USA Today* did a study. I don't remember the exact number, but they sent out tax questionnaires to CPAs, tax preparers, and IRS agents. They gave them a number of tax situations and tax questions, and asked them to solve them and send it back within three months.

11

Choosing Your Professionals

When the responses were evaluated, they found the CPAs did the best, but something like 64% of all their answers were wrong. I'm not saying right, I'm saying wrong. Incorrect! Tax preparers were about 72% incorrect, and the IRS agents, approximately 68% incorrect. Basically, two-thirds of all the advice we are getting from these professionals could very well be wrong advice.

A little while ago *Money Magazine* did the same thing. They sent out questionnaires to CPAs and tax attorneys. 99% of all their answers were wrong. Phenomenal! We're going to these people for advice? So let me tell you a couple of points on choosing a professional wisely.

I want to find someone who is going to give me advice who has been there, who is experienced with business. For example, consider a CPA who also owns five or six rental properties, if you are going to get into the rental business. How about a CPA that has his own staff and has to meet payroll and make payroll tax deposits. He is worried about cash flow just like any other businessman. See, I'm very leery of whom I get my advice from.

People come up to me all the time and they ask, "Mr. Cook, may I give you some advice?"

"Let's talk about this," I respond. "You want to give me some advice? Please tell me how much money you're making with your advice." Why should I listen to someone who is making $25,000 or $35,000 a year give me advice when that is not even close to what I make? See my point?

Let's also talk about stockbrokers. How many of you have gotten a phone call from a stockbroker in some boiler room somewhere, that's got a new, hot stock or a new, hot IPO they want you to buy? Now, I'm so kind and polite on the phone—I have a hard time being really mean to people. They start telling me about some new, hot company that I should buy stock in and I say, "Sure, that sounds great. Can I buy 10,000 shares of that stock?"

After the guy falls off his chair and picks himself back up he says, "Sure you can."

I say, "Okay, here is what I need: I need you to send me copies of the last three years of your personal tax return and I need a copy of all your personal orders for stock in this company. Show me all that, then I'll buy 10,000 shares, or I'll buy as much as you've purchased." Do you see what I'm doing?

I don't want to be rude to them and hang up the phone. I'll tell them I'll buy stock in their company. Then he'll ask, "Why do you need to see my tax returns?"

"Why should I follow your advice?" I'll ask. "You're calling me, telling me to buy this stock. I buy stock all the time and I make really good money. Why should I follow your advice? How much are you making?" The guy usually hangs up on me and won't have anything to do with me.

I'm really big into having good, solid professionals around you, and it's really tough to find really good ones. So the only advice I can give you is to make sure the people do what they are teaching. Make sure that people are running businesses and doing real estate or are involved in some of the same things that you're involved in so that you can take their advice and use it comfortably.

There are so many angles to insurance that I'd like to share with you, but I'm just going to share a few things about life insurance in general.

12

Insurance

Number one, I don't think life insurance should be called life insurance. I personally believe that in most respects it should be called death insurance.

Whole life insurance is insurance that basically has cash value building up as compared to term life insurance which has no cash value. You have combinations: universal life with variable annuities and all kinds of combination insurance packages, but the two basic plans are term and whole life (or permanent insurance).

Term insurance is usually bought for a certain period of time. It has a YRT, Yearly Renewal Term, or Annual Renewal Term, or decreasing term. Now, a lot of you who need life insurance need to get term insurance because you can get a large amount of term insurance for less money.

For example, if you are 30 years old you could buy a million dollar policy for $400 or $500. If you want to spend $400 or $500 on permanent insurance, or whole life insurance, you'd buy about a $20,000 policy.

What happens, though, is that you're buying a smaller amount of insurance, but they're taking some of that money and using it for investments. Then you have some cash value building up, so that at the age of 65 you may have some cash. Cash value is derived from the overpayment of premiums and then based on the quality of the company's investments.

If you look at all the charts and diagrams, you'll realize two things. Your cash value is building, which sounds great because you can borrow the money at a low interest rate. However, your actual amount of insurance is decreasing. You still have, for example, a $20,000 insurance policy, but as the cash value builds, if the cash value is $12,000, then the insurance is only $8,000 to make up the $20,000.

Insurance companies talk about dividends. I really think that's a misnomer, it's really not a dividend. When you pay your premium to an insurance company and they do a good job of putting insurance on the books or a good job with their investments, then at the end of the year if their expenses don't come up to your whole premium level, they are going to give you back part of that amount, and call it a dividend.

It is really a return of your premium. It's a return of an overpayment. Now, the internal rate of return on a cash value built up in a whole life policy or permanent policy is usually around $2^1/_2$ to 3%. From an investment point of view that's not a particularly profitable investment. There is a place for whole life, or permanent insurance, and I'll share that with you later in the book.

I was selling insurance from my mid-twenties to about thirty years old, and I was a really good insurance agent. I enjoyed doing that. I had a friend named John who received a raise at work. I had another friend who was also a life insurance agent, and we both happened to hit on John at the same time.

"I just got a $200 a month raise," he said. "I'm going to take $100 and I'm going to buy life insurance. Now Wade, you buy me $50 a month worth of insurance, and George, you buy $50 worth of insurance." We both went out and placed a policy.

Here is what happened: I took the $50 a month and I bought an incredible twenty-year life policy; it was going to be all paid up in 20 years and he would have this permanent insurance from then on. It was going to be the great deal. I bought him a $20,000 policy.

One night I had a dream, and the next morning I woke up in a cold sweat because of this dream. In my dream he passed away and I was so proud because I got the $20,000 check from the company and I was to hand deliver it to his wife. I took that check out there and was so happy and proud.

When I got there I met the other agent leaving. We passed and he had just dropped off his check. I walked in and I was so proud about this $20,000 check and I spent the next two hours explaining to his wife why my check was only $20,000, when my friend had bought a $500,000 term policy for his life for the same amount of money. That dream had an impact in my life.

What you need, everyone, if you're young, is more insurance. Insurance, life insurance in particular, is what we call an instant estate. Kind of like instant cocoa or coffee.

The point is you can buy it when you want and make adjustments later on. You can, if you're married with a couple of kids, create for your family an estate so that your wife could pay off the mortgage, pay off all the bills, and support herself.

My philosophy is that you need $150,000 worth of life insurance for every dependent. You add to that amount any liabilities and subtract from that amount any assets you have. So, if you have a wife and three kids, that would be about $600,000 in life insurance.

Let me run the numbers on that for you. If you have a $600,000 policy and your wife invested at 5%, or at 10%, which is pretty easy to do, $600,000 will produce about $60,000 a year. Without you, the bread winner (or bread eater), she could probably live on $60,000 a year and support the family.

You need to have the amount of money that will let your wife and your family live the life-style that they are accustomed to. The only way I would say that permanent insurance, or whole life insurance is good is, as you get older, you may become uninsurable at some point in time. So, when you're 35, 45, or 50 you can buy, as you can afford it now, some kinds of permanent insurance.

13

Living Will

When I teach at my seminars, I see everybody sitting up tall and, all of a sudden, we talk about a living will and everybody starts slouching down. A living will is basically a document that could really save your family a lot of unnecessary expenses.

For example, you can determine different things in a living will. You can decide if you want to be an organ donor. You can also determine right now if you want life support systems terminated and under what conditions you would allow that to happen.

Now, you understand that if you were to get into a car accident today and end up in a coma with no chances of coming out of the hospital, it could literally destroy your family's finances. Three, four or five months later you could be wiped out. Your family could be looking at bankruptcy. A living will would prevent that. Now, there are a lot of cautions with a living will. You need to meet with a good attorney and talk about all the ramifications, but a living will can save you and your family a lot of expenses.

*Publisher's note: the following point is an excerpt from the first chapter of one of Wade's newest books entitled **A+**.*

14

Base Decisions On Solid Principles

On many radio and TV interviews of late, there has been a constant barrage of questions, yielding a stream of statements from me about the use of the Bible in everyday life. It's as if people have given up on the Bible. Do you see it, too? All around us Biblical messages are disparaged. Its concepts are swept under the table in the name of modernism. It is ignored.

I made a statement in a radio ad that "there is in one place a collection of wisdom, thoughts, laws and principles which could help people make millions, even billions of dollars." Another time I mentioned the wealth of the ancients, how great it was. By today's standards, our billionaires do not hold up. Many main characters of the Old Testament had land and flocks—riches, as far as the eye could see. Brought forward to our times and adjusted for inflation you would see how paltry our fortunes are today. Yes, we have conveniences they did not have, but the volume of their wealth would surpass anything today. That comment was made because, in my search for great financial principles to use and share with my employees, my students and all who will listen, is simple: if you want happiness, peace, financial prosperity, a great family—then seek out the best principles, the best minds. "To whom are you listening?" has been a constant theme and question asked at my seminars.

The desire to share these ideas like everything else in my life (when I stick out, when I go against that which is politically correct), has led to a barrage of criticism, even vehement ridicule. It seems odd, doesn't it? The Bible is there for all to see and read. For the most part, its teachings are easy to read and understand. There is spiritual help in the form of prayer, inspiration and church leaders and Bible schools to help us. In short, it is easy to put to the test.

I have tried to do so. I'm not perfect and have never made a claim to be so. I have said often, "I am a practicing Christian, and I am going to keep practicing until I get it right." My point in bringing this up here is this: why, oh, why do we not use the Bible more? Why do we use it on the Sabbath and not every day?

For many years I tried to incorporate principles of the Bible into my seminars. I went easy at first, not wanting to offend anybody. I was amazed at the comments. Oh, I got a few people rolling their eyes, but the huge majority commented in word and letter their appreciation for my using these precepts in my business, my lectures, et cetera.

Emboldened by these comments I actually started quoting a verse or two. I picked logical concepts and showed how it worked for me. I talked about not gleaning the fields in both my real estate and stock market seminars. I told stories of Abraham, Isaac, and Job. From time to time I quoted Malachi and talked about tithing. I told many stories of Jesus—especially the young rich man and the ten talents. Usually though, I would rush over them on the way to another point. I did not want to offend anyone. I did not want to turn the seminar into a Sunday School class.

For the most part I still don't. I don't want to be anyone's spiritual advisor. I want to be the best financial educator in America.

I am head of a huge publicly traded company. We have many subsidiaries—including our seminar company. If I were to find a really neat angle on "Writing Covered Calls," my students would want to hear it. Now, by the thousands of comments, they appear to want this blending of scripture with everyday business and other activities.

It seems that internal truths strike a common and familiar chord. It's as if our own spiritual lives get disregarded or ignored, or at least out of tune. The ways of the world—greed, selfishness, distrust, and dishonesty play hard on our souls. They feel bad. They are discordant. Then with even a simple scripture the good feelings come back.

I have never seen anything like the response I have had to **Business Buy The Bible** and **Don't Set Goals.** The comments have been overwhelming and very humbling. It seems some people in this materialistic world just need a nudge to get back to the Bible. That's the point: it is a great book. It has what we need to build relationships, to succeed, to find happiness. God loves us and has given all scriptures for a help in our journey.

Think of it. As you send your kids off to college, or to get married, you write, phone—you keep in touch. The Bible, prayer, inspiration and revelation are God's way of helping us keep in touch.

Here are what other people have said about the Bible.

I have always believed in the inspiration of the Holy Scriptures, whereby they have become the expression to man of the Word and Will of God.
—Warren G. Harding

The morality of the Bible is, after all, the safety of society.
—Francis Cassette Monfort

A loving trust in the Author of the Bible is the best preparation for a wise and profitable study of the Bible itself.
—Henry Clay Trumbull

The Bible is a window in this prison of hope, through which we look into eternity.
—John S. Dwight

SECTION TWO

It's time to move on to real estate. I think it's good to take an old fashioned look at this once in a while to see why anyone in their right mind would want to own real estate. By doing this, I'll share with you how I made a lot of money and how you can too.

Cash Flowing Real Estate

It seems I'm always talking about cash flow, tax write offs and growth. There are basically three benefits of owning any type of investment. Let's go back over those again: cash flow (or income from an investment), the tax write offs (tax deductions or depreciation expense), and the growth.

15

An Old Fashioned Look At Real Estate

What has made real estate so good? All forms of investments look for those three things. Why is real estate the answer? Because with real estate you can get all three of these benefits of ownership at the same time, and you don't need a lot of money to get started. You can get started with virtually nothing down.

I don't teach "nothing down" seminars. There are plenty of the nothing down seminars around. The real world has taught me that usually when a property is selling for nothing down, it means there is something wrong with it. It needs fixing up. The banks get really weird and you will have to jump through all kinds of hoops. There is a reason a person is trying to get rid of it for nothing down. Don't get me wrong, I've bought a lot of really good nothing down deals, but usually there is something wrong.

Let's take a look at real estate from a different perspective: what you want to get out of it. You must consider the future and why you are buying property before you look at that duplex or that triplex down the street. Should you be involved in big properties or small properties? Should you be involved in them as an individual doing all the work yourself? Should you invest passively, through a limited partnership, a REIT, or something like that?

One of the seminars that has come and gone talked about "ideal," real estate as an ideal form of investment. They put the word "ideal" up on the screen and they attached a word to each one of those letters, creating an acronym. The "I" stood for Income, the "D" stood for Depreciation, the "E" stood for Equity buildup, the "A" stood for Appreciation, and the "L" stood for Leverage. Now, if you think about these five aspects of it, we come back to the same thing—cash flow, write offs and growth—it really is an ideal form of investment.

When we get to my style of real estate, my Money Machine way of creating cash flow, you will see how effective an investment real estate is and how well it works. I think it's good to put it in perspective and see how the money machine concept compares against the competition. Well, the competition is the old standard—go out and buy a house, a duplex, a fourplex, or a twenty unit apartment complex. For many, many years there have been two ways of doing real estate. One way was to buy a piece of property and hold on to it forever. The other way was to go out and buy a property, fix it up, and sell it; then go buy a duplex and repeat the process, moving to a fourplex, an eightplex, a sixteenplex, and so on. Pretty soon you have a 100 unit apartment complex and you retire off of it. Those have been the two seminars. I just want to put those behind us because those are the two old fashioned ways of doing business. However, within that, I want you to see an example. Let me go through the following diagram with you.

I realize that some of the prices that I'm going to talk about may be low for your area of the country, or they may be high. I try to get in that $100,000 range, like buying a property for $80,000 or $100,000. The properties where you live may be selling for $150,000, or $200,000 or $300,000.

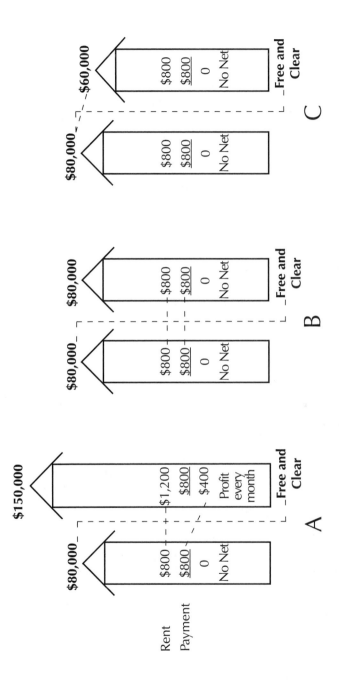

There are still many areas of the country where you can buy properties for $40,000, $50,000, and $60,000. In some of my Wealth Academy classes we have students whose minimum prices where they live are $250,000 and they are sitting next to someone who is buying houses for $8,000 or $14,000. Price, obviously, is relative to the area where you are living. So, let's stay in the $80,000 to $100,000 range.

If you buy a house for $80,000, we know that it is going to grow in value. After all, it has for the last 1,500 years since they started measuring real estate. So, over 15, 20, or 30 years the value of this house is going to grow, and it might eventually be worth $150,000, almost double in value. The payments coming in as rent are $800 right now and the payments going out, the mortgage on the property, is $800. Currently we're not netting anything. We do know, because rents have continually gone up, that the rents are going to increase from $800 up to $1,200 or $1,300; however, the payments are going to stay the same. So, even though you may not be making a profit right now, down the road five or 10 years you could start making $400 or $800 a month. We also know that this $80,000 mortgage on the property, or whatever the balance is after your down payment, is going to pay off. (This is example A of our diagram.)

You'll see that the loan is paying off, and at the end of the 15, 20 or 30 years you have a property that's free and clear. Let's just slow down here and think about this. Everything I'm saying has been true for many years. Properties go up, rents go up, loans go down.

What if I made a mistake? What if you made a mistake? What if you got involved in a property and it did not go up at all? For the next 20, 25, or 30 years that property just stayed level. I mean it just stayed at $80,000; what do you have in 25 or 30 years? Well, the loan is paying off, so you'd have a free and clear property. You'd also have $80,000 in net assets in 20, 25, 30 years. Could that put a child through college? Yes, and if one property wouldn't support a child through college, maybe you should own two or three. By the way, you could even put the property directly in the name of the child so that it's earning income in their tax bracket. Now, what if I'm also wrong about the rents. What if the rents don't go up at all? You don't make one penny on this property. It stays at $800 a month; the payments going out are $800 a month. You don't make a dime on this property for the whole 25 or 30 years. Well, what do you still have? You still have the rents coming in paying for the payments going out, and you have a property free and clear.

Let me summarize that: real estate is the only form of investment that buys and pays for itself. Now, we could talk about owning stock in the stock market, like owning stock in a certain company with dividends coming in. If you own stock in that company you may be able to share in some of those profits and, in a way, you could say that those dividends are going to pay for your investment. Usually, you call those a return on investment. But now think about real estate. Real estate, on a monthly basis, has money coming in from an outside source, from a third party. This is because there is a constant influx of new money that has nothing to do with you and your other investments. This new money has specifically to do with the property, and you get the rent checks which, in turn, cover the expense of the monthly payments. Even if the property doesn't grow in value, and even if the rents do not go up in value, you still have done a really good job with this because you're going to have an $80,000 property free and clear. (This is example B of our diagram.)

By the way, what if I'm really wrong? What if the rents don't go up and the property does not grow in value? What if they go down in value? What if that property goes down from $80,000 to, say, $70,000 or even $60,000? What do you still have? At the end of the 25 or 30 years you still have a property worth $60,000 free and clear. At its very, very worst it is still great. (This is example C of our diagram.)

One of the things I've done around the country is to be involved in many after-seminar seminars. I know that sounds weird, but a lot of speakers would go in and do the nothing down seminars, and I would come through two, three, or four weeks later and train their students. I would always show them my Money Machine concept. A whole new way of looking at real estate which would get them really excited, because a lot of people just are not cut out to be landlords. They were really excited, though, at the very beginning, about rental properties. I've had to clean up a lot of messes made by people getting involved in rental properties who just couldn't handle them.

Let me tell you what I did at my seminars: I used to ask people at my seminars, an audience of 50 or 100 people, how many of them had between zero and three properties? A whole bunch of people would raise their hands. Next I'd ask how many of them had between three and ten? How many between ten and twenty? The hands would go down. If there were a hundred people in the room, between zero and three properties there, might be 70, 80, or 90 hands. Between three and ten properties there would be three or four hands. Between ten and twenty properties, there'd be two hands, and over twenty properties usually no hands, or sometimes one.

I was teaching at a big convention in Orlando, Florida and had about 400 people in my seminar. These were real seminar groupie types—they went to seminars all the time. These people traveled the country going to real estate seminars, paper seminars, yield seminars, whatever, and they were really into real estate. When I went through the list of questions with those 400 people, like every other time, between zero and three properties a whole bunch of hands went up. The decline began with three and ten and continued with ten and twenty. When I got to over twenty there were still about 22 people that had their hands up. I said, "Whoa, I've never had this many people with their hands up when I ask that question. Now could I ask a favor? Would you 22 people stand up?" And they all stood up. I counted them and there were 22 people. Then I said, "All right, now I've got to ask a question. I want all the rest of you to watch this."

Usually when I was doing that little presentation I would say, "Okay, where are all the hands? I mean if real estate is so good, where are all the hands? If they make it sound so easy and real estate is so easy where are all the hands?" But this time there were still 22 hands up out of 400, which was really quite amazing.

I had all the 22 people standing up and I said, "This is great. You 22 people, standing up right now, who have over 20 pieces of real estate. Is that correct?" Everyone of them was nodding their head yes.

"Would you please sit down now if you have been able to retire off of your real estate," I said. "If your real estate is getting you enough positive cash flow, your rental properties are getting you enough positive cash flow, would you please sit down."

Guess how many sat down—just one! One out of the 22 sat down.

A couple of the rest of them shouted out to me, "Wade, we're having to work extra jobs to support our rental properties. We're having to get part-time jobs."

See, the point is that the properties were not supporting the people. Well, I'm here to make a case that rental real estate, in it's traditional format, is probably not the best way to go for a lot of people. It can make some people really, really wealthy, but most people don't have the stick-to-it-iveness. They don't have the persistence, the consistency, and the tenacity to make it work.

There is another way of doing real estate if you don't want to do it yourself, if you don't want to hassle with these problems. You can do it through a group of investors, like a limited partnership. You join as a limited partner, and there is a general partner who's really knowledgeable and professional at handling all of the day to day affairs of the partnership. You just tap into it, and get some of the tax write offs, some of the growth, and some of the cash flow of these investments. That's probably the best way to go. When I do rental real estate today, that's pretty much all I do. I do it as a limited partner because I don't want to have to take my time and energy to do it.

16

Wrapping Properties

This is where my excitement begins. As I mentioned before in the introduction, the Money Machine wasn't called that when I was doing it. We called it flipping properties or wrapping properties. I was 29 years old and retired before I ever heard these big words describing what I had done. I'm going to give you an example of what I did.

I'd buy a house for, say, $84,000 with $4,000 down. There's a $60,000 first mortgage on it, so I would want to assume the first mortgage.

The seller's remaining equity of $20,000 has to be dealt with. Now, the seller may want cash, and please understand if he absolutely demands cash, I'm not interested. I want to find someone who really wants out of their property. Perhaps they are behind on their payments, the house is run down, they don't have the money to fix it up, or something like that. Then I convince the seller that taking monthly payments is better than taking cash. By the way, I personally believe that it is.

I would never take cash for a property if I could take monthly payments. If I have $30,000 to $40,000 equity in a house and I'm going to get cash, I have to pay taxes on the cash, and the money disappears. If you had a note on the loan, what you took in would be worth a lot more in the long run because of all the interest. I get a higher interest rate than I could get at a bank, and I got to spread out claiming my profits because of installment sale. You would use IRS Form 6252, the installment sales computation. You can spread out claiming your profits for 30 years.

Also, people tend to fritter away large sums of money, buying things that don't last. For example, if you have $20,000 equity in your house or a rental house that you're thinking about selling, if you get cash and go buy a car, the cash then goes into the car and your money is gone. In five years you have a five year old car and it is yours free and clear. But what would happen if you took a $20,000 note at $200 a month? You could make a nice car payment with $200 a month and it amortizes it. So you got a $20,000 note making you $200 a month, you buy the same car, and make a car payment instead of paying cash. What do you have in five years? In five years you have a paid off car. Right? The payments have paid off the five or six year car loan and what do you have? Well, you have a $20,000 loan that is only amortized down to $19,200 and you still have $200 a month coming in for the next 25 years.

Why would you ever want cash? When you get cash, it just disappears. My recommendation is that you take monthly payments. I believe so strongly in this that I have a small book, **Owner Financing**, for people to use to teach buyers or sellers about taking payments. You can get **Owner Financing** by calling 1-800-872-7411.

All right, let's go back through this again: $84,000 with $4,000 down leaves $80,000. There is a $60,000 first mortgage which we assumed, and now we asked the seller to take back his equity, the $20,000, at $200 a month. Now, hopefully we could get him to take $50 a month for the first year, then $100, then $150, then $200. Maybe even pay $250 a month after four or five years on a graduated payment basis. This way we could make a profit on this deal right now every step of the way. But, nevertheless, let's just stick with $200 so you can see how good this plan is. The seller receives $200; $600 pays the first mortgage, the bank loan we assumed, totalling $800. Now we can rent this property for say, $600 or $700 a month, and we lose $100 to $200 a month. Would you like proof of that?

I don't care what price range you're talking about in most of your neighborhoods. Wherever you live, unless you make a tremendous deal on a bargain property or have a big chunk of money to put down, the rents coming in will not cover the payments going out.

So, let's continue with this example. We have $800 going out, but instead of renting it—this house is really run down, beat up, needs paint, and needs carpeting—let's sell this house as a fixer-upper. Let's clean it up a little bit, wash it up, and turn around and sell the house next week. By the way, I run a lot of ads in the paper. One of the ads I run says "I sell houses, no bank qualifying, I'll finance," and it lists my phone number. My phone rings like crazy, and I get people calling me trying to sell me their house. But I also get calls from people trying to buy houses from me from the same ad. So, I may have five, 10, 15, or 20 people trying to buy houses from me and three or five calling me, trying to sell me their house or give me their house, or let me take over their payments.

Well, we can just mix and match these callers. By the way, you could legally buy a house at 10 o'clock in the morning and sell it at 2 o'clock in the afternoon. Technically, I don't know if that's possible with all of the details to be completed, but legally you could do that. What if you make only $5,000? What if you made only $8,000 on the deal? Not bad for one day's work. You see, quit thinking big in million dollar chunks. Think big in bite size pieces.

Try to find properties that have the older FHA loans. (Newer FHA loans, like the ones after 1994, have due-on-sale clauses in them. Other than these, all FHA loans are assumable, but now they require qualifying by the new owner. You want to find the older, non-qualifying loans.) Another mortgage you want to find are the ARMs—Accelerated Rate Mortgages. They usually require some qualifying, but they are assumable. If you can, find private mortgages, people who've sold houses to other people. There is owner financing deals around and those, too, are usually assumable. You want to find, take over, and assume the existing mortgages so you can get the lower interest rates, the lower payments, and get control of the first mortgage on the property. The hard part is getting a seller to take monthly payments for their equity.

Okay. Let's look back at our first example. We bought the house for $84,000 with $4,000 down and a $60,000 assumable mortgage. This house is worth $105,000, $110,000, or $120,000, if it were all fixed up, but it is really run down. Let's sell it for $100,000 with $10,000 down, and let's sell it as a wrap around. Our new buyer, the guy buying the house from us, owes us $100,000 minus the $10,000 down payment, leaving $90,000. To do this on a wrap around, in most states, you're going to use an All Inclusive Trust Deed, an AITD. In some states you're going to use a land contract, or a uniform real estate contract.

Let's explore a wrap around mortgage or deed of trust. A wrap around leaves the bottom loans alone. Which means that I owe the $60,000 first mortgage to the bank and I owe the $20,000 second mortgage to the seller. I keep making the payments on them. The new owner now owes me $90,000 and I continue to owe $80,000. His payments coming in to me are about $920 a month; my payments going out are $800 dollars a month. We put $5,000 into the property ($4,000 down payment plus a little bit of fix up cost), plus closing costs. We sold it for $100,000 with $10,000 down. We got back our $5,000 down plus $5,000 more cash. Now, after all the closing costs we probably put about $3,000 to $4,000 cash net in our pocket. And the person still owes us $90,000. We owe $80,000. His payment is $920 coming in. Our payments are $800 going out.

I use a professional escrow company—some real estate companies do this, a lot of title companies, some banks now do this, too—they'll collect my note payments and make the mortgage payments for me for a $6, or $7 fee a month, depending on how many loans you have going out. You've got $920 coming in, $800 going out, $7 service fee per month. You've got $113 in your pocket every month which may not seem like a lot, but its for the next 28 years!

Well, after you do this once, or twice, or three times you get good at it. It's not that it gets easier, it's that your ability to do it gets better. Pretty soon you turn into a money machine. Remember, the bottom line key to wealth is duplication. If I walked into your life and I told you that I have a type of investment that you can get involved in—you only have to put up $5,000 or $10,000, but you're going to get your money back quickly, and you're going to have a $10,000 or $20,000 equity sitting on your financial statement making you monthly checks for the next 25 or 30 years—what would you say? Well, everybody gets excited about that. Here you have a way of knowing your exit before you go in the entrance. You can make sure that you're only buying properties that are going to resell right away. You may possibly only be buying properties when you have five, 10, or 15 people waiting to buy the house or houses from you, and you can turn this thing into a little business.

Remember the cash flow, tax write offs, and growth? We're not going to get any tax write offs here, but we're going to get some tax deferment by selling them on installment sales and spreading the income out over a period of time. And, by the way, I'll mention this later on, but a Pension Plan can go out and do the Money Machine. It can go out and buy and sell properties and create a substantial amount of wealth with huge monthly incomes for a great retirement.

This is the Money Machine, and I love it because it's the greatest way to get started in real estate. You don't put the emphasis on inflation which you can't control. You don't put the emphasis on Washington, D. C. and what they are going to do with the tax write offs, which you cannot control. You do put the emphasis on that little house in the back of a cul-de-sac in some neighborhood that you drive by every day. Can you buy that and sell it and make a small profit on it? Bite sized pieces.

Look, I've even seen people buy houses for $84,000 and sell them for $84,000 and still make money on it. How? Because you buy it for $84,000 at 6$^1/_2$% interest with payments of $675 a month. You sell it for $84,000 with 8, 9, or 10% interest and the payments coming in are $875 a month. You make $200 a month for the next 25 or 30 years, but you have hardly any equity tied up in the property, which is the difference between the receivable and the payable.

In my Real Estate Cash Flow System home study course, over half the documents and tape sets and forms are all about the Real Estate Money Machine. Buying and selling, building up a huge amount of net worth just to the point where you have a lot of cash flow coming in can be incredibly profitable. You can spend it. You can literally retire in … well, I want to say nine to 12 months because that's what some people do it in, but that's for you fast people, you people that really grasp this and go for it. You slower people, it'll take you a little longer. And you skeptical people—there's no hope for you. Don't even try the thing because you need to have some enthusiasm for it to make it work.

You don't particularly need any knowledge. I can train you. For example, if you don't know how to buy a house, I have a tape in my Real Estate Home Study Course. You just put this tape in the car. If you don't know how to find good deals, you just listen to the tape while you're driving in the car and I will tell you right on the tape when to stop the car. You'll say, "Stop, stop! There's the house he's talking about right there." Then you put in tape number four which is about analyzing the property. Listen to the tape on your tape recorder while you are walking through the house and I'll show you how to analyze a property to determine if it's a good deal. You can just get out there and get going. If you need a little help, these courses can really get you going.

17

Buying Paper

Many people are going to say, "Why would I want to buy paper or mortgage notes if you just showed me how to sell paper?" That's a great question; I want you to think about that. In the Money Machine you buy and you sell and you usually get your cash back, so you can get on to the next deal. The key to this system is getting on to the next deal.

What are we talking about here? Second mortgages, deeds of trust, contracts, debt instruments against properties. For example, let's say that someone has a property for sale for $150,000. The interest rates are fairly high and the new buyer has $20,000. $150,000 minus $20,000 is $130,000. There is a $100,000 first mortgage on it, which he's going to assume and the seller of this particular property will allow the buyer to give him payments for the $30,000 difference. So, the seller owns this $30,000 mortgage and he's going to take in $250 to $300 a month on the for the next 25 years. Not only does he have the $30,000 note on his financial statement, but he also has a $300 a month income. He got the $20,000 cash down minus his closing costs which probably put $12,000 to $16,000 in his pocket.

He goes along for a year or two and then all of a sudden his situation changes. Perhaps his kids need dental work, he wants to go back to college, get married, whatever. His situation changed and he does not need the monthly payments as much as he now needs the cash. Is the $30,000 second mortgage, second deed of trust on this property a marketable item? The answer is, "Yes."

Now, these $30,000 mortgages will sell for $15,000, $18,000, or $20,000 all the time, depending on the yield. A lot of investors when they discount paper for cash, measure the monthly payments coming in and they are happy with a 12, 14, or 15% yield. Well, not me. I want to make sure I'm yielding at least 22 to 28% if I decide to hold on to the note.

When I go to other paper seminars and listen to them, I usually sit in the back of the room and I say to myself, "My goodness, if these people in the audience do what they are being taught, they are going to pay 60¢, 70¢, or 80¢ on the dollar for these notes." I have not paid over 54¢ on the dollar for a note in the last nine years. Why? Because I found various ways of finding the lower prices. Now, while everybody else is finding them and having to pay 80¢ or 90¢ on the dollar, for a $30,000 mortgage at a discount they pay $27,000. I'll find that $30,000 mortgage for $15,000, $13,000, or $16,000. I want to just quickly run through a list of how to find these and if you really want more information on this call 1-800-872-7411 and ask for The Real Estate Cash Flow System, more specifically ask about Paper Tigers.

You don't need to learn about how to get every one millionth of one percentage point out of a yield. You don't need to learn future values. What you need to know is: are you going to make good money, and is it worth trading your cash for that? Well, you can buy an expensive calculator like one of the Business Analyst Calculators to figure out yields and internal rates of returns. I have a $6.95 calculator from Kmart and I use that one, because I have found that it's really tough to go wrong at 50¢ on the dollar and I can divide anything in my brain by two. So if it's a $30,000 note, I'm willing to pay $15,000. If somebody doesn't want to sell it for that, I just get on to the next deal.

There are still a lot of deals out there, but not like there used to be. When the interest rates got up to 16, 17, and 18%, a lot of owners had to sell their properties at a discount, or get the full price, but then help the buyer take back monthly payments. The buyers couldn't afford to get a new bank loan at 17% interest, because the payments were too high. There were second mortgages everywhere. Well, now that everybody has refinanced their properties in the last five years, there's not many really good second mortgages around that are well secured. You've got to be very, very careful with this. Right now we buy about one out of nine second mortgages that we are presented with. By the way, when we get notes from California we buy about one out of 13. That means that we reject 12 out of 13 notes. We're very, very careful. We really do our homework.

Here's a quick list on how to find second mortgages:

1. Run ads in the newspaper.

2. Go to other real estate seminars that come through town and hand out your business card.

3. Talk with the service companies that service these loans to see if they're willing to let you put an advertisement in their mailings that go out to the people that have notes.

4. While you're out doing standard real estate deals you might come across a rental that has a second mortgage on it and you may be able to negotiate a deal on that; maybe have your Pension Plan buy it.

5. You can also go to the courthouse and look up the notes. Now, I don't like going to the courthouse, by the way, because there are too many other people doing it. Other seminars do not have a list of seven ways of finding notes, they have a list of one way—go to the courthouse. There is too much competition. You may be fourth or fifth in line and competing against people who have a lot more money than you have.

6. Do the real estate deals, create a Real Estate Money Machine.

7. This is the best way: if you want to know how I'm getting them at 50¢ on the dollar, it's by working with real estate agents.

Real estate agents sometimes carry back notes (not all of them, mind you, but a lot of them will carry back a commission from time to time on a property). In the real estate business it's always feast or famine. They may have sold a house for $120,000 with an $8,000 commission note from which they're getting $80 a month. But then all of a sudden situations change again. They don't need the $80 a month, they need some cash, and they're willing to sell this $8,000 note for $3,000 or $4,000. Why? It's a small note. In the note buying business, the people that are professionals want to buy the $50,000, $100,000, $200,000, $300,000, and $400,000 notes. There are not that many people buying the small $4,000, $8,000, and $12,000 notes. Those are the ones that I like the best. So, I can constantly find these by just letting a lot of real estate agents know that I am willing to put up cash and buy notes.

Once you find them, whether you run ads in the paper, check the courthouse, or whatever, you've got to do your homework. Check out the property and make sure that everything in the property is right. Is the value there? Because you do not want to buy a note on a property that's over valued. This is one investment where you can measure the yield before becoming involved. The second thing you want to do is check out the title to make sure that it really is in second position or in third position, and that you're paying a fair price for it. You have to understand everything that's in front of you in the chain of title. Request a title report. You're looking for the truth. What is the real truth of this note? Where does it stand in the chain of title?

One of three things that is going to happen in the note buying business. One is that the note will run the course. Another one is that the note will be refinanced. The third one is that something will go wrong, the people will quit making the payments, and you're going to end up with the property back. Now let me make a quick comment on that.

Don't ever buy a note unless you are willing to own the property. This is why I buy notes only close to home where I can drive by and check out the property.

By the way, what are you really buying here? Yes, you're buying a $30,000 note, but what are you really buying? You're buying the cash flow from the note for the next 25 or 30 years. You're trading cash for cash flow. Now, you had better make sure that your yields are up in that 12, 15, or 20% range.

And, by the way, it hardly ever happens, but when we have to take a note back, and foreclose on the note, our yields usually pop up to 150 to 300%. Because, now we're not just dealing with the note. Now we've got the whole property and we have all the extra equity on top of the note, so we can sell the property and make a really big profit.

There are four ways of making money in the note buying business:

1. Buy and hold these notes. I think this is where many of you would like to be: to have enough cash right now to retire and continue to live off these mortgages. Think about this: every time you buy a mortgage, every time you spend money, you increase your asset base, and you increase your cash flow. That is one way to go, but a lot of you are not there yet. Most of you don't have enough cash to buy the number of notes that you would need to support yourself.

2. Buy and sell these notes. You could put up $15,000 cash on a $30,000 note, and turn around and sell it to somebody else who's happier with a lower yield for say, $18,000 or $20,000. In some states you have to have a license to do this, so you need to check with an attorney, a real estate broker or mortgage broker on what kind of license you need to have to do this.

3. Buy notes with a partner. If you don't have enough cash right now, chiropractors, dentists, and other professionals often have money. You can find money

everywhere. You've got a $30,000 note you can pick up for $15,000. Let someone else put up the $15,000 and then give them an even bigger portion of the $300 income. Let's say they get $200 out of the $300 a month to pay back their investment and their profit, and then you get $100 a month. You received $100 a month and you have no cash tied up. Documents are easy to draw up. This is not a tough deal to do.

4. Buy a note and restructure it. Now this is where the excitement begins. Before I give you the details of this, let me explain what I'm saying. Everyone else teaches you to look at what is. Well, not me, I want to look at what could be. Here's the point: find a note and make it better. Let's buy this $30,000 note for $15,000, then go to the person now making us a payment. We own the note and someone is living in the house who is making us the $300 payment. Let's go to him and say, "Hey, look, you're paying $300 month. Do you know that if you could pay $400 a month, I'll lower the interest rate from, say, 11% down to 8%? And if you can pay $500, a month I'll lower the interest rate down to 2 or 3%." What did we just do? The yield that we had, which was a good yield at $300, is excellent at $400 or $500 per month. We've substantially increased our yield, and we're doing substantially better at cash to asset to cash. *Find a note and make it better.*

If the person living in the house looks really good financially, they could refinance the property. They're credit worthy and the house has a lot of equity, why not get the person in the house to go down and refinance it and pay you off?

"George, I just bought this note. You owe $30,000 at 11% interest. Do you know that you could possibly beat that today and get a better interest rate? If you'll go down and refinance this note, George, I'll give you $1,000 cash, and I'll even pay most of the closing costs."

Now, closing costs could be one, two or three points on the $30,000. If he goes and refinances in two or three weeks you're going to get your $30,000, minus the closing cost of $1,000, minus the $1,000 going to George. You get $28,000. You put up $15,000 weeks ago and now you get back a check for $28,000. You just made $13,000 profit for the two or three months. And how many of these a month could you do? If you don't have that much cash, then you can get your investor, or whoever else to put in the money so that you can expand exponentially.

The note buying business is a wonderful way to go, and I must confess to you that I do a lot of this. I'm so busy traveling the country with the seminar business and book tours that I don't have a lot of time to buy and sell houses anymore. However, I love these notes because they have a steady check coming in. And if you're really busy with your job or your career it may be a good way for you to go.

18

Positive Cash Flow

I'm going to just give you a couple of quick ideas here on getting you to cash flow your properties. This means you have positive cash flow. An old term in the real estate business was an alligator—negative cash flow. A property that had a $1,000 a month rent coming in and a $1,200 monthly payment going out was an alligator. One of the ways to stop negative cash flows is to look at rental real estate in a different light. You're probably asking, "Why are you talking about rental real estate after just bad mouthing it awhile ago?" The answer is long term capital gains. If you hold the property for a certain period of time, you'll only have to claim and pay taxes on part of the capital gains. I believe there are many properties in this country held by people who want to sell, but who will get killed on taxes. The hope that we're going to get better treatment on long term capital gains tax breaks is why I'm going to go over this.

I'm talking specifically about lease option, or a lease purchase. Instead of selling the house outright, and instead of just renting the house, let's lease it and give the person leasing the property an option or an opportunity to buy the property. Why do that?

Well, first of all, a lot of people don't have the whole amount of the down payment. Let's go back to our example from #15. Let's say that we bought the house for $84,000 with $4,000 down. We want to sell it for $100,000 with $10,000 down, but the buyer doesn't have the $10,000. How about this—we sell it to him for $110,000, but we'll give him two years to come up with the $10,000. You see? We'll settle on a price right now. By the way, I don't like settling on prices down the road, that is, we'd sell it for $100,000 right now, but if it goes up in value, then we get an appraisal and we'll split the difference. I don't like that method. Most people walk away from those kinds of deals because they're just too complicated and uncertain. Let's settle on a price right now, say $110,000 with $10,000 or $12,000 down.

Now, where's the person going to get the $10,000? Let's say we would rent this house to them for $700 or $800. How much more than the rent do you think this person would be willing to put up on a monthly basis if that extra money went toward the purchase price in the future? I've found that you could get about half again the amount of the rent on a good day. So, if the rent is $700, you could probably get $1,000, or $1,050, or maybe even $1,100.

How much option money could you get up front right now? The person doesn't have the whole $10,000, but he may have $2,000 or $3,000. So, let's get $2,000 or $3,000 option money up front right now. The question is: "Do you have to claim that money as income?" The answer is "No." That $1,000, $2,000 or $3,000 is option money. You don't have to claim it until the deal is consummated in two or three years. You'll have to claim that money in the future when one of two things happen: either the person walks away from the deal, or the person goes through with the deal. At that point in time, in that year, you'll have to claim that $3,000 as option money and pay taxes on it the next April 15th.

The rent coming in would normally be $700, but the person is paying an extra $300. You do have to claim the rental income as income, but you don't have to claim the extra $300 as income until the person walks away or goes through with the deal. These lease options are phenomenal. A lot of you that have rental properties could get a positive cash flow, or get more money coming in from those rental properties, if you're willing to give the person a chance to buy the property in the future.

Let's go through seven quick reasons for doing these lease options:

1. The up front lease option money is not taxable at this point in time.

2. The monthly option money is not taxable at this point in time.

3. It gives you a chance to check out the person living in the house. I mean, if you're going to sell this house to a person, and do business with this person for the next 30 years, this would give you a chance to check them out for the next year or two to make sure they make the payments on time.

A quick point: we have the person pay the $700 and the $300 no matter what, but the only way the $300 applies to the option payment in the future, toward the purchase price in the future, is if it's made on time. Ever since we implemented that about eight or nine years ago, our rent checks have come in right on time.

4. Make the person living there responsible for the fixing up of the property. One of the worst things about being a landlord is fixing toilets at two o'clock in the morning. Well, you make the person living there responsible for all incidental repairs. And, by the way, that even includes the appliances, say, up to $250.

What we're trying to do is to get the person living in the house to act like an owner. And how do you get him to act like an owner? Well, you either sell him the house so he actually is the owner, or you give him an opportunity at ownership.

5. Who still owns the house? You do. So you still get the depreciation expense. Nice deal.

6. It gives you a chance to cash flow the property. A property that was losing you money before can now make you a profit.

7. The long term capital gains tax breaks are why we started this discussion. If long term capital gains are being adjusted and you have a two or three year option, when you do have to claim your profits upon the sale of this property you'll have capital gains but you'll only have to pay taxes on part of it.

19

How To Increase Your Cash Flow

This strategy is about other rentals and how to get bigger cash flow. I've only done it a couple of times, but a lot of my students have done this and have become very, very good at it. I'm not really big into rentals from any source, but if you're going to play the rental game then why not do it right? When I was teaching seminars and doing my real estate deals at the same time, I ended up, mostly by accident, renting some of my properties to different churches who would place battered wives in them, or families that just needed a temporary place to stay. They were willing to pay $40 to $50 a day. Now, this is a house that I would have rented for $400 or $500 a month, and these people pay $50 a day for it. However, I needed to provide pots and pans, the bedding and linens.

Well, someone else told me that you could fix up that house for handicapped people; like putting in doorbells where the lights go on for deaf people, and a gadget that thumps on the side of the bed if there is a fire, and a phone with a light and so on. There are quasi government agencies or private agencies (every area has a different one), that will put people in there and pay really, really nice rents. For example, a house that would rent for $800 will rent for $1,200 or $1,300. You just picked up an extra $400 or $500 a month for having spent $1,000 or $2,000 to get the house equipped for the deaf. They'll even want to do it on a long term basis, like ten or fifteen years, and if the deaf person moves out for awhile, they'll even continue to pay the rent to keep it in their program. They're looking for houses like this. Every time I teach that, I get some of my students to go out and do it with a 20 unit apartment building, and put people in there. So this is another way of getting some really, really good rents and doing a good service at the same time.

20

Picking Up Foreclosures

With this strategy, I will briefly explain how to pick up foreclosures. In the beginning I didn't go out looking for foreclosure properties because I didn't know they even existed. After talking with different homeowners, and realizing the problems that many of them were getting into because of their house payments, I realized this might be a profitable investment avenue. Because of various problems, people wanted to unload properties, and unload them with excellent terms.

I started to realize that if I was going to make big money on any one property, it was going to be in some kind of distress sale. There are three main types of distress sales. First, the owner needs to relocate immediately. This is usually due to a job change. The second type of distressed property is a house that is in need of repairs, and the owner has run out of energy, time, or even the money to do the repairs. The third type of distressed property is when people come up against some kind of financial difficulty in their lives and are on the verge of losing the property because payments haven't been made. Once I started looking into this, I realized there was an active foreclosure market.

I started to call on people who were about to lose their property at some kind of foreclosure sale. I found them by simply reading an advertisement in my local paper. In most cases, even though the property was listed in the legal notices, there was nobody living on the property. As I tracked down people to find out all I could about these properties, the system became easy. I was able to pick up many of these properties at great prices.

The sheer leverage of getting into these properties by picking up just the back payments and a few of the court costs to that date, made them extremely good deals. It also helped the people who were losing their houses; they would not be foreclosed on and it would save their credit rating. It would also stop the banks from bugging them. They might have lived in the house for up to a year without paying any monthly payments. Now they were able to walk away and not have to worry about how it was going to affect them in the future, because I stopped the foreclosure.

After dealing with these types of properties for several years, I realized that the best time to pick them up is before they are on the auction block; before anything drastic takes place and they are given back to or taken back by the bank. I have also learned that because you are dealing with people who are going through a bad part of their lives, you need to approach them with a great deal of care. My philosophy is that the only kind of properties I would go after would be vacant properties. They were very numerous. As a matter of fact, there were more houses going through foreclosure in which the people had already moved out, than there were ones that had people still living in them.

I developed a step by step process for not only locating these properties, but finding information about the properties and the homeowners. Public announcements (legal notices in your local newspaper and legal records of your community), attorneys who are trustees for banks, and real estate agents are a few of the ways to locate properties. If you want more information on this powerful strategy, my book **How To Pick Up Foreclosures** is available at bookstores everywhere. Once you have located the property being foreclosed, the following list will help you to determine if it is one for you to get involved in.

1. Look at the property. Do not use up any of your time processing the legal work until you've seen the property. Until you do that, you don't know what the neighborhood looks like, if it's vacant, or the condition it is in.

2. Call the Trustee. Don't feel bad if you don't get all of the information you need right away.

3. Check with the bank. Now is the time to put the finishing touches on the information gathering system. Go to the bank and check into 1) the exact loan balance, 2) the exact monthly payments and if there will be any changes, and 3) the legal documents that you will be signing.

4. Get a title report. Go to a title company or to the courthouse and look closely at the title status of the property. Also, check the person's name to see if there are any liens, et cetera against him that might cause a problem when he conveys it.

5. Contact the homeowner. There are only a few ways of changing ownership of property from one person to another. One way is for some government entity to sign it over. Another way is for the homeowner to sign the deed himself. This deed needs to be signed by the parties that have the legal right to convey the property.

6. Have the homeowner sign the deed. Any simple quit claim deed will do. Get one from the title company

or an office supply store. Remember his, her, or their signature(s) must be notarized. Do this properly so there will be no problems.

7. Contact the bank and the trustee to finish. Hopefully, the bank and the trustee will not be out in the cold as you have been doing all this. They should know you are coming.

Once you have all the proper forms signed, take them to the attorney (or whoever is handling the case), with a cashier's check for the amount needed to cure the property. They have nothing to do but accept it—the property is already yours. You have a deed with your name on it. Ask if there is anything else they need, and if not, leave and go have a party!

I have said time and time again, if a person wants to become an expert, real estate is probably the best area in which to gain expertise. Not only is it fun and exciting, but real estate also has a very high rate of return. If you choose real estate, become an expert in finding good value. In all of my years of investing, I have found the largest values can be found in foreclosures.

Owner financing existed long before bank financing. For years, people have been selling property and receiving payments or some kind of trade items for their property.

21

Owner Financing

Along comes the government and heavy bank financing. The banks can loan money and be protected with FNMA, FHA and VA loans. The whole emphasis in the market for the last 50 years has changed to bank financing. Banks have been controlling interest rates. They have been controlling who qualified, et cetera. Now all of a sudden, banks are finding that they are out of control because people can't live up to the bank's standards.

But people haven't changed—they're still looking for homes to purchase and other ways to finance those purchases. Looking down the road, all I can say is that if the interest rates are high then there's going to be a big demand for owner financing. I think this is creating a new awareness in all of the real estate industry as it deals with real estate agents, brokers, investors, and the average home buyer and seller. They're realizing that bank financing is not the only way.

From the seller's point of view, owner financing is also a means of generating income. Let's say, for instance, that we want to avoid taxes and we sell a property on an installment sale. We earn $10,000, but spread out the taxes over the whole length of the time we receive it. Also, let's say that we take nothing for a down payment and we just have a $10,000 contract with $100 a month coming in. Suddenly our situation changes. We need a little bit of cash. We can take that equity contract to get a loan, which is borrowed money, and we pay no taxes on that money.

A contract can be used effectively for collateral purposes. Be sure, though, to keep the ownership of the contract in your name. If it is going to be pledged as a security, it should say, "The assignment of this contract is given for collateral purposes only." Also, if you're getting a loan from the bank and the bank wants to receive the payments from the contract, have the money deposited into your savings account and then drawn out to make the loan payment.

Whatever you do, make sure that all the wording stays in your name and that there is no real assignment to the bank. If there is an assignment to the bank, the IRS might deem it a sale and make you claim your profits at that time.

There are several reasons why you would want to sell a property using this method. If a person selling a piece of property thinks that he can make a fair profit, the tax advantages of the installment sales method (being able to claim profits as received) is incentive enough. Let me give you an example: suppose a property has a high negative cash flow, meaning that a person has a property and the rents coming in are less than the payments going out. He can sell that same piece of property and receive higher monthly payments from somebody else buying from him. It would be in his best interest to sell the property, alleviate the negative cash flow (which can be a real burden), and get a down payment and some kind of monthly payments coming in so that he can take the money and reinvest it in still other properties.

It does not even have to have a negative cash flow. Some people may be tired of rental headaches and would rather have a steady monthly income, letting someone else worry about collecting rents. Other times, people may be moving and can't care for their local rental. A nice check in the mailbox once a month is no worry at all. For more ideas on this call 1-800-872-7411 and ask for my **Owner Financing** booklet.

$\mathcal{22}$

Total owner carry-back is what this strategy is all about. Suppose you find a property you would like to acquire with a fair market value (FMV) of $50,000. It has an existing assumable mortgage of $30,000 at 8% interest per year, with payments of $245 per month. The seller's equity in the house is $20,000.

Papering Out

You offer the seller the basic no money down deal. You tell him, "I like your house very much and I really want to buy it. It's worth $50,000, and I'm willing to give you that much for it. But I can't give you that much all at once. I can do this, though. I can go ahead and assume your mortgage for $30,000 with the bank. I'll start making these payments to the bank immediately. I know that you have $20,000 worth of equity and I will buy your house if you will let me pay it off in monthly payments. I'll give you a $20,000 second mortgage on the house at 11% interest per year. I will be making payment to you of $200 per month."

At first the seller is shocked by your offer. He says, "I want my $20,000 *now*! I can't afford to wait around and let that $20,000 dribble in at a rate of $200 a month!"

You reply, "There are three reasons why you might rather have this paid off in monthly payments as opposed to getting the $20,000 all at once. The first reason is that you could save yourself a lot of money on taxes."

"If I pay you $20,000 cash right now, you have to declare the whole thing on your income taxes for this year. Do you know how much tax you would have to pay on that? Remember, it would jump you into a much higher tax bracket, so you would be paying a higher percentage on your regular income for the year, as well as the $20,000 extra for the sale of your house."

"You're right," he says. "There really would be a big advantage as far as taxes are concerned. What are the other reasons you mentioned?"

You continue, "This will give you a regular steady monthly income. You can use this steady monthly income to help you with your retirement, or use it to buy something you want—a car, or furniture, or anything else you would like. You could use these monthly payments to make monthly payments on something else you would like to buy."

"That's true," he admits. "It would be nice to have a steady monthly income."

"And the third reason is this: this money will not pay off quickly. At $200 per month, I will be making these payments to you for twenty years or more. You will end up with far more money in the long run than if I gave you $20,000 cash right now. You will end up with something more like $60,000 than $20,000."

He makes his decision. "All right, you've got yourself a deal."

Congratulations! You've just bought a house with no money down!

This is really the ultimate in no down payment financing. It is called the "Paper-Out." The name comes from the simple reason that the seller wants to "get out" of his property so desperately that he is willing to take a note, or "paper" from you, with no down payment in the form of cash.

Why would any seller do this? You can rest assured that he has a very pressing reason for selling the property. He is called a "Don't Wanter." It is the term used to described a highly motivated seller. He has some kind of ownership problem. When you come to him with your offer, you will replace his ownership problem with a steady positive cash flow from your paper.

You can even do better than this. You may even be able to set up the deal so that you will not be making any monthly payments at all for awhile. My book *101 Ways To Buy Real Estate Without Cash* contains 101 ways to work these deals. It's available at bookstores everywhere. The secret is negotiation.

Let's put to rest the concept that your only asset for starting an investment plan is the equity in your house. It's there all right, and I'm not going to ignore it, but I will put it in proper light.

23

Equity In Your House

Here is your house, the one you're working so hard for. The following sentence makes very little investment sense until you look closer: "I want my own house to be free and clear." Ostensibly it looks like you're not maximizing the potential of mortgaging your house to the hilt for the purpose of leveraging into other properties or investments.

Once you look deeper, you realize how important it is to have this one nest egg, this one piece of earth that is yours. Therefore, if the equity in your home must be used, try to do it only temporarily. If you feel that your personal residence is your only source of investment funds, there are a few ways to free up the money.

Banks will let you refinance your home up to a certain percent of it's fair market value. Eighty percent is common these days; however some lending institutions are offering higher percentages. This move could free up some cash for you to use. However, there is a negative side that should be looked at. This new loan means three things may change: 1) the amount of interest will go up, 2) your monthly payments will increase, and 3) the terminology of the new loan papers will probably change, more than likely in the bank's favor.

Are you willing to pay the price? Do you want to trade what you have for this new set of figures? The answers to these questions need to be put in perspective, and the best way to do that is to ask another question: what else could you do with the money?

This is an important question that needs asking frequently. It helps to prioritize many things:

1. Can I make more money with what I'll get out?

2. Am I willing to pay the price in the meantime?

3. Can I pay off this excess loan with my profits?

4. What happens if the expected profits aren't there, or are longer coming in than anticipated?

5. Do I need the whole amount, or can I get by with less?

If you can safely answer these questions, you may proceed in several ways. All of the ways involve some type of additional mortgaging of your house. You could:

1. Refinance with a new loan for the whole amount.

2. Place a second or third mortgage on the property. (Note: the terms of this type of loan are usually more stringent, but these terms only apply to the actual amount of this loan. The first mortgage remains intact with no change.)

3. Create notes and mortgages to yourself as a lien against your property and then use them as down payments on other properties.

4. Sell your house, thereby receiving the full equity. Part may be used to move into another house with the balance going to investments.

5. Trade your property for other property.

Any lending institution can help you prepare these documents. That's the easy part. The hard part is making the decision to go ahead. Before you make that decision, I suggest you consider the following:

1. The first consideration in purchasing any property should be its investment qualities. Yes, it's important to look at the tax implications, but your first analysis should be to determine if it's a good investment.

2. Making small amounts of money do large amounts of work is a main ingredient of successful investing. You must use the Law of Leverage. We all talk about leveraging, but unless it becomes an integral part of our investing philosophy, this successful law is wasted.

3. It is a revelation to some that they do not have to take out all of their money to accomplish a lot. In reality, it is a relief for them to know that they will

not have to commit to a whole new life-style because they have taken out a large loan. You can take a little cash and test the waters with different types of purchases and learn what to do when you get larger amounts.

4. Create tax write offs. Learn as much as you can about the tax laws; become familiar with NOLs (Net Operating Losses), Section 179, property tax credits and many of the other ways to help your money grow by decreasing your tax liability. Because investing in real estate is so profitable, the tax implications need to be taken into account at every step.

We're about finished with this section, but I want to make one last point. If you don't do any of these strategies yourself, you can definitely tie in with limited partnerships, or REITs—Real Estate Investment Trust units. You can tie into companies, either private little partnerships or large publicly traded partnerships, where they are investing in these kinds of properties, buying and selling, buying for cash, renting, going for the tax credits, or going for the tax deductions. If you can't do it yourself you can get the benefits of ownership. Usually not quite as extensive and pervasive in your whole tax situation, but you can get a lot of the benefits of real estate by doing it passively.

That about wraps up this section. I wish you good luck and I hope you give some serious thought, once again, to real estate investing. I'm here to help you.

SECTION THREE

Sections Three and Four are all about stock market investments. You're going to read some wild things, as you read about my strategies. I'm obviously aware of many of the strategies available, but I have found some that really work for me.

We're going to start off with the basics, the fundamentals. Then we'll move on to cash flow strategies. Some of these are very aggressive strategies for making a lot of money. Some of them are going to be kind of laid back.

Peter Drucker said it the very, very best. He said—I don't like the word "conflict" so I'm going to change his word of conflicting opinions to contrasting opinions—that "our decisions should be based on contrasting opinions," and I agree. If everything and everyone is saying, "Yes, yes, yes," you ought to be saying, "No." Hold back until somebody says, "No," and throws a bucket of cold water on you, because nothing is as clear cut as when there's a second side to the story.

Stock Market Strategies

Part One

When choosing companies to invest in, make sure that the fundamentals are very, very strong. What we're interested in is the story line of the company. Most of these investment ideas that I'm going to tell you about are about buying equities or stock in the company. Let's go back to the story line. Who are the competitors? How easy would it be to copy the product? Is it really a good market niche to be in? Is it cyclical? Is it dependant upon a lot of other things? Is it retail oriented where it creates a lot of sales, or is it wholesale oriented where it is dependent on other companies using its product? See, I want to know about the company, and then I need also to trust my own feeling. Let me kind of segue into something to think about in regard to your own feelings.

24

Very Strong Fundamentals

Once I've learned all about a company, if I'm not excited about it I just don't buy it. I really trust my own feelings with most companies. Let me tell you what happened awhile ago. When I was living in Scottsdale, a Michael's craft store opened. My wife went into the store a couple of times and I didn't think very much about it. One time she said, "Come on in with me. I want you to help me pick out a frame." I'd sat out in the car reading my books the other times she'd gone in the store. This time I walked in the store and I could not believe it. Everywhere I looked there were people buying this and looking at that and waiting in lines; it was just unbelievable. I had no idea that the craft business was so strong. Here's a company that attacks that whole marketplace. I'd never seen anything like it. So I checked out a couple more Michael's in the greater Scottsdale area and they were all the same. They were all busy and they were all making money. I checked out the stock and it has been a great investment for me. I just trusted my feelings.

Another time I went with my feelings was with TCBY. My wife really likes frozen yogurt. We went into this one yogurt company and I said, "Man, this is really good frozen yogurt. I wonder if the company is publicly traded?" I checked it out and sure enough it was.

I personally love to go to movies. I work really hard, but I usually try to go to one or two movies a week. I mean, I work really hard in the mornings then in the afternoon I like to go to a matinee. If somebody in my office wants to know where I am at two or three o'clock in the afternoon, I'm usually at a movie. Because of that, I've grown to really like this one theater chain. "I wonder if they are publicly traded?" I said. They were, and I started buying stock in the company. I'll tell you more about that one when we start talking about Rolling Stocks, but the point is that you can be your own best researcher by investing in the solid companies you frequent.

Whenever it comes down to you deciding whether you want to buy a stock or not, you need to check out the basics of the company. Get their prospectus, get their annual reports, and really look at the fundamentals. For example, how much debt do they have compared to their income? How much debt do they have compared to all their assets? Are they financially strong? Who are they run by? What is the reason that those people are there, running this company? How much of the company's stock is publicly traded? Now, these are just a few basic things, and any of you that have a good broker can find them out. A good stockbroker friend can get information, reports, insider tips on a lot of companies out there, but if the fundamentals are not strong, if it's thinly traded, if there's too much debt, then avoid that company like the plague.

Before I move on to point 25, I just want to mention something about what I've read, and that I'm sure that you're familiar with. If you've read any kind of stock market news-letters or any of the business pages in your local newspaper or the national business newspapers, there always seem to be tips about market timing. Trying to predict when it's go-ing to go up; when it's going to go down. Whether you should sell short or not, and this and that. Well, I have a real prob-lem with that. It's like trying to predict which way the wind is going to blow. You just cannot do that. Every time I see some kind of new trick on the stock market, it reminds me of going to Las Vegas and learning some trick on how to win at blackjack. I just don't see very much of that working consis-tently.

I know that there are some with good track records for three and four years, and I've read those. Don't get me wrong, I do read some of those newsletters from time to time, but I don't use them as my primary rationale behind investing in a certain company or a certain mutual fund. What I do is use them as just another source of information. I don't base very much of what I do on them. They're just another spoke in the wheel to help me get a well-rounded education about the market or a particular company.

Choose the advisors that you use wisely. Now, let's just take time out and talk about the three kinds of broker-age accounts that you can have. There are thousands of brokerage accounts out there and they all have their different rates, their benefits, and their good and bad points. But let's narrow it down to just three basic kinds of stock brokerage com-panies.

25

Choose Advisors Wisely

The first one is going to be a full service broker. These are the Merrill Lynchs, the Dean Witters and a lot of others that just give you full service. They will prepare reports for you, they'll do all kinds of things, they'll call you up with stock market tips et cetera.

Now, if you don't need that kind of full service broker, then the next one is a discount broker, like Charles Schwab, for instance. These brokers can get you information when you ask, but they won't be calling you with tips.

Finally, you can also go to deep discount brokers where you can get stock traded at 3¢ a share with $30 minimums and the like. These discount brokers charge some incredibly low, low commission fees for trading stock, but they offer no services.

Believe it or not, I have accounts at all three of these types of brokerage companies. But, I don't use information from one to go buy stock from another. I know a lot of people do that, but I feel too much loyalty to my stockbrokers. If my stockbroker for my full service account calls me up with some really good stock advice and I want to buy the stock, I buy that stock from him. I don't hang up the phone and go buy it from another company. You can do what you choose, that's just the way I am.

I probably shouldn't give a plug to another company— but I personally like Charles Schwab. They are very user friendly, and with Charles Schwab I have their Street Smart Program. It's amazing the things that you can get from this program. If you have a computer with a modem, you can become your own stockbroker. You can get reports and up-dates; you can even get a pie shaped graph on your account. You get almost immediate information. It's not like an on-line trading service where you're seeing exactly what is going on with the trading of the company, like the bigger boards or the bigger computer programs have, but it's very user friendly. I've never, ever been disappointed with Charles

Schwab. They've just done a very good job, and I pay them a lot of money in commissions, but I think that they've well earned that money.

I also have accounts at some really super discounted brokers. I've got some problems with them, even though I get really good commissions rates, they're not very user friendly. You know that's all they do, they give you a good commission rates, but man, I tell you it's like pulling teeth to get information on how to work your accounts around. For example, some of these deep discounted brokers insist you have the cash in your account before they let you do anything. Some companies are just fun to work with and some companies are not fun to work with. I choose, though I pay a little bit more money sometimes on my commission, to work with the mid-priced ones, mainly because I like the information that I get. I like working with them.

One last thing on choosing an advisor wisely—you can read reports yourself. If you are not already, you need to be subscribing to *Forbes* and some of the other newsletters that provide you with information about companies. Specifically, in *Forbes*, towards the back of the magazine in the Street Walker section, there are all sorts of articles. Now, what I like to do myself is to pick up a current *Forbes* magazine and read what is going on, but I also like to pick up one that's three or four months old and see the stock that they were recommending back then.

One of the best things you can do yourself about getting information is to get a stock guide. (I'll go into more detail about that later on.) Get a stock guide so that you can look up the ticker symbols, or trading symbols of a company. I'll look up the stocks that they were recommending three or six months ago and see how they've done—see if their advice has paid off. Half the time it does and half the time it doesn't. And that's okay, because I really want to trust my own feelings anyway with this. I want to be my own best advisor, and the only way I can do that is to be educated myself. Therefore, I don't invest in hundreds of companies at a time.

Some of the stocks I buy just because I want to own them, like Disney and Toys R Us. On some of the other ones I'm doing my Rolling Stock, Covered Calls, or other strategies. I'm investing in a few turnarounds. I've got quite a bit of money in these brokerage accounts for several different corporations and retirement plans.

I want to get my own information. I don't want to rely on other people. I especially don't want to rely on people who get a cut of the money I make if I follow their advice. That's why if you follow my advice, buy a book, or a home study course from me, I don't get anything out of what you do. I don't get any commissions. I don't get any percentages. I don't get a part of your profits. Everybody else that touches you after you get done reading this book, every stockbroker that tells you to buy a stock, every real estate agent that tells you to buy a property, are going to get something out of what you do. Therefore, they have a biased reason for telling you to buy something or to sell something, because they get a commission. Not me. I'm the only guy in your life that will get nothing out of what you do.

26

Margin Accounts

If you want to get wealthy very, very quickly, one of the ways to do that is to leverage your money. In real estate it's easy to talk about leverage—you can buy a $100,000 property with $10,000 down. Starting up a small business you can start with a small amount of money, and you can leverage it into a huge business and hardly have any money of your own tied up at all. What about stocks? How do you buy stock with leverage? With a margin account.

A margin account simply means that the broker where you have your account will loan you money to buy more stocks. So, for example, if you put in $10,000 cash and it's on margin, they'll usually loan you $10,000, and let you buy $20,000 worth of stock. Now, what they get out of that, obviously, is a commission on a higher stock purchase, and because they're loaning that extra $10,000, they will charge you an interest rate usually at 6, 7, or 8%. It's usually not too high, but they will earn interest on it. If the stock goes up in value, the next day you call in, or a couple of weeks later when you call in, you may have more buying power. For example, if the stocks that you purchase at $20,000 become worth $22,000 over a period of time, then you could possibly buy another $1,000 worth of stock because you have more collateral, more leverage. Now, if the stock goes down in value, say from $20,000 to $18,000, you're going to get a phone call asking you to bring in some more money. You have to bring it in because your account balance has gone down, the value of the stock has gone down, and you're going to get a margin call.

It's almost impossible to get into trouble because they call you up and hound you every day if you're short on your monies, so you really can't get too far behind. They will not allow you to lose that much money. Once you've had your account for awhile, many brokers will allow the percentages to float a little bit. Instead of being 50% it may even go down to 40 or 30%, so you can expand and grow very quickly.

Here's another quick point. If you set up a Pension Plan at most companies around the country they are not designed to be able to have margin capabilities. If you use my company to set up your pension account, written right in the documents in the master plan that has been approved by the IRS is the ability for you, with your pension money, to invest it in margin accounts. I hope you consider using us to set up your account. We have state of the art, cutting edge Pension

Plans and pension trusts for you to use, so that you can really maximize all these potential earning devices to get ready for a great retirement.

27

Mutual Funds

I don't have a lot to say about mutual funds because I don't invest in that many of them myself; although I have in the past. Mutual funds can be a great way to diversify your holdings because they specialize in certain areas. For example, if you have a high need for growth to increase your wealth for the future, and you don't need a lot of extra money right now, you can invest in a mutual fund that's a growth fund. If you need cash flow, if you need income from your fund, then you have funds that are specifically for that. If you want a mix, a blend, then you can do that, too. You can get cash flow and you can get growth. There are also funds that have tax write off type investments, or tax savings type investments, like municipal bonds. You can invest in government securities or municipal bonds or anything like that. You can get as many different mutual funds as you want to, as you have the money to do, and have all kinds of diversification.

I recommend that you decide what you really want out of life. I'll make a case here that what you probably should do is get more cash flow. Even if you're getting ready for retirement, and you think you need some growth for your retirement, try to get growth along with cash flow or income. There's just no trade off for cash flow. If you have more cash flow from the mutual fund or the stock right now, that allows you to purchase more of that type of investment in the future.

Another quick point: if you buy and sell mutual funds, you're going to have capital gains. If you take the dividends, the earnings from the mutual funds, and you reinvest in more of that specific mutual fund, it adds on to your basis, and you don't have to pay any tax consequences until you actually sell out of the fund. So you can reinvest the dividends and not have it hurt your tax situation from year to year. That's one good advantage of doing mutual funds.

May I also recommend that you get more information on these? You should subscribe to Morning Star or another rating service. I haven't seen any rating service that compares to Morning Star. If you're going to invest in mutual funds, they are the monitoring company. If you want to check out the rating, to check out how they stack up and what the ten best are at any given point in time, you can get that information from Morning Star. Get their individual reports or subscribe to their full service and really get some information, so that you're loading up with knowledge to choose the mutual fund that you want to do.

I think that I can beat the average mutual fund out there, and I've been doing it for many, many years. When I first started in the stock market I realized that there are just a bunch of guys sitting there in New York, or Kansas, or wherever they're based out of, and they're choosing stocks to buy. While they're doing their research, I could do my research. They may be invested in 120 to 130 companies, and have fund managers or even mini managers within a fund who are gathering up information, but I don't need to have that many. I don't need to have 120 shares of stock in my own personal mutual fund that I'm creating. I could do the 15, 20, or 30 stocks that I'm happy with. Some I hold, and some I'm buying and selling. I can build up my own mutual fund because I have the time to do that. At the very beginning I wanted to make sure that I could really make good money with my stock market investments. Now that I'm making really good money there, and with some of the other projects that I've got going on, I'm a little bit chicken sometimes. If I have several hundred thousand dollars in one account, I don't want to stick it into one or two or three stocks. So, I may take $100,000 of $300,000 and play an aggressive game with it, but the other $200,000—simply put, I don't have time to manage it in an aggressive manner. So now, years later, after I've been doing my own buying, selling and building up accounts that have a lot of different stocks in them, I'll put that money into good blue chip stocks and mutual funds.

Publisher's note: Wade Cook Seminars has developed some extensive seminars on blue chip and mutual fund investing. Call 1-800-872-7411 for a listing of events.

There are a lot of funds out there that you can look at that'll get you at least 14% returns. If you're getting anywhere under 10%, you ought to get out of that one and get into one where you can make some really good money.

28

Investing For Dividends

This is about investing for dividends. Please refer to the example of the Corporate Dividend News on page 88. This provides information on when a company is going to issue a dividend. With this, you have a date that the company announces the date of ownership. So, for example, a company will make an announcement that it's going to pay a 28¢ dividend on May 28th for people who own the stock (shareholders) as of May 15th, or something like that.

I speak Japanese, and I met some Japanese investors in a hotel in Los Angeles once. We were talking about money-making strategies. They said they had come here with almost $100 million, and they were looking for companies that were getting ready to pay a dividend.

Now, you have to really measure this out—whether buying stock in the company and paying a commission is worth it or not. Which, by the way, if you're doing three percent commissions, is not very much. If you own 1,000 shares of stock in a company and there's going to be $1.28 dividend, then you are going to capture that dividend and you can buy that stock the very day or even the day before the day of ownership. You own the stock on the day of record of ownership, and you get the dividend paid out to you in two, three, or four weeks. You could sell the stock the very next day, but every shareholder as of May 15th is going to receive the $1.28 dividend, even though they're not going to get paid until May 28th. Now that's a great play.

If you learn about the right kinds of companies, which ones you can get involved in that don't require a lot of cash as a percentage of the dollar you're putting up for the dividends you're getting back, you make a fortune. These Japanese investors had come here with $100 million, and about a year and a half later they had $200 million. Over double their money in a year and a half just by playing this dividend game.

Let me tell you just a couple of other things that I've noticed since I started doing this. I started buying these stocks for dividends, and I noticed that almost immediately after they announce the dividend, especially if it was a dividend that was a little higher than the projections, the stock would go up. So, I'd buy stock in a company for $20 that was going to pay an 82¢ dividend; however, the very day of, or around the time, it made the announcement the stock would go up to, say, $23 or $24.

Now, here's my play: I would not only go in and capture the stock for the dividend, but I would wait for it to jump a dollar or two, and then sell the stock. So I'd almost get a double and triple whammy, because the cost of buying the shares at 3¢ a share was minimal compared to capturing it. A lot of times, two, three, or four weeks later, the news is over and the stock would float back down to the $19 or $20 range—just waiting for the next dividend.

I put this angle on it because I noticed in all the companies where I would buy for the dividends I was always tempted to sell immediately. Then I noticed that the stock would jump up a dollar or two, so I'd wait for it to do so. As soon as it went up, in two, three, or four days, then I would

CORPORATE DIVIDEND NEWS

Dividends Reported August 25

Company	Period	Amt.	Payable date	Record date
REGULAR				
Cass Commercial Corp	Q	.13	9-15-97	9-5
Central ME Pow3.50%pf	Q	.87½	10-1-97	9-10
Cincinnati Finl	Q	.41	10-15-97	9-12
ConsumEnr $4.16pf	Q	1.04	10-1-97	9-5
ConsumEnr $4.50pf	Q	1.12½	10-1-97	9-5
ConsumEnr $7.45pf	Q	1.86¼	10-1-97	9-5
ConsumEnr $7.68pf	Q	1.92	10-1-97	9-5
ConsumEnr $7.72pf	Q	1.93	10-1-97	9-5
ConsumEnr $7.76pf	Q	1.94	10-1-97	9-5
ConsumEnr $2.08pf	Q	.52	10-1-97	9-5
ConsumEnr 8.36%TOPrS	Q	.52¼	9-30-97	9-26
Dimon Inc	Q	.15	10-13-97	9-6
Duff&Phelps Credit	Q	.03	9-11-97	9-5
1stCommCorp Ark	Q	.24	10-1-97	9-15
1st Midwest Finl	Q	.09	10-1-97	9-15
Knape & Vogt Mfg	Q	.16½	9-12-97	9-5
Mahaska Investment	Q	.20	9-15-97	9-8
MainStreet BankGroup	Q	.14	9-26-97	9-5
Natl Gas&Oil Co	Q	.06	9-29-97	9-15
RelianceSteel&Alum new	Q	.03½	c9-10-97	c9-2
c-Corrected dates.				
Untd Illuminating	Q	.72	10-1-97	9-11
USBancorp Inc PA	Q	.35	10-1-97	9-3
IRREGULAR				
American Business Finl	Q	.01½	9-15-97	8-31
FUNDS - REITS - INVESTMENT COS - LPS				
Amer Govt Inco	M	.03	9-24-97	9-4
Amer Govt Inco Port	M	.03½	9-24-97	9-4
Am Insd Mtg Inv'86	M	m.08	11-3-97	8-31
m-Includes $.01 extra.				
Am Insd Mtg Inv'88	M	.10	11-3-97	8-31
Am Insd Mtg Inv'85	M	.10	11-3-97	8-31
Amer Muni Inco Port	M	.062¾	9-24-97	9-4
Amer Muni Term III	M	.04¾	9-24-97	9-4
Amer Muni Term Tr	M	.0542	9-24-97	9-4
Amer Muni Term II	M	.0517	9-24-97	9-4
Amer Opport Inco	M	.037	9-24-97	9-4
Amer Select Port	M	.08½	9-24-97	9-4
AmStratIncPort II	M	.08¼	9-24-97	9-4
AmStratIncPort III	M	.08¼	9-24-97	9-4
AmStratIncPort	M	.08	9-24-97	9-4
AmericasIncoTr	M	.05½	9-24-97	9-4
Australia WEBS Index Ser	–	.3291	8-29-97	8-27
BRE Properties	Q	.34½	9-25-97	9-5
Belgium WEBS Index	–	.7256	8-29-97	8-27
Canada WEBS Index Series	–	.1688	8-29-97	8-27
Colonial IntermHi	M	.057	9-12-97	c8-29
Colonial MuniInco	M	.04¼	9-12-97	c8-29
c-Corrected date.				
ConAgraCapLC pfB	M	c0.1376	9-2-97	8-29
c-Corrected amount.				
France WEBS Index Series	–	.353	8-29-97	8-27
Germany WEBS Inx Ser	–	.1314	8-29-97	8-27
Highlander Inco Fd	M	.094	9-24-97	9-4
HongKong WEBS Inx Ser	–	.5906	8-29-97	8-27
Italy WEBS Index Series	–	.3544	8-29-97	8-27
Malaysia WEBS Index Seris	–	.0265	8-29-97	8-27
Managers Bond Fd	M	h.12	8-27-97	8-25
Managers Int Mtg	M	h.08	8-27-97	8-25
Managers Short & Inter	M	h.09	8-27-97	8-25
MaunaLoaMacadamia	Q	.07½	11-14-97	9-30
Mexico(Free)WEBS Inx Sr	–	.5006	8-29-97	8-27
MinnMuniIncoPort	M	.063⅛	9-24-97	9-4
MinnMuniTerm II	M	.0492	9-24-97	9-4
MinnMuniTerm	M	.0509	9-24-97	9-4
Neth WEBS Index Series	–	.8279	8-29-97	8-27
One Liberty Prop pf	Q	.40	10-1-97	9-17
One Liberty Props	Q	.30	10-1-97	9-17
Prud Global Util A	Q	h.12¾	8-29-97	8-26
Prud Global Util B	Q	h.09½	8-29-97	8-26
Singapore(Free)WEBS Inx	–	.0541	8-29-97	8-27
Spain WEBS Index Series	–	1.0895	8-29-97	8-27
Sweden WEBS Index Series	–	.7555	8-29-97	8-27
Swtzland WEBS Index Seris	–	.5696	8-29-97	8-27
UK WEBS Index Series	–	.5739	8-29-97	8-27
STOCK				
Alliance Bancorp Inc	s		9-26-97	9-12
s-3-for-2 stock split.				
Cooperative Bkshrs	s		9-22-97	9-8
s-2-for-1 stock split.				
Harris Corp	s		9-26-97	9-4
s-2-for-1 stock split.				
Merrill Corp	s		10-15-97	9-30
s-2-for-1 stock split.				
Natl Gas&Oil Co	2%		12-22-97	12-1
PepsiCo Inc	c		10-6-97	9-19
c-Correction; 1 shr of Tricon Global Restaurants, Inc common for each 10 shrs held.				
Robert Half Intl	s		9-26-97	9-5
s-3-for-2 stock split.				

	INCREASED	--Amounts--		
		New	Old	
ANB Corp	Q	.17	.15	9-30-97	9-12

Stocks Ex-Dividend August 27

Company	Amount
ABN AMRO HldgADS	.2544
AEGON N.V. ADS	.6708
AetnaC LLC mipsA	.197916
Allmerica Secs	.21
Allstate Corp	.24
AmerFirst PrepFd2	.1089
Amer Bankers Insur	.22
AmerGenlCap pfB	.169271
AmerGnlCp pfAmip	.176042
AmerGenlDel pfAmip	.25
Am Insd Mtg Inv'86	.08
Am Insd Mtg Inv'88	.10
Am Insd Mtg Inv'85	.10
ArgentBank	.14
Arizona Land Inco	.25
ArizonaPubSvc un	.208333
Arm Finl Group	.02
ARM Finl Group pf	.59⅜
Armco Inc $2.10pf	.52½
Armco Inc $3.625pf	.90⅝
Armco Inc $4.50pf	1.12½
Ashanti Goldfields	.12½
Badger Meter Inc	.12¾
Barclays Bk ADR E	t.50
Barnes Group	.167
Best Buy Cap LP pf	.27083
Brit BrdcstgADS	.3873187
CIM Hi Yld Secs	.06
CL&P Capitl LP pfA	.19⅜
CNF Trust $2.50pf	.55½
Cabot Corp	.10
Cagle's clA	.03
Carnival Corp	.11
Centura Banks	.27
Chart Industrs new	.06
Citizens Util clA	1%
Coastal Corp	.10
Coastal Corp pfA	.29¾
Coastal Corp pfB	.45¾
Coastal Corp pfH	.53⅛
ColonialHiIncoMuni	.0455
Colonial Interm Hi	.057
Colonial Muni Inco	.04¼
Comdisco pfA	.55
Comdisco pfB	.55
CommercialBncshrs	.30
Comml Intertech	.13½
ComsatCpl LP mips	.16927
ConAgraCapLC pfC	.194791
ConAgraCapLC pfB	.137552
ConAgraCapLC pfA	.18¾
CorningDel LP mips	.25
CrossTimbers Rylty	.1473
Crown Amer Rlty	.20
Crown Amer pfd	.9931
Cullen/FrstBkr	.25
Current Inco Shrs	.21½
DLJ CaptII8.42% pf	.17542
Dana Corp	.27
DeKalb Gen clB new	.03½
Delta & Pine Land	.03
Deltic Timber	.06¼
DevelopersDivR pfA	.59⅜
DevelopersDivR pfB	.59
Dominion Resources	.64½
DomResBlckWr un	.692395
Donaldson Co	.09
Dover Corp	.19
Duff&PhelpUtilInco	.06½
Duquesne Cap pfd A	.174479
EastAmNatGasTr dep	.4569
Eastern Co	.11½
Empire District El	.32
EnergyNorth Inc	.32
EnronLLC 8%mips	.166667
EnronCapResLP pfA	.18¾
EnronGlb Pwr&Pipe	.25
EntergyGulf deppf	.9688
EntergyGulf$5.08pf	1.27
EntergyGulf$4.52pf	1.13
EntergyGulf$8.80pf	2.20
EntergyGulf$1.75pf	.43¾
EntergyGulf$4.40pf	1.10
Enterprise Oil pfB	1.61½
FPL Group Inc	.48
Federal-Mogul	.12
FerrellgasPtnrs un	.50
Finova Group	.28
1st Aust PrimeInco	.07
1st Commonwlth Fd	.08¼
1st Union Corp new	.32
1st West VA Bncp	.20
Franklin MultiInco	.064
Franklin Princ Mat	.06½
GTE DelLP pfA	.192708
GTE Del mipsB	.182291
Geon Company	.12½
GeorgiaP CapLP pfA	.18¾
GulfCanRes adjpf1	b.017

Company	Amount
Hartford Life Inc	.09
High Yield Plus	.07
Honeywell Inc	.27
HoraceMann Educatr	.13½
Huntco Inc clA	.03½
ITT Industries Inc	.15
IIIPwrCapLP pfAmip	.196⅝
JCPLCpLP pfAmip	.178333
Kellogg Co new	.22½
LSB Ind 2ndpfC	.81¼
LTC Prop pfd A	.1979
Leggett & Platt	.14
LoewenGpCp pfAmip	.196⅞
Lone Star Ind	.05
MCN MichLP pfA	.195313
Mart Marietta Mtls	.12
May Dept Stores	.30
Maytag Corp	.16
McDonald's Corp	.08¼
Media General clA	.13
Mercantile Stores	.30
Meredith Corp	.12
MerrLyn 6% strp	.34¼
MerrLyn 7 1/4%str	1.0218
Mesa Royalty Tr	.315622
Met-EdCapLPpf9%mip	.18¼
Mid-Atlantic Rlty	.24
Mid-Amer Apt pfA	.1979
Midland Bk ADR C	t.57031
Midland Bk ADR A	t.55469
Midland Bk ADR B	t.64063
Midland Bk ADR D	t.59688
MissnC 8.5%mps B	.177083
MissC 9 7/8%mps A	.205729
MorganStan HiYld	.11
NthCarolina NatGas	.35
Nuveen (John) Co	.23
PLC CpLLC pfAmips	.18¾
PNC Bank Corp pfC	.40
PNC Bank Corp pfD	.45
PWG Capl pfd	.172916
PWGCpTrII 8.08%pf.168333	
PECOEngvCp pfAmip	.18¾
PenelecCap mips A	.182291
Pennzoil Co	.25
PermianBasin Rylty.022739	
Phoenix Duff&P pfA	.37½
Phoenix Duff&P	.06
PIMCO CommlMtgSecs	.09⅜
Providian Fincial	.05
Providian pf mips	.184896
PSE&G Cap mipsB	.166666
PSE&G Cap mipsA	.1953125
RayonierTimber clA	1.24
Republic Group	.09
SBC 7 3/4%DECS	.767734
SanJuanBasin Rylty.071436	
SeaCont $1.4625pf	.365⅝
Sears Roebuck	.23
Sonat Inc	.27
SWPubSvcCapItrupsA	.49⅝
Sprint 8.25% decs	.6573
StPaulCapLLC 6%mps	.25
Station Casinos pf	.87½
Stepan Co	.12½
SturmRuger&Co	.20
Sunbeam Corp	.01
Sunsource LP clA	.091666
Sunsource LP clB	.03
SuperValu Inc	.26
Temple-Inland Inc	.32
Templeton GlobIGvt	.05
Texaco Cap mips A	.143229
Texaco Cap pfB	.12½
Thiokol Corp	.20
TimesMirror peps	.417
Tompkins County Tr	.32
TorchmkCap LLC pfA	.19⅛
Transam Del LP mip	.1901
Transam Inco Shrs	.16
TriNetCorp pfdA	.5859⅜
TrinetCorp pfdB	.57½
UGI Corp	.36
USX Captl pfA Mips .182291	
Utd Cap Fd LP pfA	.20052
US Surgical Corp	.04
Unum Cap 8.8%mids .183333	
UtilicpCappfAmip	.184895
VirginiaEP $5pf	1.25
WPS Resources Corp	.48½
WeiderNutriIntl A	.03¾
Wellman Inc	.09
Wisc P&L 4 1/2%pf	1.12½
Wiser Oil Co	.03

t-Approximate U.S. dollar amount per American Depositary Receipt/Share before adjustment for foreign taxes.

sell the stock at that point in time. By the way, I've gotten burned a couple of times, in that I'd buy for $20 and I'd sell for $23. Then the stock would go up to $25 or $26. But it's important not to get greedy. I'm always happy if I get the goal I shoot for, and I try not to lament that I could have made more, because I could lose more too. I pick an exit and stick with it. I'm putting in my money, getting a huge return, and when I say huge return I'm talking about a 5 or 10% return, but in three days.

Now this one is going to make a few of you a little bit angry, and I hope so because what I'm going to tell you right now sounds almost criminal—even though it's not. It's a weird deal. I noticed that a lot of mutual funds, and a lot of big portfolio managers who have hundreds of millions of dollars in their stock portfolios, would do something toward the end of November and December every year.

29

Year End Strategies

Here is what they would do: they would get rid of all the little stocks in unknown companies and companies that they had invested in back in the last part of January or February hoping that they would grow—some of them had. Some had grown a lot in value; some doubled and tripled in value in a year or two. But they would get rid of the stocks. Why were they doing that? Well, it's for window dressing. They're going to send all of their fund investors a stock report as of December 31. You've seen these big booklets that they come up with, and they include a list of all these companies. You tell me, when you look down that list of companies, do you like to see the big heavy hitters? For example, the IBMs, the 3Ms, the Hersheys, the Disneys, the Toys R Us, all the big companies. Yes, we all like to see those there. It makes you feel good to say, "I own part of this, I own part of that." That's kind of nice. We like to see that.

So, the mutual fund managers get rid of a lot of their little no name stocks, and they start accumulating these huge blocks of stock in big companies. Ironically, they're going for companies that are trading at like $1 to $10 a share, and they're now buying companies that are trading at $40 to $100 a share, which has nothing to do with anything, except that it's a lot easier as a percentage of growth if you have a company that's at $2 and it goes to $4. You've doubled your money. If you have a company that's at $52 and it goes to $54 you only made $2. Well, you've got a small percentage, but nothing like doubling your money. Oh, and by the way, what happens right after the first of the year?

As soon as the new year begins they start getting rid of a lot of the big name companies, not always though, because the last couple years I've watched them and they've really held on to certain stocks. Then they start buying a lot of the little start ups, little IPOs, turnaround companies, the ones that they think they're going to double and triple their money on in the next year. Because they want their portfolio to grow as a percentage, and the only way to do that is not in the blue chips. Now, you'll get some good returns in blue chips, but not the kind of returns that you can get on some of these smaller companies.

So how do we take advantage of this? Well, it's really quite simple. Towards the end of the year, when all these big funds are dumping their stocks in these little companies, it's time to buy them. You'll see their stock drop from $6 down to $4. And it's a great buy, but it's only been two months and all of a sudden it's $4. This is what I did last year with a couple of huge companies, like Boeing, and I noticed that their stock dropped. I got rid of all of my stock in some of those companies right there in December, and sure enough the small ones that I was buying went up in value after the first of year. The big ones that I had, I was able to sell because the prices were really driven up high, and those big ones went down after the first of the year. So, you see how you take advantage of that?

At the end of any given year, you look for small companies you could buy that are at discounted and wholesale prices. After the first of the year you start buying the bigger companies' stock because the values are down. Now, I don't think you're going to make a fortune on this strategy, but it's good to know so that you don't get caught up in buying at the wrong time and selling at the wrong time.

Before I go into the strategies of point number 30, let me give you a little background on it. I do some trades all the time, and I'm pretty excited about it. My wife and I talk all the time about the different companies that we're doing this with. It wasn't until just a few months ago that I started teaching this. I've heard there are something like 6.8 million people in America that own a second property like a rental house; whether it was given to them or they purchased it. There are, though, over 28 million Americans who have brokerage accounts. So, obviously, for the ease of investing, the ease of getting involved and handling your money and the liquidity of your money, it's a lot more appropriate to a lot of people to have stock market accounts.

30

Rolling Stock

I started noticing also that there were a lot of different people coming to my seminars. They were not the old tennis shoe crowd of people trying to get rich and doing it in real estate. All of a sudden we were getting some very sophisticated people that not only wanted to learn about the stock market, they also wanted to learn more about Nevada Corporations, Living Trusts, and Pension Plans. One day, out of the blue, I made about $13,000 on a little stock and I didn't have that much money invested. I was teaching my Money Machine one day seminar and I asked, "Do you want to know what I did yesterday?"

Everybody responded, "Yes." I told them about what I had done. Well, it generated so much excitement that I told people how I learned about it, so let me tell you.

This is called Rolling Stock. I made up that name because I kind of figured it out by myself. The only part I learned elsewhere was from a stockbroker, and then I made it more sophisticated by what I did with it. Let me tell you what happened. I got a phone call one day from a stockbroker who asked me to come in and talk with him. He told me about a company that was trading at $50 a share, and over the last two or three years it had rolled from $50 up to $60 and back down to $50 again, sometimes two or three months at a time.

"Let's buy 100 shares," he said, "that's $5,000 plus a little bit for the commission, and put in an order to sell as soon as it hits $60."

And I said, "Okay, let's do that."

So sure enough, about a month and a half later the stock went from $50 to $60, and the computer triggered a sale. I had a sale of $6,000 cash back in the account, which was $60 times 100 shares. After the commission I still had about $900 profit on this deal. Then I put in an order to buy it again at $50, and about a month later it rolled back down to $50. I put in an order to sell whatever I had purchased when it rolled back up to $60.

Now, I did this for a couple of years—$50 up to $60 down to $50 back up to $60. Sometimes the stock would drop down to $45, $46, or $47, and once in awhile it would get up to $62 or $63, but not very often. It would go between $49 and $50, and about $60 and $61. So I just kept my limits at $50 and $60. Then I started thinking, "What if I could do this with companies that are in the $5 to $7 range? I wonder if there are any companies rolling between $5 and $7 dollars. I wonder if there are any companies rolling between $1 and $2, or between 50¢ and $1." Then the light just started clicking on.

I started noticing what the stock of many companies that I was investing in was doing. I mean, I'd buy a stock at $2 a share and it rolled up to $4, and I'd be all excited about it, but all of a sudden I'd look in the paper about two weeks later, and it's back down to $2.25. "Why don't I just buy more at $2.25 and I'll start selling it at $4?" And that's what happened.

I got a call from one of my stockbrokers one time, and he asked, "Have you forgotten about us?"

I said, "No, why?"

"Because you put $2,000 into an IRA, and it's just been sitting there for the last couple of years," he said. "There's like $2,200 in your money market account."

And I said, "Wow, okay. Well, let's get going with that. Why don't you buy 2,000 shares of this stock at $1."

Now, I bought an airline stock that was in bankruptcy at that time. I bought it at $1, put in an order to sell at $2. When it got up there to $2, the computer triggered a sale, and I had doubled my money. Now, that took about three or four weeks. I waited for it to roll back down a couple weeks later to $1, and I bought a bunch more and I sold it at $2. One time I bought a bunch at $1 in the morning, and I put in an order to sell it at $2, and it hit $2 that afternoon.

Now, can it do that? Well, can a big company go from $50 to $51 in a day? Can a small company that's getting ready to go, a new IPO or a turnaround company, or a company that's in bankruptcy, do that?

Just this morning, before I came in to the studio to do a tape, I was talking to my stockbroker and she said she'd send out some reports on a couple of companies I was questioning. I just found out about them over the weekend, and I wanted to do some stuff with them. Before I start buying and rolling this stock I wanted to know what was going on.

If you have a computer with a modem, give us a call to log on to WIN—Wealth Information Network—our internet subscription service (www.wadecook.com). I can't sell you any stock because I'm not a broker and I won't give you advice or take any of your profits. What I will do is tell you what I'm doing, and which companies I'm doing deals on, and what the ranges are. I've got stock reports and I've got tax reports, all kinds of Q & As, real estate questions, all kinds of things for people to make money on and ways to keep more of what they are making. We want to make this information more accessible to a lot of people. Then you can go out and find your own companies. I'd like you to visit my website and tell me about companies that you're rolling, and what you've been doing.

You know, almost every time I do a TV show or a radio show, somebody calls in to the station afterwards and talks to me, and they've been Rolling Stock since 1938 or they've been Rolling Stock since 1960. One lady makes about $40,000 a year. She's got about $80,000 to $100,000 in her account at any given time, and she only does it a couple of times a month, because she's retired. She makes $40,000 just buying and selling stock. And any time she wants to buy a new car she gets really aggressive at it. She buys and sells, buys and sells, buys and sells, makes $25,000, and goes and buys a new car. People have been doing this since before I was born, but I stumbled across it and put it in an educational format, and I'd love to share that with you, because it's made us a lot of money. One of my trusted friends, Gregory Witt, just published a whole book called *Rolling Stock: Making Money On The Ups And Downs*. This is a great teaching guide and resource for anyone who wants to make money by Rolling Stock.

Now, one last thing before we move on. My recommendation is that you do this type of investment activity in an IRA, a SEP-IRA, a corporate Pension Plan, or a Keogh plan—some kind of retirement account. You'll get so good at it, and you'll make so much money at it, that you'll get killed in taxes. So you want to do this in an account that has no tax consequences.

You need to do your investing within different types of entities. I just hinted at that in point number 30, and I'm going to get more specific now. You can have a corporate account or you can have an individual account. Let's talk first about a corporate account. Do you know that if you have a corporation and you have a brokerage account, and you get dividends, that you can exclude from taxation 80%, with some corporations only 70%, but 70 to 80% of the dividends that you receive can be excluded from taxation. You get to forget about them. Ignore them as if they never happened.

31

Types Of Entities

What I'm talking about is called the 70% Exclusion Rule. Corporations can do this. You cannot do this as an individual. By the way, I don't really like S Corporations which we'll talk about later, but S Corporations do not qualify for this 70% exclusion rule. That's why I like a regular, ordinary C Corporation. So, you can do it individually and have your own brokerage account. You can do it as a corporation. You can do it as a retirement account.

Now, you have four choices there, plus you have a SEP-IRA, and an IRA which everybody can have. Whether you can deduct the $2,000 or not, you can still have an IRA, and put in the $2,000 if you're working. You can have a Keogh plan if you're self-employed, or a corporate Pension Plan if you are a corporation. The corporate Pension Plan, by the way, gives you the most latitude and the most flexibility. It is just substantially greater than any of the other plans because you can borrow the money, you can do a variety of things that you cannot do with a regular Keogh plan, even though they've come to parity in the amounts of money that you can put aside.

Why would you want to take investing for dividends, Rolling Stock, Range Riders, which is point number 32, or any of these ideas and invest in an account where you would have to pay full taxes? Because you're just constantly fighting this thing with Uncle Sam, and if you're constantly sending off part of your profit, it really cuts down on your future profits.

R ange Riders is another strategy that I have. Ironically, a lot of you have seen these little graphs on TV financial

32
Range Riders

programs. Sometimes a broker is there, and he's showing you all these little zigzag lines. For example, a stock is going to go from $10 a share to $30 a share. But as you look at how it got there, it went from $10 to $12 and back down to $11, up to $14 and back down to $13, and then down to $12, and then up to $15 and back down to $10, and then up to $17 and back down $12. You've all seen this sort of thing. I mean, the road to wealth is not a freeway; it's a pretty rocky road.

A lot of you would think that if you can get a stock at $10 and have it grow to $30, that you've made a lot of money. But what about this: what about riding the range? When that stock goes up to $12 or $13, why not put in a sell and sell it right there? Now, hopefully, it's going to go back down to $11. Again, buy some more at $11, and then sell it at $14, and then buy it at $12 and sell it at $15. Now, I'm going to do a combination of things here with Range Riders and Rolling Stocks, so if you can, just keep these two together in your head for me.

At the last Wealth Academy there was a gentleman named Kurt. When I finished talking about this Rolling Stock, he went home and ran a report on this one company that was trading between $2¹/₂ and $3¹/₂. All these little zigzag lines were going up and down, up and down.

This is a company I was buying at $2^1/2$ and selling at $3^1/2$. And after we got done teaching this, one of the people in class said, "Look, Wade, that's not true what you said. It takes four months for it to go from $2 to $4."

"No, hold it, hold it," I said. "You guys are missing the whole point here. I'm not buying this stock at $1.75 or $2 and waiting for it to go to $4. I'm buying this stock in the mid range all the way through here. I buy it at $2^1/2$ and I sell it off at $3^1/2$. I make $1 a share, minus a little bit in commissions. And then when it goes back down to $2^1/2$, I buy it, and when it goes back up to $3^1/2$ I sell it. I even put in a computer order so I don't have to be there when it hits $2^1/2$. It may go to $3.75 or $4. Don't get greedy. I made my money at $3^1/2$."

Over the four year period I think it did it 38 times—38 times it rolled that $1. Now, you could have made 38 times however many thousands of shares that you own over that same period of time. If you bought the stock at $2 and waited for it to go to $4, you'd be really disappointed. But you can ride the range up and down and up and down, or you can do the Rolling Stock, and it just keeps working over and over and over again.

Find your own companies, call me or get on WIN (Wealth Information Network, our internet service), and find them. Come to the Wall Street Workshop. We spend time in class talking about these because this is a lot of exciting information. I love hearing about these companies, and sharing what I'm doing.

I've seen some people make a tremendous amount of money. Let me tell you about two of those people. I did an all day seminar in Sacramento a short time ago. A lot of people signed up to come to the Wall Street Workshop.

At the program there was a lady named Monica and a man named John. John called me up on Wednesday and said, "Wade, I should have done it. I should have listened to the cab driver."

"What happened?" I asked.

He said, "Well, I went to call my stockbroker and he wasn't in, so I put the order in with the secretary to buy $30,000 worth of that stock you were telling me about."

"And what happened?" I asked.

He called me back a little bit later that Monday morning and said, "You don't want to buy that company. Who are you listening to on that? You don't want to buy that company's stock."

John said, "Wade, it went from your buy price to the higher price. By Wednesday, I would have made $32,000 profit—in two days."

This is ironic, because the following week he was talking to Monica, the lady who had been at the seminar in Sacramento. She had gone out on Monday, bought the stock at $30,000, and on Wednesday sold it and actually made the $32,000. This really ticked John off, because he had listened to his stockbroker. I'm telling you right now, everyone, you've got to make a choice whether you're going to listen to this cab driver, who can show you how to make money, or listen to your CPA or your attorney or your stockbroker. Our advice will always be different. At some point in time in your life, you're going to have to make a choice on who's advice you want to follow.

Now, I'm just going to mention a few things here about what I do with global investing, and if you want to do that then maybe some of my advice can help you. First of all, I'm really worried about global investing, because a lot of the funds that I see invested in South America or Southeast Asia, while they heat up very, very quickly,

33

Global Investing

you'll notice that they also cool down very, very quickly.

Their stock markets take a big tumble. So when I do global investing, I don't particularly want to get involved in a certain region. I'm also not particularly fond of getting involved in a certain sector of the market place; for example health and pharmaceuticals.

I want to invest globally in a mixed fund that is after growth, cash flow and appreciation, from these companies. I want to invest in a fund globally that has some European funds, some Southeast Asian funds, some Pacific Rim companies—a real mix. I've had the most fun with those, and the most luck with those.

My advice is that you take a well rounded approach to this. It's just too hard to tell which regions are going to heat up and slow down. It's too hard to tell from a cyclical basis which of the sectors is going to increase, so the best thing to do is get with a good portfolio manager—there are a lot of them. A lot of the big funds have international funds. You can get the reports and see whether they are sectors, whether they are regions, and then get involved in a well rounded fund. Some of those funds, by the way, are getting 12, 14, 16, or 18% returns, and have done so for many, many years.

If you want to take advantage of the global economy and you're not ready to do all the research yourself, then you can get going by doing this through these mutual funds. They also have debt funds just like any other kind of investments.

Also, just one last thought, if you travel and know about companies, you may want to have a brokerage account on the NEKA exchange in Tokyo. If you've got that kind of sophistication, if you're traveling, if you're learning about companies, then go ahead and invest.

One other way to invest in these companies worldwide is when they bring their investments and list it over here. These are called ADRs—American Depository Receipts. You can call any stockbroker about a particular company and ask about an ADR. Like everything else, do your homework.

That's my problem. I can't do my homework as extensively on global companies, international companies, as I can with companies here in the United States. So I really have to trust the fund managers to do the research for me.

34

DRIPs

This is about getting involved in companies with low entry costs. Specifically I'm talking about DRIPs—Dividend Reinvestment Programs. A lot of companies will allow you to reinvest the dividends in their particular company without any commissions, so that all of the money that is coming from the dividend is going right back from the dividend is going right back into the company, and 100% of it is being invested. Now, this is a low entry cost, which just makes sure that all of your money gets going. There are about 800 companies that do this right now. Any stock broker can get you a list.

35

Bet On The Jockey

My wife and I raise Arabian horses on our little farm. Our kids show them in shows. We breed, buy and sell, and even make a little bit of money sometimes. But we've learned a lot about horses by being involved in this business. And there's a really simple rule—you bet on the jockey.

You know, the horse is important, but you bet on the person in control. Let me get more specific from a business point of view.

If you have an "A" Team working at a company, just a really great group of managers handling a project, but the product is a "C" product, they're going to get great results from that product, or dump that product and get something else.

Conversely, if you have an "A" product, just an incredibly great product, but you've got a "C" group of managers, you're going to end up with mediocre results. I cannot stress this enough.

It's the quality of the management that you should be investing in, specifically if it's in a limited partnership. Traditionally in limited partnerships there's a limited base, there's a limited number of people. There's really no secondary market place to sell all of your units in a partnership, and if you do, you usually have to take a big hit. In a limited partnership, because you're very limited, you've got to make sure that the general partner, the people handling the company, are of top-notch character and quality, and have good experience. So, you bet on the jockey in the company.

When I'm reading about any company that I want to invest in, I'm always reading about the managers. And, by the way, that's one of the reasons why I like to read *Forbes* magazine, because I'm always reading about people in there. I'd much rather read about the people behind the company than the company itself, because that tells me so much about where it's going, what their drive is, what their ambition is, what their priorities are, and what their future will be.

36

Stock Options

This strategy is about stock options. In order to give you a good comparison I want to use a real estate example. Let's say that you find a property that could be worth, if it were all fixed up, $150,000 to $160,000. You could pick it up right now for $120,000, but the seller wants $50,000 down. You don't have the money now. So you propose a different alternative.

You get an option to buy the property. You say, "How about if I give you $3,000, or even $5,000 cash right now, and I will buy the property from you within six months for $130,000." Well, he was willing to sell it for $120,000 right now, but can he wait six months and get $130,000? He's willing to do that. Plus, you're paying him $3,000, or $5,000 for that right. Now, if the option time comes and goes and you don't buy the property, you forfeit your $3,000 or $5,000.

There are really two plays here—one play would be for you to take possession of the property, or just to scrape together the financing or whatever to buy the property, within the allotted time. The second play would be for you to sell your right to buy the property, or to sell your option to someone who does have the money right now.

The way this would work would be something like this: somebody else, maybe a builder, a remodeler, someone who wants to buy that property is willing to pay you cash to take over your option. You paid $5,000 for the option, and now someone is willing to give you $10,000. So they give you a check for $10,000. You assign your option and you're out of the deal. An option is a right to buy something within a certain period of time at a specific price.

Let's talk about stock options. When I talk about stock options don't get turned off by the word "options." We're not talking about pork belly futures. We're not talking about cattle futures. We're talking about options on a particular stock. I'm going to demonstrate two ways of making money with this, and also two ways of keeping out of trouble, which is the other side of that same coin.

Before we can do this I need to give you a quick little vocabulary lesson about options and I'll define that word again: it's the right to buy or sell a stock at a set price (called the strike price) before a specific date. Here are some other words to define. The word "call" means the right to purchase a stock at a fixed rice. A "put" is the right to sell a stock at a fixed price. So, when we talk about calls and puts, now you know what we mean. A call is the right to buy. A put is the right to sell.

Now for a little strategy: you buy a call on a stock if you think that the stock is going up. You buy a put if you think the stock is going down. For example, let's say Ford Motor Company is trading around $25 a share, and you think that it's going to $30.

We could spend 25¢ per share right now for the right to buy Ford stock at $30 before June of this year. Let's say that's two or three months away. What you've done now is you've paid 25¢ to buy the stock at $30. If the stock goes to $33 or $34, you make a killing, because you have the right to buy the stock at $30. You're paying a small amount of money to get the right to buy a stock at a set price.

Now, a put is exactly the opposite. Let's say that you think Ford is going to go down, so you sell a June put for 50¢ at $25. If the stock goes down you have the right to sell or put it to someone else. And that's the exact phraseology that's used. To "put it to someone." If the stock goes down to $22 you've got the right to sell it to someone at $25. You see the point? You make the $3 difference per share.

The next thing we need to discuss on options is that all options are done in 100 share increments. These 100 share increments are called a contract. So, in our example, when I say 25¢ I really mean $25, because it's always times 100.

So every time I mention a penny number, $1, $1.25, $1.35 or whatever, you always need to add a couple of zeros to make it 100 shares.

The "strike price" is the price at which you agreed to buy it or sell it. The word "premium" refers to money that you receive or spend in purchasing the call or in selling the call. The expiration date of an option always refers to a particular month, and your option expires on the third Saturday of the month. The stock market is not open the third Saturday, so it's effectively the third Friday at 4:00PM Eastern time, when the stock market closes. That will be the expiration date for all intents and purposes.

Let me show you how this works. You, with a small amount of money, want to purchase Ford stock. Now, I'm going to show you a couple of ways of making money. One way of making money is new. You hear that Ford is doing really, really well, or you hear that the sales are really, really bad, and you think that the stock is going to go up or down. If you think it's going to go up you may buy that Ford $30 call at 25¢. Remember that 25¢ is $25, and that controls a contract of 100 shares. Let's say that you bought ten contracts—ten times $25 would be $250. So you spend $250 right now, and Ford starts to move. It goes from $25 to $26 to $27.

Another quick point: sometimes there's a small movement in the stock based on market sentiments. Let me give you some background on market sentiments. Options, obviously, are risky. If you purchase stock in Ford, that's called a long position. Whether the stock goes down to $23, or up to $26, or whatever, you still own the stock.

With an option, because it expires, it is what is called a fixed time investment, or fixed time security. Because they're highly risky you may not even be able to trade them in your account. For example, you can't do options in IRAs. Now, you can sell Covered Calls, which is covered in point number 38, but you can't be out there risking a lot money with IRA money, with other Keogh plans, or Pension Plans.

Okay, so Ford goes from $25 to $26. Guess what? Your option also went from 25¢ to 50¢, to 75¢, up to $1. When there's a small movement in the stock, and if there's still plenty of time before the option expires, then the option is going to move in a magnified amount either up or down. So when Ford goes up only $1, from $25 to $26, if there's still plenty of time and there's a lot of market sentiment that it's really going to go well. If new earning reports are going to come out and the company is going to fly, then the option's worth may go from 25¢ to 50¢ to 75¢.

Well, Ford only went up $2, but your option went up from 25¢ to 75¢. Let's go back over our numbers—you bought ten contracts at $250, if the option goes up to 75¢ you have just tripled your money. If you sell, you get back $750. So you have a $500 profit.

I am not going to go over all the different option strategies here. There are more advanced courses that we offer if you're really into the stock market strategies. Then you may want to buy some tape sets and other books that I've put together to help you really get into this, because there are some really cool ways of making money.

I have only a small percentage of my money invested in options at any one time because options are risky. For example, three months ago I had about $5,000 invested, and lost $4,000 on different plays, but I made $18,000. Last month I had the $5,000 invested, and I lost $2,000 and made $22,000. I am constantly looking for news driven options.

Another quick point, this time regarding margin accounts. You know, this is where you are able to put $10,000 into a brokerage account with your stockbroker, and then have the right to buy $20,000 worth of stock. Well, you can't margin your accounts with options. Cash on cash, dollar for dollar.

By the way, options trade into your account in one day. So, when you buy options you have to have the money in your account within one day, and when you sell them, you get the money back into your account in one day.

$\mathbb{I}$ was teaching seminars about Rolling Stock, and people were getting really excited. In one class I had a person who

37

Rolling Options

would said, "Wade, we subscribe to WIN—Wealth Information Network—your internet subscription service, and every time we read about you doing Rolling Stock, we do Rolling Options on that."

I started looking, and I said, "Well, let's look at this." Think this one through: what if you have a stock that goes from $6 to $8, like a Rolling Stock? We've had several of those that have done that. One gold mining stock dipped down around $5.

Let's run through some numbers. Let's say you buy 1,000 shares at $5. That's $5,000. The stock goes up to $5.50 or $6, and then you sell it. It may even go back up to $7.50 or $8. But you sell it for $6 a share and you profit $1,000, minus your commissions. Instead of buying the stock, let's consider buying some options on the stock.

Options are sold in $2.50 increments up to $25. They start at $2.50, then they go $5, $7.50, $10, $12.50, $15, $17.50, $20, $22.50, and finally $25. After $25 they go up in $5 increments—$30, $35, $40, $45, $50, et cetera. (Once in awhile, if there's a lot of stock being traded and options being traded, you may see an option for $27.50 or $32.50, but not very often.)

The stock is around $5 and you buy an option to buy that stock at $7.50. Let's say right now that the option costs 25¢. Again, 25¢ times 100—remember we always do it in 100 share increments—is $25. Let's buy 20 of them. I want to give you a comparison here.

In our first example we spent $5,000; let's spend $500 and see the difference. So, we buy 20 contracts at 25¢ each—$500. Remember, when there's a slight movement in the stock there's a magnified movement in the options, so you watch this now.

The stock goes from $5 to $5.25 up to $5.50. Now, the stock is only budging. It's only moving up a little bit—$5.50 or $6 a share. But now the option goes from 25¢ to 50¢ to 75¢. Well, let's say it hits 50¢, goes on to 75¢, and you sell the option.

Now, you're not really buying the option so you can buy the stock. You're really just playing the option. Just like we did back in real estate, you're going to buy the option and sell the option. So you sell out at 75¢. Remember, the stock only went from $5 to $6, so you made $1,000 profit on doing the stock.

Your 20 contracts at $75—75¢ times 100 equals $75—which equals $1,500. Now, you take away the money that it cost you to buy the option—$500. You now have $1,000 profit, minus your commissions. And, by the way, commissions on options are really small.

Either way you've made $1,000, but what's the advantage? Obviously, in options, you spent $500 to make $1,000 profit, as compared to spending $5,000 to make $1,000. This is the strategy that we use called Rolling Options. Why? Because we can watch a stock rolling up and rolling down. We get familiar with it. We know where it's heading. We get charts and diagrams on it, so we can really see what's happening, and we go in and leverage our money.

By the way, you can do both. Why not? If you have the cash, why not buy a couple thousand shares of stock, and also spend $500 or $1,000 on the options, and do both plays. I've made a lot of money both ways. Comparatively speaking now, I've made just as much money, or even more, rolling options as when I was just rolling stocks.

38

Covered Calls

This probably gets more excitement on the radio and TV talk shows that I've been doing recently, and at my seminars, than any other topic that I've ever covered. Because it is a cash flow topic, it literally means getting money hitting your account, bam, bam, bam. Every three or four weeks you've got more cash into your account. For all of you that have existing stocks, this is really good information.

By the way, I have become a student of this over the last several years. I spend hours upon hours studying writing Covered Calls, and I'm going to show you here what I actually do.

Many of you already own stock. What are you doing with it? You are owning it for what? Are you willing to sell it? Let's say you bought some stock at $14, $15, or $16 a share. Once in awhile it gets up to $18 or $19, but then it drops back down to $15, and you buy a little bit more.

Then you think it's really going to go because you hear some good news about the company, and it even gets up to $19.50 or $20, but then it drops back down to $17. I think we've all been there. I've been there on too many occasions.

I was buying a lot of this computer networking company. I owned 3,800 shares of this company at around $15, $16, and $17. I saw this company go up to $21 a share, back down to $19, then down to $18. It went back up to $20 again, and then went right back to $16 and $17, and I bought a bunch more at $16 and $17.

Quite awhile ago I said to my broker, "The next time this stock gets up to $20 I want to sell everything I have. It's not really a good Rolling Stock because it costs too much. The next time it hits $20 I want to sell it."

He said, "Wade, if you're willing to sell it at $20, then why don't you write a Covered Call on it right now?"

I'll say this right now, I'm going to say it in the middle, and I'm going to say it again: this strategy is so safe you can do it in an IRA. Now keep in mind, you can do no mismatches in an IRA. You can't do commodities, you can't do futures contracts—you can't do anything like that in an IRA, but you can write Covered Calls in an IRA.

Now, you obviously have to have a brokerage account to buy and sell stock and to buy and sell options. Remember, a call is the right to buy and a put is the right to sell. Expiration dates—remember all those words that we talked about—are all going to play right now because what we're going to do is sell an option. We're going to sell a call. We're going to give someone the right to buy our stock, and they're going to pay us cash for that right. I'll give you some actual examples here.

The company I'm talking about is Novell Computer. (Whether it's good for you at this point in time, whether it's a good company or not, I don't know. I don't make any recommendations at all. Call your own stockbrokers. Check out these companies. Do your own homework on these companies.) I bought this stock at $16 and $17, as I said before, and I was willing to sell this stock at $20.

And I asked by broker, "How much will it cost me to write an April call on my 3,800 shares?" Now you see, I'm not buying a call. I'm going to sell a call, and I'm going to receive cash in my account for that.

He said, "You can get $1 a share."

I said, "What? Hold it. You're telling me that I can get $3,800 cash for my 3,800 shares right now and sell a call and give someone the right to buy this stock from me at $20? I'm willing to sell it at $20 anyway."

Now, if you own a stock that you're not willing to sell, if you think a stock is really going to fly through the roof and take off, then you ought not to be doing this. You're locking in and giving someone the right to buy the stock from you at $20.

You don't know who's actually buying your stock because it's part of a big lottery, but the point is that I get $3,800 cash in my account now. It hits there the next day.

The word "covered" means that you actually own the stock, and the word "uncovered" means that you don't own the stock; what is called "going naked." I'm not really recommending that here at all, I'm talking about writing a Covered Call, which is just about as safe as anything you can do.

So let's review this: I bought a number of stocks at $16 and $17, and I am willing to sell them at $20, but right now, into my account, I can get paid $3,800 without selling them. That is $1 per share for the 3,800 shares that I own (minus a small commission) and gives someone out there, in Duluth, Minnesota, or Tallahassee, Florida, the right to buy the stock from me at $20. I'm perfectly happy to sell it at $20. What is my risk, and what is the risk of the other person?

My risk is that the stock could go up to $25 or $30 a share. See, my risk is what is called an "opportunity lost" risk. I risk losing out on some of my potential profits. But I was willing to sell the stock at $20. I don't care if it goes to $24 or $25.

Hundreds of millions of dollars are made by wealthy individuals and corporations writing Covered Calls.

The premium that is paid is yours to keep no matter what. If the stock goes up and you get bought out at $20, fine. If you bought the stock at $16, you sell it at $20, you have another $4 profit right there. Plus, you get to keep the $1 per share that you made as a premium for writing the Covered Call. If the stock goes down and you don't get exercised, or don't get called out on your stock, you still get to keep the premium. Let's say the stock drops down to $15 or $16. You're not going to get called out at $20. So you just get to keep the $1 per share.

Now, what is the other person doing? Why is somebody else buying these calls? You see, from somebody else's perspective, this Novell company is going to fly through the roof. They think it's going to go to $22, $23, or $24. They paid $1 for the right to buy this stock in a certain month at $20.

If the stock goes to $24 or $25, they've made a killing. They can buy a lot of the stock now at $20, their option is worth a lot more and the stock is worth a lot more. It's worth $24. See the point? Their risk, their gamble, their hope is that the stock is going to go up in value. It doesn't matter to us, because we're willing to sell the stock at $20. We're willing to get called out no matter what.

Let me explain a couple of strategies in regard to this. Strategy one is that you buy the stock on dips. Whenever the stock takes a little dip, you buy the stock, and then you wait just a little bit, and you sell the call on strength. See, with Novell, for example, if the stock is at $16 and $17, you'd buy it around $16, but as the stock gets to $17, possibly $18, and gets close to that $20, then the price of the option is going to go up. When you write the Covered Call, when you sell the call, you get a lot more money for it. So you buy on dips or weaknesses, and you sell on strength.

Another strategy: you could also write calls on stocks you own which you know are rolling. By the way, pretty much the only stocks that are optionable are over $5, so you're not using penny stocks. You can do this with many stocks that are over $5. The big companies, all have options available at different strike prices, at different expiration dates.

So you can shop around and you can say, "I want to write an April, or a May, or a June call." They're all on different cycles. Stocks don't have options available on every month of the 12 months, but you can pick months. You can pick your strike prices and you can shop around to get the premiums that you want.

I love Covered Call writing because it gets cash into the account. Before we go on, I've got to tell you about a couple more strategies. If you only have $10,000, or even only $1,000 or $2,000, you can get started doing this. And remember, even if you only have $2,000 in an IRA, you could start buying stock and then writing Covered Calls on the stock, getting paid cash to buy the stocks.

Now, from my experience over the last several years you only get exercised on your options 15% of the time. Now, if you're writing calls that are above where you bought the stock, then that's another profit center for you 15% of the time.

Let's talk about "in the money" calls, "out of the money" calls, and "at the money" calls. Let's say that you bought a stock at $6, and you were willing to write a call on this stock at $7.50. That would be an "out of the money" call. You see, you're out of the money by $1.50. You bought the stock at $6. You're willing to sell it at $7.50. That's an "out of the money" call.

However, you may think that this stock is not going to go very high. It's probably not even going to go to $7.50. I've done this, by the way, with several companies. You think the stock is going to go down to $5.50, or stay right around $6, or even go down to $4.50 or $5. So you buy the stock at $6, and instead of writing a $7.50 call, you write a $5 call.

Think about this. You're giving someone the right to buy the stock from you at $5. What are they willing to pay for that? They may be willing to pay $1 or even $1.50. Now, I sold a bunch of them recently at $1.25 on an airline company. Whether the stock was up or down, I get to keep the $1 or $1.25.

Let me give you an example: I buy 1,000 shares of stock at $6 a share—that is $6,000. Then I turn around and write— two or three weeks from right now—a call for $5. So, this is an "in the money" call. You see, the stock is already at $6, the call is at $5, so it's in the money by $1. I'm giving some-one the right to buy the stock from me at $5. They're willing to pay me $1.25 for that right. So if I get called out, if I get exercised on, the worse that can happen is that I'm at break even.

What happens if I don't get called out? I did this on about 18,000 shares of stock, and I got called out on 500 of them. So on the other 17,500, all the contracts I wrote, I got to keep the $1 on all those. I do this almost every month.

If you have a little bit of money to invest, like $20,000 to $40,000, and if you're not making $8,000 to $10,000 a month, then you're just not following this strategy. I really recommend, first off, that you get the booklet, *Characteristics and Risks of Standardized Options* by the Chicago Board Options Exchange Incorporated. It's a great little pamphlet. You need more information. You need to get into these words and the terminology, so you really have the information. An even more powerful source of information on options is the High Octane Options seminars by Steve Wirrick. These seminars teach you more about stock options than almost any-where else. You can get a seminar scheduled by calling 1-800-872-7411.

I'm going to show you a couple of strategies here, and work these numbers for you—this is the Wade Cook for-mula for doing Covered Calls. You see, I like to get 15 to 20% monthly returns. This is no joke, absolutely no joke. I get 20, 30 and 40% returns all the time. Let me give you an example. I'm going to walk you through several strategies here because this does involve having a margin account. Remember, in a margin account, if you have $6,000 worth of stock, you only had to put in $3,000 cash, because the brokers loan you the other half of that, the other $3,000.

Example A
Say there's a computer company out there with stock at $9.50 a share. Let's buy 1,000 shares of that. It's a lot of money, again, but let's buy 1,000 shares—that's $9,500. Now

you divide that by two. This is my formula. You take the stock price, times however many shares, you divide it by two because that's your margin account. You have $4,750 in your account—$4,750 plus a little bit in commissions.

You turn around and write a $10 call on that, for say three or four weeks from right now. Your $10 call premium is $1.25. You have 1,000 shares, so that lets you write ten contracts. You take ten times $125, remember, $1.25 times 100 times the ten contract equals $1,250. You spend $4,750 today, and you get back into your account $1,250 tomorrow. Now, this represents about a 20% return for three or four weeks.

Example B
Let me give you another one of my formulas: we bought a stock at $5.25. We bought 1,000 shares. So that's $5,250. (You have to have $2,625 in your margin account. Again, $5,250 divided by two equals $2,625.) Then I wrote a call on this company. Remember, I bought the stock at $5.25, but I wrote a call on this stock at $5, and I got $1.25 for doing so.

Yes, that's right, a phenomenal amount. So take a look at this again: $1.25 times 1,000 shares. If you want to do it the other way, you take ten contracts, remember that's 1,000 shares divided by 100 is ten contracts, but each contract is worth $125. So I got back into my account $1,250 on this account, which represents about a 45% return.

Now, if I do get called out on this second example, then I have to give back 25¢ of my profits. Remember, I bought the stock at $5.25, and I'm now selling it at $5. Again, this is writing a Covered Call, selling stock that you already own. Now let's go back up to example A.

In example A, where I bought that computer company, if I did get called out at $10 (remember, I have 1,000 shares), there'd be another 50¢ of profit. Right? Fifty cents, because I bought it at $9.50 and I'm selling at $10. Well, 1,000 shares times 50¢ is another $500. So instead of just having $1,250,

I now have $1,750 profit on my $4,750 investment. So, the worst thing that can happen is that I'm only going to make a 20% return, but the best thing is that I can make a 28% return on my money.

What's my risk? My risk is that the stock that I bought at $9.50 may go to $12, $13, or $14, and I've given the right to someone to buy it from me at $10. But hold it, I made a profit. Don't write Covered Calls unless you're going to make a profit.

Now, if you do these on margin, you can consistently, as long as the stock market stays fairly stable, make 15 and 20% monthly returns. I've given you two examples here. These are real examples of stocks that I have done. By the way, the way to get those 20% returns is to do it on margin.

Quick point: you can't do IRAs on margin. That still means that your $2,000, month after month after month, is going to earn you about $2,000 to $2,400 a year. I'm very serious about this. I took one IRA with a couple thousand dollars in it, and over a few years made $19,000 with $2,000. This is very real, and I do this all the time.

When I hear people arguing over getting 4% annual returns or 5% annual returns, and I'm showing them how to get 200 and 300% returns, it gets quite remarkable. Now, I'm going to give you a little assumption here, for all of you who are reading this and saying, "What is this all about?"

If you had $10,000, maybe even $15,000 or $20,000 that you could scrape together, and put into an account that could generate a 20% monthly return, that would generate somewhere between $2,000 and $3,000 a month. The average American family can live on about $3,000 a month. What I'm saying is that if you had $20,000 that you could put aside, and were consistently getting 20% monthly returns, you'd generate $4,000 a month in income, and you could quit your job. You could retire.

Think about having $20,000 and getting a paycheck every month. By the way, once the option date expires, then you could just tell your broker, "I need that check for $4,000." He sends it, and he's still got the $20,000 in there, so you write another Covered Call for the next month, and you pick up another $3,800 the next month, and another $4,000 the month after that.

If the stock goes up and you get called out, you even make some more money there, and now you can take that money and invest it in other accounts. I really like stocks in the $5 to $20 range. I've hardly ever been able to make Covered Calls work on stocks over $20. If you want 20, 25, or 28% a month returns, you need to stick to the lower priced stocks, not the $50 and $80 stocks.

I hope I have peaked your interest with Rolling Stock, Rolling Options, writing Covered Calls, Dividend Capturing, and some of these other great stock market strategies. Everything I teach is about building up your monthly income, because isn't that what you want more of? The income to spend more time with your families, income to give more to your church, income to do with your life what you really want to do.

I hope you will give some serious thought to the educational materials that I've mentioned here. I've put together more extensive and detailed stock market strategies including the Wall Street Workshop. You can come and spend some time with my instructors in class and see the actual examples and the actual confirmation orders. Also, read good books from people who are doing the deals. See the available resources for a suggested reading list. It will give you more in depth and detailed understanding of these strategies so you can immediately put them to work for you. Call 1-800-872-7411 for more information, so that you can get these strategies working for you.

SECTION FOUR

Section Four, like the section before it, is full of stock market strategies. These strategies are designed to help you create cash flow, increase your assets, and keep that wealth for your heirs and/or beneficiaries. Most of the ideas found here will not be found in other stock market books. These are strategies that I make incredible returns with and that I know work. If, after reading these sections, you want to learn more about my investment strategies, refer to the suggested resources at the back of the book.

Stock Market Strategies

Part Two

39

Investing In Corporate Bonds

This point is about investing in corporate bonds. If a company decides to raise money it has two choices. One choice is that it can give up some of its equity, or sell stock. The other choice is that it can go into debt. If it chooses to go into debt, once again, it has two choices. It can go into debt by doing a bond offering. The other option is borrowing money from a bank.

For many years now the banks have gotten very, very picky, and have even wanted a piece of the action. A lot of companies said, "Hold it. We would rather just do our own bond offering, and control the terms of this debt." Now, if a company does a bond offering, it, once again, has two choices. A bond offering can be with collateral, or it can be with no collateral.

Bond offerings with no collateral are called junk bonds. In order to entice people to invest in a bond, or debt that has no collateral, they would have to give a high rate of return. A lot of people would substitute security for these incredibly high yields on their investment, sometimes up to 16 and 17%. Now traditionally a collateralized bond is going to be in the 4 to 8% range, and a noncollateralized debt, or junk bond, will be in the higher ranges, like 9 to 13%. Now, think this one through because a company can change its position.

Let's say a company raises money with a junk bond, but it does really, really well. It builds up the asset base of the company. Then the debt becomes collateralized at some point in time, because there is enough equity, enough collateral in the company, to support the debt. Conversely, a company that has plenty of collateral could do a very, very poor job, go down in value, and the bonds that it has could become junk bonds in the future.

This is something that you have to weigh out, whether you want to invest in high quality corporate bonds, or junk bonds. I have made just about as much money in both. I haven't had any junk bonds that I've purchased that I lost money on. Some of them have gone down in value a little bit, but they went back up.

I like nice high grade corporate bonds, and yet this is not where I make a lot of money, because you're so limited on the yield that you can get. I would much rather make money taking more of an aggressive approach.

Make some basic decisions on what you will accept as collateral or security, and what you will not accept. Decide what kind of rates of returns you want to get, and what you're willing to trade off for that. Always remember to research the company before you buy any bond.

A city, like a corporation, may want to raise money. It has two choices. A city can give up some of it's equity: a city

40

Municipal Bonds

doesn't have any stock for sale, but it does have land and property for sale. A city can also go into debt. Now there's a dilemma. If a city goes into debt, to whom does it owe its allegiance? To the citizens of the city, or to the debtors? Cities did not want to pay a high interest rate to raise money on their bond offerings that they were going to impose on their citizenship. So they appealed to Congress many, many decades ago and got a special dispensation, wherein there would be no taxes on interest paid on these municipal bonds, or city bonds.

Some states even got into the picture. If you're a New York resident, you can not only get out of paying your federal income taxes on the income from New York State's bonds, but also your state income taxes. Some cities even have city income taxes; it's like a triple whammy now, because you can get out of paying taxes at the federal, state and city levels. As a result, municipal bonds have become very, very popular.

You can now even borrow on zero coupon municipal bonds. My recommendation is that you give some serious consideration to these municipal bonds, especially at a time in your life when you have high income and a need to get out of paying a lot of taxes. For example, in your 40s and 50s you may find yourself in the position of making really, really good money. You want to replace the asset base, for example your career or your job, with some investments. So the higher your tax bracket, the greater the yield on an investment.

Let me explain. A bond that has an interest rate of 5% could have a yield of 8 to 9%, depending on the tax bracket you're in. And, obviously, if you're in a tax bracket close to 40%, the yield is substantially higher. If you're in the 15% tax bracket, obviously, these municipal bonds are not that attractive as a form of investment, because the yields are not all that great. If you're happy with those kinds of yields, then go for it.

By the way, I'm going to ask you an interesting question. What do you say about just having $200,000 or $300,000 in municipal bonds, and not having to pay any taxes on all the income that you make from those bonds? That's your only source of income. Now, you may have to worry about some alternative minimum taxes, and things like that, but I just wanted you to think about that, because a lot of you are saying, "Wow, that would be nice."

How would it be to have $40,000 or $50,000 a year in income, and enough to pay your basic bills, and then not have to pay any taxes at all? You really ought to give a second thought to municipal bonds.

41

Invest In Debt

You can also invest in other kinds of debt. I've done these from time to time in the past, and I've made some pretty good money on them. I'll tell you where I make money on them.

For example, you can invest in mutual funds that buy bonds, and you can invest in mutual funds that buy government securities. You can invest in Fannie Mae and Ginnie Mae directly, and get returns on your money that way. There are companies out there that go after, in a factoring manner, receivables. I suggest you buy those. There are also some publicly traded companies where all they do is buy debt.

You could extend your reach by investing in companies that specialize in investing in debt. They collect paper, receivables and other kinds of debt. I do a lot of that, but not as much as I do in the stock market. When I say a lot of it, probably 2 to 4% of my portfolio right now is currently with debt, which is non-note debt, associated with real estate. I still like buying second mortgages and deeds of trust, and I have a few percentages of my whole portfolio invested in other kinds of debt, only because I like to have a balanced portfolio.

This one gets really exciting, especially for me as a real estate investor, and because I'm buying paper—you understand that paper is debt. Here I'll be discussing zero coupon bonds. These are United States Treasury Bonds that I'm talking about, specifically, and I'll tell you why in just a minute. For many, many years the United States would put out bonds, and across the bottom they would have a tear-off portion to return for the interest that was due for that three month, six month, or one year period of time. It was a coupon that you could turn in to a government agency or to a bank and get your money for it. Many brokerage houses in the 50s and 60s started cutting off these coupons and keeping the interest, and then they would sell off the bonds at a substantial debt.

42

Zero Coupon Bonds

So, for example, on a regular treasury bond you could buy a $20,000 bond for, say, $16,000. Over a 25 or 30 year period of time your $16,000 would grow and become worth $20,000. Now, if they take out all of the interest, this $20,000 bond could sell for as little as $2,000. I purchased some a short time ago for 8.5¢ on the dollar, which means I bought a $10,000 zero coupon bond for about $1,700. It will grow in value over a period of time.

Let me tell you why I like these. First of all, they're not getting that great of a return, you know, 7, $7^1/4$, $7^1/2$% returns on the money. As the returns go up, the bond prices go down, so sometimes I buy a bond for $1,500 cash. Then I wait for the yields to go down, and I can sell it for $1,800 or $1,900 and make a little bit of money that way. However, that's not my major play. Let me tell you why I use them. Let me show you one of the problems with them, and then I'll tell you how I use them.

First of all, if you buy a $20,000 zero coupon United States treasury bond, for $2,000, you need to watch out for something called phantom income. The IRS considers these liquid, because you could turn them in and get cash at any point in time. Therefore, they're going to make you claim the interest on the bond every year, even though you did not receive it.

You buy a bond for $2,000. It's going to be worth $20,000 at maturity. You're going to make $18,000. Let's say it's out there 30 years, just so we can keep the arithmetic simple here. If it's out there 30 years, you divide the $18,000 by 30 years, and you get $600 a year. You just take a standard, flat $600 a year, each and every year, and you have to claim and pay taxes on that, even though you did not receive the $600. Now do you understand why they use the term phantom income?

It's a bad deal, and it shouldn't be happening. So, the only good part about it is that at the end of the time, after you've paid taxes every year, 25 or 30 years down the road when you sell this bond you've already paid the taxes on it. If you're in a 15% tax bracket, maybe that's not going to hurt too much if you don't own too many of these. However, if you owned $200,000 up to $500,000 worth of these bonds, that could really be quite a substantial amount to pay in taxes every year, and you did not get any cash out of your investment to pay the taxes with. That's why they call it phantom income.

Where and how do you buy zero-coupon bonds? I like buying these bonds for my kids because they can be taxed in their tax bracket. I really like buying bonds in my IRA and in my pension accounts. I get a nice yield for some of the money that's there and not doing too much else, but one of the places that I really like them is for incentives or for kickers.

Now, I know that this is going to be tough for some of you to understand, but I'm a negotiator. I may be out buying a $20,000 second mortgage on a property, and the guy wants $10,000 cash or he wants even $12,000 or $13,000, but I'm offering $10,000 cash. He says, "No, I really want $15,000." And I say, "Well, how about if I give you $8,000 cash, and a $7,000 United States Treasury Bond. As you know, it's not worth that right now, because it'll pay off over a period of time. You'll get your whole $15,000—$8,000 cash right now and $7,000 in 15, 20, 30 years down the road."

You'd be amazed at how many people take this offer. By the way, please don't get me wrong. I've never traded a bond for somebody's equity in their house. I've traded a bond for *part* of somebody's equity, but it's hard trading bonds, which is debt, for equity—it's easier to trade debt for debt.

Sometimes people would rather have debt in the United States Government than on the second mortgage of a house in Albuquerque that they're leaving and they never plan to go back to. So, I like bonds as kickers.

Let me tell you about another one I saw a Cadillac dealer in Southern California do. (This could make some of you angry, but I found it interesting.) This Cadillac dealer was selling Cadillacs for $33,000 to $40,000, and he had an advertisement that said if you come in and buy a Cadillac this weekend he'd give you a $5,000 United States Treasury Bond, a zero coupon bond.

Now, customers would come in and negotiate on a $38,000 Cadillac. If they negotiated in good faith, with cash or whatever, with financing, they could probably get that Cadillac for $35,000. He wouldn't budge off the price, but he would give them a $5,000 bond if they bought the Cadillac—it only cost him $500 or $600 for the bond. So he paid $500 or $600 for the bond, gave it to the customer, and sold the Cadillac for the full price.

I've done this with my employees. I've had some sales contests, and instead of giving them a $500 or $1,000 bonus, I'll give them a $5,000 United States Treasury Bond that cost me $865 to buy. So I'm buying $5,000 for $865. Instead of giving a $1,000 bonus on a big sales contest, I'll give them a bond. So, I like bonds for incentives.

I also like them for one other thing—my retirement account. I love having bonds in there. Now let me tell you one angle to that; I think that those of you who are in your 50s and 60s will appreciate this. Understand that you can buy these bonds at different maturities.

Once you buy a $5,000 bond, you can buy in any increment you want at $1,000 levels. So you can buy a $13,000, a $9,000 bond or whatever you can afford, but there are $5,000 minimums, with $1,000 increments. If you're 50 years old, you can buy a bond that will mature at the age of 65. Now, this could be in your IRA. You could buy a bond next year, or even another one this year that will mature in fifteen years, when you're 66. And then you could buy another bond for $20,000, $30,000, or $40,000 that will mature when you're 67. This would provide income each year.

If you want to be a millionaire, you could go out and buy a million dollars of United States Treasury Bonds for, say, $100,000, and you will become a millionaire. Now it may take you 25 or 30 years to do that, but you will become a millionaire. Now, I don't know what the money is going to be worth at that point in time, but you will be a millionaire.

I also like the bonds in conjunction with my retirement accounts, because it gives me a lot of strength to realize that each year that I'm retired, I'm going to have a sum of money that will mature, and I won't have to pay any taxes on it at that point in time. If I take that bond out of my IRA and have not been paying taxes on it in that manner—the phantom income is not effective in an IRA— then I'll have to pay taxes when I pull it out of my IRA. Even with that, it's a great way to go.

Safe blue chip investing—I think everyone knows how to do this. You can just invest in the big companies, the blue chip companies. One time I went out and bought all 30 of the Dow Jones Industrial Average stocks; they change all the time, but I bought the 30.

43
Safe Blue Chip Investing

Most of the money that I make on a rapid basis, I make in rather small companies, but you can do safe blue chip investing. By the way, huge utility stocks of blue chip companies, have a great rate of return over the years as compared to smaller companies, mid-capped stocks, and the like. So you have to decide how aggressive you want to be. If you want to have very little worry with your investments, then invest in these kinds of companies. They have a tendency to continue to go up, because there are so many people that want to invest in them. It's a safe and good way to go, especially if you don't want to worry a lot or take a lot of risk. I like to own stock in big companies just for a safe portfolio.

Turnaround involves a little bit more of a risk and a little bit more gain, obviously. When I say turnaround, I mean a company that has been in existence for awhile, and for some reason—change in management, a change in market conditions, or whatever—has gone down in value. Usually it results in a lack

44
Turnaround

of sales, and the company goes down. You can find these companies all the time. Matter of fact, you'll have so much fun doing this.

Let's look at the following example of the New York Stock Exchange Composite Transactions. This can be found daily in the Money and Investing section of *The Wall Street Journal*.

NEW YORK STOCK EXCHANGE COMPOSITE TRANSACTIONS

	52 Weeks Hi	52 Weeks Lo	Stock	Sym	Div	Yld %	PE	Vol 100s	Hi	Lo	Close	Net Chg
	27 1/8	25	CarolPwr QUICS	CPD	2.14	8.1	...	14	26 3/4	26 1/2	26 1/2	– 1/8
	48 1/2	32	CarpTch	CRS	1.32	2.9	14	378	46 3/16	44 13/16	45 1/2	+ 11/16
	6 3/8	3 3/8	CarrGottstn	CGF		...	dd	15	4 15/16	4 15/16	4 15/16	+ 1/16
	32 1/4	23 1/2	♣ CarrAmRlty	CRE	1.75	5.8	29	791	30	29 3/4	29 15/16	+ 1/8
n	17	7 1/4	Carson A	CIC		...	...	26	12	11 3/4	11 3/4	– 1/4
	36 3/8	23 1/4	CarsnPirSct	CRP		...	19	389	35 13/16	35 1/8	35 3/4	+ 1/4
	19 3/4	10 7/8	CarterWal	CAR	.16	1.0	28	591	16 1/4	15 15/16	16 1/4	+ 1/8
	19 3/4	11 1/2	CascadeCp	CAE	.40	2.2	14	14	18 1/8	18 1/16	18 1/8	+ 1/16
▲	17 1/2	15 1/4	CascadeNG	CGC	.96	5.6	21	134	17 11/16	17	17 1/16	– 7/16
	71 1/2	45 1/8	♣ CaseCp	CSE	.20	.3	14	2349	68 3/8	67 1/4	68 3/16	+ 1 1/8
	11 3/4	6 7/8	CashAmInt	PWN	.05	.5	18	396	11 1/4	10 11/16	10 7/8	+ 1/8
▲	17 13/16	13	CastCooke	CCS		...	cc	241	17 15/16	17 11/16	17 7/8	+ 1/4
	5 11/16	2 1/2	CatalinaLt	LTG		...	dd	56	5	4 7/8	5	+ 1/8
	60	25 1/8	CatalinaMktg	POS		...	37	483	48 1/2	46 1/4	48 1/2	+ 2 3/16
	21	9	♣ CatellusDev	CDX		...	cc	774	19 5/16	19	19 1/8	– 1/8
s	61 5/8	33 3/4	Caterpillar	CAT	1.00	1.7	15	11228	59 3/8	57 13/16	58 7/16	+ 3/8
s	17 1/2	9 1/8	♣ CavlrHomes	CAV	.12	1.2	8	509	10 9/16	10 1/4	10 3/8	+ 1/8
	45 3/8	34 3/8	CedarFair	FUN	2.50	5.6	15	115	44 15/16	44 1/8	44 11/16	+ 11/16
	11 11/16	7 1/2	CentrEngy	CX	.80	7.2	13	1177	11 3/16	11 1/8	11 1/8	– 1/8
	33 5/16	25 3/4	♣ CenterptProp	CNT	1.68	5.1	27	111	32 5/8	32 1/8	32 5/8	+ 1/2
	31 1/2	14 3/8	CentexConstr	CXP	.20	.7	14	371	29 3/16	28 11/16	29	+ 3/8
	59 3/4	29 7/8	Centex	CTX	.28f	.5	15	1462	55 3/4	54 3/16	54 15/16	+ 9/16
	28 1/8	18	CentlSoWest	CSR	1.74	8.4	10	3477	20 3/4	20 9/16	20 3/4	+ 1/16
	26 3/16	18 3/8	♣ CentlErpnFd	CEE	1.92e	8.0	...	399	24	23 5/8	24	+ 1/4
	28 1/4	25 1/2	CentlHispano prB		2.36	8.5	...	10	27 3/4	27 3/4	27 3/4	– 1/16
	28 7/8	27	CentlHispano prA		2.63	9.4	...	10	28	28	28	+ 1/16
	34 3/4	29	♣ CentlHudGE	CNH	2.14f	6.4	11	252	33 1/2	33	33 3/8	...
	29 1/4	24 3/4	♣ CentlLaElec	CNL	1.58	5.9	14	684	26 3/4	26	26 11/16	+ 7/16
	13 9/16	10	CentlMePwr	CTP	.90	7.0	11	1549	13	12 3/4	12 15/16	+ 1/4
	76 1/4	36 3/8	CentlNews	ECP	.76	1.1	23	679	69	68	68	– 1/16
	49 3/8	23 7/8	CentlPrkng	PK	.09	.2	47	506	45 3/4	44 1/4	45 1/8	– 5/8
	3/4	7/32	CnTrnpRtl	TPH		...	...	323	3/4	11/16	3/4	+ 1/16
	13 1/8	10 3/8	CentlVtPS	CV	.88	7.3	9	232	12 1/8	12	12 1/8	+ 1/16
	23 9/16	16 7/8	♣ CentrisGp	CGE	.24	1.1	9	110	22 3/16	22 1/8	22 1/8	– 1/16
	58 5/8	35 1/4	♣ CenturaBk	CBC	1.08	1.8	22	384	58 1/2	56 3/4	58 1/2	+ 1 5/8
▲	37 7/8	28 1/2	♣ CenturyTel	CTL	.37	1.0	13	1204	38	36 7/16	38	+ 1 11/16
	53 1/8	29 1/2	♣ Ceridian	CEN		...	15	7390	35 3/8	34 11/16	34 13/16	+ 1/4
	23 1/4	13 3/4	♣ ChampEnt	CHB		...	17	793	17 3/4	17 1/4	17 11/16	+ 7/16
	63 1/2	40 7/8	ChampInt	CHA	.20	.3	dd	2783	60	59 1/4	59 15/16	+ 3/4
	9 3/4	4 1/8	ChartHousEnt	CHT		...	dd	69	8 7/8	8 13/16	8 13/16	+ 1/16
s	21 3/8	10 1/16	♣ ChartInd	CTI	.24	1.2	18	179	20 15/16	20 5/16	20 9/16	+ 1/2
▲	34 3/8	23 1/4	ChartwellRe	CWL	.16	.5	13	93	34 1/2	34 1/4	34 1/2	+ 1/4
	28 9/16	16 3/4	♣ ChaseInd	CSI		...	12	12	27	26 3/4	27	+ 1/8
	115 13/16	72 7/8	ChaseManh	CMB	2.48	2.2	15	20851	114 1/16	110 5/8	113 3/4	+ 2 9/16
	29 1/2	27 5/8	ChaseManh pfA		2.63	9.1	...	115	28 7/8	28 11/16	28 3/4	...
	29	27 1/8	ChaseManh pfB		2.44	8.7	...	5	28 1/8	28	28	+ 1/16
	31 5/8	29 1/2	ChaseManh pfC		2.71	8.7	...	72	31 1/4	31 3/16	31 3/16	+ 1/16
	26 5/16	24 3/4	ChaseManh pfF		2.08	8.2	...	42	25 7/16	25 3/8	25 3/8	...
	31 1/2	29 1/4	ChaseManh pfG		2.74e	9.0	...	5	30 3/8	30 3/8	30 3/8	+ 1/8
	26 1/8	24 1/8	ChaseManh pfI		1.98	7.8	...	1	25 7/16	25 7/16	25 7/16	+ 1/16
	26 1/2	24 1/4	ChaseManh pfJ		1.90	7.4	...	359	25 3/4	25 11/16	25 3/4	+ 1/16
	26 1/4	24 1/4	ChaseManh pfK		1.88	7.3	...	48	25 7/8	25 7/8	25 7/8	...
	26 7/8	25 3/8	ChaseManh pfM		2.10	8.1	...	2	26 1/16	26	26 1/16	– 1/16
	25 1/2	21 5/8	ChaseManh pfN		1.45e	5.7	...	175	25 5/16	25 5/16	25 5/16	...
n	26 9/16	24 1/4	ChaseCap pfA		2.03	7.8	...	193	26	25 7/8	25 15/16	– 1/16
	31 1/8	23 7/8	♣ ChateauCmnty	CPJ	1.72	5.7	30	170	30 1/4	30 1/16	30 3/16	+ 1/16
	3 1/8	1/2	Chaus	CHS		...	dd	18	1 7/16	1 3/8	1 3/8	...

	52 Weeks Hi	52 Weeks Lo	Stock	Sym	Div	Yld %	PE	Vol 100s	Hi	Lo	Close	Net Chg
	26 3/4	25	Comdisco pfA		2.20	8.8	...	17	25 3/16	25	25	...
	26 5/8	24 1/4	ComEd TOPrS		2.12	8.3	...	79	25 5/8	25 1/2	25 5/8	+ 1/16
	76 1/4	48 1/8	Comerica	CMA	1.72	2.4	19	1540	73	70 7/8	73	+ 2 3/16
n	20	15 1/2	CmfrtSysUSA	FIX		...	...	467	18 1/4	17 7/8	18 1/8	+ 5/16
	38 7/8	23 3/16	ComrcBcpNJ	CBH	.80b	2.1	17	86	37 1/2	37	37 1/2	+ 1/2
n	26 1/2	25 1/8	CommCap 8 3/4%		.68p	...	...	7	25 3/4	25 5/8	25 3/4	...
	29 1/8	20 7/8	CommrcGpInc	CGI	1.04	3.6	13	113	28 5/8	28	28 5/8	+ 11/16
s▲	42 1/16	25 5/8	ComrclFed	CFB	.28	.6	21	500	44	42 1/16	44	+ 1 15/16
s	17 3/8	9 3/4	ComrclIntech	TEC	.54	3.2	13	471	17 3/8	16 5/8	16 7/8	+ 1/8
	33 1/2	27 1/8	ComrclMtls	CMC	.52	1.7	12	196	31	30 15/16	31	+ 1/4
	16 3/8	13 3/8	ComrclNetRlty	NNN	1.20	7.5	13	685	16 1/16	15 3/4	16 1/16	+ 5/16
	25 1/4	23	ComwEd pfC		1.90	7.6	...	795	25 1/4	24 7/8	24 7/8	– 1/8
	26 1/2	24 3/8	ComwEd pfD		2.00	7.7	...	103	25 13/16	25 11/16	25 13/16	+ 1/8
	26 1/4	18 7/8	ComwEngy	CES	1.58	6.3	9	209	25 1/8	24 3/8	25 1/8	+ 1/2
n	19	15 1/16	Commscope	CTV		...	...	2792	17 3/8	17 1/16	17 1/16	– 3/16
n	19 9/16	14 3/8	Copel	ELP		...	...	855	14 11/16	14 1/2	14 9/16	+ 3/16
s▲	68 3/4	21 3/4	Compaq	CPQ		...	34	89847	69	66 13/16	68 1/2	+ 3
	18 1/4	7 3/4	ComprehnCr	CMP		...	dd	80	11 11/16	10 7/8	11 1/8	– 7/16
s	32 3/8	13 1/4	CompUSA	CPU		...	32	3471	32	31 1/16	31 7/8	+ 15/16
	71 13/16	37 1/4	CptrAssoc	CA	.10	.1	66	11121	69 7/8	68 5/16	69 1/2	+ 2 5/8
	86 1/2	57 7/8	♣ CptrSci	CSC		...	29	2178	75 7/8	74 1/2	74 7/8	+ 1/2
s	**49 3/16**	**13 15/16**	**♣ CptrTask**	**TSK**	**.05**	**.1**	**59**	**1029**	**47 1/4**	**44 13/16**	**47**	**+ 2 5/16**
	10 3/8	**2 3/8**	**Cptrvision**	**CVN**		**...**	**dd**	**1304**	**2 5/8**	**2 3/8**	**2 3/8**	**– 1/8**
s	24 3/8	16 5/8	Comsat	CQ	.20	.9	dd	811	21 3/4	21 3/8	21 9/16	– 1/8
	25 3/4	24 1/8	ComsatCap pfA		2.03	8.1	...	54	25 3/16	25 1/16	25 1/8	+ 1/16
	14 5/8	6 5/8	ComstkRes	CRK		...	9	1261	12 5/8	12 1/4	12 9/16	+ 5/16
	27 1/2	25 1/2	ConagraCap pfA		2.25	8.6	...	17	26 3/16	26 1/16	26 1/16	– 1/16
	23	21 1/16	ConagraCap pfB		1.59e	7.0	...	26	22 15/16	22 13/16	22 7/8	+ 1/16
	27 1/2	25 9/16	ConagraCap pfC		2.34	8.8	...	58	26 9/16	26 7/16	26 1/2	– 1/16
	71 5/8	41 1/2	ConAgra	CAG	1.09	1.6	25	5493	66 1/2	64 1/16	66 3/8	+ 1 15/16
	9 1/2	7	♣ ConeMills	COE		...	dd	990	7 15/16	7 7/8	7 15/16	+ 1/16
	14 7/8	10 1/2	Congoleum A	CGM		...	10	51	11 7/8	11 1/2	11 7/8	+ 3/8
	24 3/4	19 5/8	♣ ConnEngy	CNE	1.32	5.4	14	43	24 5/8	24 5/16	24 5/16	– 1/4
s▲	**43 7/8**	**20 1/2**	**Conseco**	**CNC**	**.50f**	**1.1**	**20**	**13888**	**45 15/16**	**43 1/2**	**45 7/8**	**+ 2 7/8**
▲	**154 1/4**	**77 5/8**	**Conseco PRIDES**		**3.00**	**1.9**	**...**	**129**	**155 7/16**	**151**	**155 7/16**	**+ 9 7/8**
n	26 5/8	24 7/16	Conseco TOPrS		2.29	8.7	...	52	26 1/4	26 1/8	26 1/4	+ 1/16
	35 7/16	21 1/2	ConsolCigar A	CIG		...	25	170	33 3/4	33	33 7/16	+ 5/16
	32 1/8	25 7/8	ConEd	ED	2.10	6.7	11	3430	31 1/4	30 5/8	31 1/4	+ 5/8
	74 3/4	66 1/4	ConEd pf		5.00	6.8	...	1	73 1/2	73 1/2	73 1/2	– 5/8
	25 3/8	23 3/4	ConEd QUICS	EDL	1.94	7.7	...	202	25 1/4	25 1/8	25 1/4	+ 1/16
s	53 1/2	10 13/16	ConsolGraph	CGX		...	50	353	49	48 5/8	48 7/8	+ 3/8
▲	59 3/4	47 3/8	ConsNatGas	CNG	1.94	3.2	19	1424	59 15/16	59 1/16	59 15/16	+ 7/8
	60 9/16	47 1/8	ConPaper	CDP	1.68	2.8	19	304	59 1/4	58 7/16	59 3/16	+ 7/8
s	19	12 61/64	ConPdts	COP	stk	...	19	192	18 3/16	17 15/16	18	...
s	40 3/4	22 15/16	ConsStore	CNS		...	40	3287	38 1/2	37 13/16	38 3/8	+ 15/16
	61	49	ConsEng pfA		4.16	7.2	...	1	58 1/8	58 1/8	58 1/8	...
	26 7/16	24 1/2	ConsEng pfI		2.08	7.9	...	203	26 77/256	26 1/4	26 77/256	– 1/16
	25 3/4	24 1/4	ConsEng TOPrS		2.09	8.3	...	17	25 7/16	25 5/16	25 5/16	– 1/16
	40 1/2	26 3/8	Contifnl	CFN		...	13	315	33	32 7/8	33	+ 1/8
	40	21	ContlAirln A	CAIA		...	6	17	37	36 7/8	36 15/16	+ 5/16
	40	21 1/8	ContlAirln B	CAIB		...	...	3402	37 1/4	36 3/4	36 13/16	+ 3/16
	23 15/16	10 3/4	ContlCan	CAN		...	15	246	20 5/16	20	20	+ 3/16
	23 3/4	15 3/8	ContlHomes	CON	.20	.9	6	836	23 5/8	23 1/16	23 3/8	+ 3/8
n	21 11/16	13 3/8	CntrldrCom Gdr	MCM	.14p	...	...	241	21 1/16	20 1/4	21 1/16	+ 15/16
	28	6	Converse	CVE		...	cc	1368	12 1/4	12	12 1/8	– 3/16
	13 3/8	9	CookerRestr	CGR	.07f	.7	14	288	10 11/16	10 3/16	10 1/2	+ 5/16
s	66 7/8	26	CooprCamrn	RON		...	dd	1430	66	64 5/8	65 7/8	+ 1

You'll look in the high and low column—the 52 week high and low. (I don't think that the 52 week highs and lows tell you very much, because you don't know what the company was doing 53 weeks ago. You just don't know that much about it, but it's a start. It's a start, telling you that there's something interesting going on with this company.)

If you see a company that has a high of $18 and a low of $2, and it's currently trading around 2\frac{1}{2}$, that is when you start doing some research. The company's obviously had a lot of growth, because it's been up to $18 before. Why is it at 2\frac{1}{2}$ a share right now? Maybe it's in bankruptcy, or has been; maybe it's had a lot of problems, and it's working out of those problems. I look for companies to turn around.

What I look for, again, is the story line. What are the fundamentals? What's the management like? What's the debt like? What is the cash flow? What's it doing? How is it expanding? How is it growing? And, ironically, sometimes when you see these companies turning around, they expand by going into debt.

Now, you would think that when a company announces that it's going to buy 30 more planes, or expand two new gates, or when a company is going to open up 17 new stores, that the stock would immediately go up. Usually the opposite is true. Usually when a company makes an announcement that it's going to expand, the stock goes down. Why? Because usually, not always, but usually it incurs debt to do that, and when a company incurs debt, a lot of the investors get worried and discount the stock.

Let's go back to these turnarounds. If you look in the newspaper and you see a high and a low of $18 and $2, respectively, and the stock is currently at 17\frac{1}{2}$, you see that there's not much room to grow. That doesn't tell you very much, because you may buy it at 17\frac{1}{2}$, and it may grow to $20, $25, or $30, depending on where the company is heading. Do you have a better chance of making money by buying it at 2\frac{1}{2}$ and hoping it goes back up to it's high, or even half of its high? You could double, triple, or quadruple your money. I like turnarounds; I go looking for turnarounds. I subscribe to newsletters that talk about turnarounds because I want to get involved in the excitement and the enthusiasm.

I like companies that are in Chapter 11 bankruptcy. They're news driven companies. The value of the stock usually has nothing to do with where the company is, its asset base, or anything else. It has to do with the news of the day.

A bankrupt company is going to get a new loan; boom, the stock goes up. Well, the loan didn't go through; boom, the stock goes down. They're going to do a merger with this other company; boom, the stock goes up. The judge didn't like the deal, so he disapproved it and boom, the stock goes down. Do you see what I'm saying? They're news driven.

In *USA Today* if you see a little "vj" in front of the company name, that means that they're in Chapter 11 bankruptcy. You can also talk to your stockbroker about different companies that are in Chapter 11 bankruptcy. I'm not saying to exclusively invest in these, because they are a little bit scary.

The stock could drop out, and they could go to Chapter 7, and you could lose everything. But still, and I must admit that I don't invest in companies unless I've watched them for six months, I don't run out and buy it just because somebody tells me about a company that's trading between $2 and $4 a share.

Let me give you an old farming analogy. In the farm lands, when they would harvest a field and burn off the field, they would light the fire out in the middle of the field, so it would burn toward the edges. The heat is always on the edges. The heat is always in the expansion. Now, in real estate this meant to me that you would go to a downtown area, and as it died off, there would be suburbs being created, suburb after suburb after suburb, growing and expanding—the heat or growth was always on the fringes. Not until somebody would go back in and refurbish or redo the whole downtown area, would the fire start all over again in the down-town area and spread back out again.

I want to know about the companies that are on the fringes, that are heating up again. I enjoy watching compa-nies that are doing that—companies that have been very, very powerful before. They are a little bit slow right now, but they're coming up with new products, new ideas, new man-agement, and they're ready to make a rebound. I like turn-arounds. Sometimes a lot of them had to go through bank-ruptcy to get to the point that they were turning around to the level that I like them.

IPO strategies are also a great way to make money. Sometimes it's difficult to find information about IPOs—Ini-tial Public Offerings though, so they're a little more challenging. I've made mini-fortunes investing in these. I didn't make a fortune on any one company, because sometimes the stock is limited.

45
IPOs

Now just let me walk you through a process here. An IPO—it could be a secondary or tertiary offering on the com-pany—is an Initial Public Offering of that stock. So, a stock may be publicly traded, and the company wants to raise an additional 200 million dollars. To do this, it's going to sell off a couple million more shares of stock at $10 or $100 a share, or whatever. This is considered coming out with a new offer-ing. If you could buy that offering—it may also be a new class of stock—they usually, but not always, have a tendency to go up. There is a tendency, if it's been properly promoted, for the stock to go very high in value. So, a company coming out with an offering at $10 could have that stock, within a day or two, go up to $20 or $30.

When the company is private, and getting ready to go public, the insiders of the company, the President, Vice Presi-dent, and founders of the company, usually have a lot of stock in the company. Usually they have a total of about 50%, sometime as much as 80 and 90%, of the company's stock. This is called restricted stock, as compared to free trading stock, or registered stock. The stock that is free trading has been registered, and they can either do an IPO to raise money, or just register certain amounts of stock that the company has.

Wouldn't it be nice to find out about a company getting ready to go public and be able to be one of the insiders—one of the initial investors? You've probably heard about all those companies in Sunnyvale, Santa Clara, and San Jose, California—Silicon Valley—going public. What got them to the point they could go public? Well, what got them to that point was a lot of investors, or sometimes as few investors as three or four, putting up huge amounts of money. These investors would then own 30 or 60% of the company. The company would then go public, and these investors would be rewarded with sometimes five, ten and fifteen times their original investment in the company. Sometimes even more.

It'd be really nice to get involved in a company in the early, early stages of the going public process. Now, if the company is publicly traded and doing a new stock offering, then there are ways to find those, too. One way to find them is to read your local newspapers. If you have publicly traded companies in your local area, it's amazing how the newspapers find out they're getting ready to do an IPO. If they are getting ready to do an Initial Public Offering then you can contact your broker about getting some of the stocks when the IPO comes out. Another way is newsletters. There are a lot of newsletters that report on companies doing public offerings.

My experience with IPOs is that when the stock comes out, it immediately goes up for a day or two, sometimes three or four, and then it comes crashing back down to usually right around the offering price. A stock that comes out at $10 can immediately jump up to $20, but within a week or two you find it back down around $10 or $8 or $12 a share—somewhere around the initial. So, there are two times to get involved: one time would be the initial, when it does the run up, and the next time would be after it runs back down. Once it settles in at a price, start buying the stock again, at that point in time, watch whether it's going to roll, whether it's going to continue to grow in value, whether you have to worry about it or not, or whether you need to take an aggressive stance or not. Just remember, they go up, then they go down, and then they start climbing back up again, a lot slower than the first time around.

W hen a big company wants to spin off a smaller division or subsidiary company, you can get involved and make a lot of money. How do you find out about them? Well, you find out about these in some of the major newspapers. Obviously, your local newspapers will have the information if there's a large national company that's headquartered where you live, and they're getting ready to spin off one of the divisions. Usually that information is very, very common to a lot of people in the area. So you can find these companies in a variety of ways.

46

Spin Offs

Why are they good? Because that spin-off company almost always has experienced management, and the parent company spinning it off usually keeps a substantial amount of stock. They want it to do well, so they put proper and effective management in place, and usually that company is being spun off because it, in and of itself, has established a market niche. It knows it's competitors, it knows the good, the bad, and the ugly of the business world, and the parent company is ready to fly high and be a bigger company, realizing that one of it's children is ready to go. I've probably been involved in about 50 of them. I really go looking for spin-offs, because of the ease of making money with them.

47
Watch The Insiders

Learn to watch the insiders, the owners of the company. There are even newsletters that are insider watch dogs. If the insiders of a company start selling the stock, what does that tell you? Conversely, if the insiders of the company start buying the stock, what does that tell you? Well, obviously, when they're selling you want to be selling, and when they're buying you want to be buying. Why are they buying? Why are they selling? That's what you've got to find out. Is it just that they need money? It could have nothing to do with anything, except they need to raise some personal money. But when the insiders, based upon their percentage of ownership, start selling their stock, it'd be good to know that.

Would you want that information if you were getting ready to buy stock in a company? Would you want to know that the owners had just sold off 10% of their ownership? Would that have an effect on your decision to buy? Would that affect your decision to do some more research on the company? So, watch the insiders. Subscribe to the newsletters that will give you insider information, because they can tell you a lot.

48
7% Rule

The 7% rule. I've read about this for many, many years in *Forbes* magazine and other places, and it's very true. I've watched it myself, and I've noticed that every time there's a drop in the stock market of around 7, 8, possibly 9%, in any two calendar months, over the next three months after that there is an incredible rise. Now, over the last umpteen years that the stock market has dipped, 75 out of 80 times it has gone back up to near it's previous value, and above that.

One of the best indexes for watching this is the New York Stock Exchange Composite Index; start reading it, and just watch the drops in the stock market. Any time there's a drop for a two-month period of time—maybe it's just a minor correction, maybe it's the beginning of a recession, you don't know that, but if it's just a minor correction, after two months, the stock market starts to go back up, this is a good time to be investing in your blue chip stocks and your Dow Jones Industrial type stocks. They're the ones that are affected by this the most. So, when it takes a dip, realize that it's just going to go right back up.

I'm really not very big into annuities, so my advice here is going to be that you can save yourself a lot of time and grief by not investing in annuities, because they are just not what they're cracked up to be.

49

Annuities

Basically, an annuity is a product, usually provided by insurance companies, that allows you to invest your money tax free. You put in $5,000 or $10,000, and all the growth in the annuity is going to happen, and you're not going to have to pay any taxes on it. If that's what you're looking for, then go for it.

There are two types of annuities: there's a fixed income annuity, and there's a variable rate annuity. A fixed annuity invests in securities like government securities; your rate of return is fixed. A variable annuity has different mutual funds and products available to you, and you as the individual investor can choose. The rate of return you're going to get on the money held in the annuity is going to be based on you. It's up to you to get a good rate of return.

Who should go for annuities? Maybe high income tax bracket people, and also people who don't have any desire to really manage their money on a day to day basis. They may want to get involved in annuities so they can get growth tax free. Not me, though, I'm not into it for that. I would rather have my money working, and pay taxes on it. I would rather get a 20 or 30% return and pay taxes, than get a 7 or 8% return and not pay taxes.

If you get involved in annuities, you also need to understand your cost of getting out. Most of them charge a substantial fee if you get out before the annuity time is up, and you need to ask the annuity sponsor if you can borrow the money. If you cannot borrow the money, you may want to consider not investing in the annuity.

There are just a lot of negatives to buying annuities. I know there are a lot of insurance salesmen right now selling them, and there are a lot of people buying them. In fact, I've probably just popped your balloon, because you thought that it was such a hot deal and I don't like them. But, if you like them, go for it. I just have not seen them as a viable alternative to other ways of making money. So my recommendation is to keep your money working and making a lot more money in other places.

50

Investing In Currency

I'm going to be very detailed on this one. I really believe that the best currency in the world to have your money in is Swiss currency. I know that sounds weird, but the dollar has gone so far down in value. If any of you are worried about our national debt, our imbalance in trade, then you may want to have some of your money, not all of it, but some of your money held in a currency that is outside of the United States.

First of all, why Switzerland? For hundreds of years, Switzerland has had a very stable economy. It's also been a stable political scene when the world scene has gone through so much turmoil. This is especially true in the European part of the world. In Switzerland, the government requires the currency to be backed by 200% of the gold standard. Now think about what I just said here—200%. As you know, starting in 1929, the United States started to go off the gold standard. In 1962 and 1972 the United States fully went off the gold standard. Our currency is not backed by the gold standard.

By the way, just kind of a little fun sideline here, starting in 1950, our money was backed by dollar certificates. Previously the $5 and $10 bills had said gold certificate or silver certificate. When it wasn't backed by silver or gold, they took that phrase off the currency, and started putting the words on the back of the bills "In God We Trust."

Now, if you can't trust the gold and you can't trust the fact that Fort Knox has the gold, then you've got to trust in somebody, so why not choose God? It's kind of funny that at that point in time, a few years after they went off the gold standard, they added the words "In God We Trust."

When you invest in Swiss Francs, you may do so in a number of ways. One way would be through stocks held in Switzerland. Another way would be through bonds put out by the Swiss government.

Another way would be through Swiss annuities. Now, if you do that, then you are going to get a rate of return based on the type of investment that you choose. And, also, your currency is not going to be devalued like the dollar, here in the United States. Do you know that if you had $1,000 in United States currency 20 to 30 years ago, today that would have a buying power of approximately $376. Now, if you held $1,000 in Swiss Francs for the same period, today the buying power of it would be approximately $998.94. That is phenomenal.

If you'd put your money in there then and you converted it back today, it may be worth so much more than what it is worth today because the exchange between the Swiss Franc and the dollar goes down about 6% a year, or almost every year. So if you want to keep your value high, you should get a bank account or brokerage account opened up in Switzerland. It's not that complicated to do.

You may want to invest in currencies, directly, which do not have a rate of return. You just stop the devaluing effects of the dollar. Or you may want to invest in annuities, because the annuities that we're talking about are tax free annuities.

51

Stock Tax Credits

Stock tax credits is our next strategy. This is one of the most fun ones I'm going to show you. I don't know what your philosophical or political aspirations are, but I'll tell you what I think—I like keeping my money at home. I like it working for me, building up my companies, beautifying neighborhoods, and strengthening jobs. Now, we don't need to get off on any political discussions right now, but I want to show you some ways that you can save some money in taxes.

This is a stock tax credit. What I'm specifically talking about is Section 29 of the Internal Revenue Code. The companies that qualify for Section 29 are into recovering energy, as in oil or coal. For example, and I don't know if this will be a good company for you to invest in by the time you read this, look at a company called Williams Coal Royalty Trust—ticker symbol WTU. I found three of them that I like: WTU, TRU—ticker symbol for Torch Energy, and BRU—ticker symbol for Burlington Resources Coal. These are New York Stock Exchange companies.

These are not corporations, by the way, they are trusts. They're royalty trusts. When you invest in these companies you are buying stock. By the way, these companies will end 20 to 25 years out. I mean, there is a definite time. But while you own the stock they produce three things for you—income, depletion expense, and tax credits.

Now, let's think about real estate. If you buy real estate, you get growth, you get income, and you get depreciation expense. Well, in these royalty trusts you get the same things—you get income, you get a depletion allowance because the well or the mine or the field is going to deplete, and you also get tax credits. A tax credit is a dollar-for-dollar write off on the taxes that you actually owe.

So if you owe $30,000 in taxes, and you get a $10,000 deduction, that will affect your income level, and you'll save money. But if you owe $30,000 and you have a $10,000 tax credit, you'll save a lot more, because the $10,000 tax credit goes right against the $30,000 that you actually owe. So we have to be out there looking for tax credits. In order for you to understand this, I want you to look at the accompanying example.

The following example is an actual 1041 that I received from Williams. Now, I've owned a lot more stock than what you see represented, but this is in one tax credit company, and I bought 200 shares of stock earlier in the year. You're going to see the 200 shares of stock showing up on the front on the different quarters. This is the actual copy of the 1041 that I received.

On the front, you see all the different information that I need to put on my tax return. And, low and behold, if you look over to the back, as nice as this company is, they send me miniature copies of my actual IRS tax forms, with arrows showing where I'm supposed to place the information from the front side of the page.

About the middle of the page you see where I received income of about $300. Now if you take away all the deductions, it comes out that I have income of $330. I did receive that income, I actually had these dividends, or investment incomes, if you will, deposited in my account. I bought this stock at about $20 a share. So, I bought 200 shares, that's about $4,000, and received a profit of $330—not bad, that's about an 8 to 9% return.

WILLIAMS COAL SEAM ROYALTY TRUST
GRANTOR TRUST FORM 1041

DEAR UNITHOLDER:

ACCORDING TO THE INFORMATION PROVIDED TO NATIONSBANK, YOU HAVE OWNED
UNITS IN WILLIAMS COAL SEAM GAS ROYALTY TRUST ALL OR A PORTION OF
1994. THE CALCULATIONS BELOW ARE PROVIDED TO ASSIST YOU IN REPORTING
YOUR FEDERAL INCOME TAX CONSEQUENCES OF OWNING UNITS. THE INCOME AND
EXPENSE INFORMATION PRESENTED ASSUMES YOU USE THE CASH METHOD OF
ACCOUNTING AND REPORT YOUR TAXES ON A CALENDAR YEAR BASIS.

UNITHOLDER OF RECORD:

QUARTERLY RECORD DATE POSITIONS OF UNITS:

02-14-94	**0**	**05-16-94**	**200**	**08-15-94**	**200**	**11-14-94**	**200**

ITEM NAME OF ROYALTY		FORM 1040			
	LINE 1	PART 1	SCH. E	WILLIAMS COAL SEAM GAS ROYALTY TRUST	
GROSS ROYALTY INCOME	LINE 4	PART 1	SCH. E	$	374.78
SEVERANCE TAX	LINE 16	PART 1	SCH. E	(	34.41)
INTEREST INCOME	LINE 1	PART 1	SCH. B	$	0.93
ADMINISTRATION EXPENSE	LINE 18	PART 1	SCH. E	(	10.48)
NET CASH INCOME				$	330.82
RECONCILING ITEMS				(	0.47)
NET CASH DISTRIBUTED				$	330.35
DEPLETION (YOUR BASIS X FACTOR)	LINE 20	PART 1	SCH. E		*
FNS (SEC. 29) TAX CREDIT	LINE 45, "FNS", FORM 1040			$	305.08

*DEPENDING ON THE YEAR THE UNITS WERE ACQUIRED AND THE QUARTERS THE UNITS WERE
HELD, THE FOLLOWING QUARTERLY DEPLETION FACTORS SHOULD BE USED TO DETERMINE
DEPLETION FOR FEDERAL TAX PURPOSES REPORTING BY MULTIPLYING YOUR TAX BASIS BY
THE SUM OF THE APPROPRIATE FACTORS:

	1ST QTR	2ND QTR	3RD QTR	4TH QTR
1994	**0.040044**	**0.039425**	**0.039322**	**0.041797**

IF THE NUMBER OF UNITS ON ANY GIVEN RECORD DATE IS NOT CORRECT, THEN DISREGARD
THE FOREGOING CALCULATIONS AND COMPUTE YOUR INDIVIDUAL AMOUNTS FOR FEDERAL TAX
REPORTING PURPOSES USING THE QUARTERLY FACTORS SET FORTH BELOW AND DESCRIBED
IN MORE DETAIL IN THE TAX INFORMATION BOOKLET:

PER UNITS FACTORS:	1ST QTR	2ND QTR	3RD QTR	4TH QTR
GROSS ROY INCOME	0.659546	0.671629	0.676872	0.525397
SEVERANCE TAX	-0.063143	-0.073748	-0.048202	-0.050122
INTEREST INCOME	0.001270	0.001469	0.001949	0.001238
ADMIN. EXPENSE	-0.011508	-0.012313	-0.025012	-0.015063
RECONCIL ITEMS	-0.001379	-0.008935	0.006971	-0.000401
NET CASH	0.584786	0.578102	0.612578	0.461049
FNS TAX CREDIT	0.503702	0.512286	0.494438	0.518701

THIS FORM 1041 IS PROVIDED FOR YOUR INFORMATION ONLY. THIS FORM SHOULD NOT
BE ATTACHED TO YOUR TAX RETURN. THIS FORM WILL NOT BE PROVIDED TO THE IRS
BY THE TRUSTEE. FOR ALL STATE TAX REPORTING, YOU SHOULD REFER TO THE TAX
INFORMATION BOOKLET. FOR ANY ADDITIONAL ASSISTANCE, PLEASE CONTACT THE
TRUSTEE AT 1-800-365-6544.

Form 1040 – Back Side

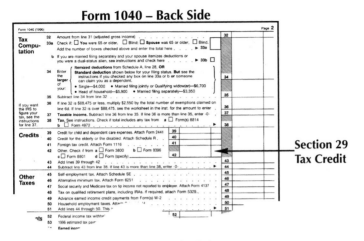

Section 29 Tax Credit

Schedule B

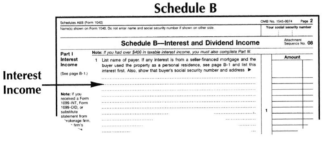

Interest Income

Schedule E

Name of Royalty Trust

Royalty Income

Severance Tax

Administrative Expenses

Depletion

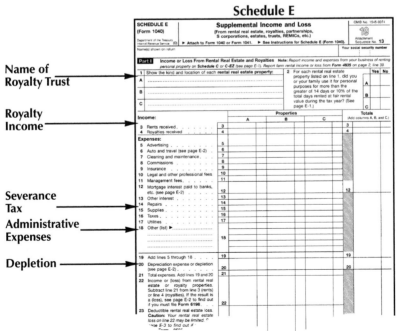

Now I want you to see the next line. Just look down a little bit further. Let's say that's you now, you're at about a 30% tax bracket—30% of $330 equals about $100. You owe the IRS $100 on the income that you received. Now just go down a couple more lines, though, and you see where it says "Section 29 credit." Well, my Section 29 credit for the same investment, based on the number of shares I own, is $305. Now think about that: I had a tax credit of $305 that I can use against the $100 that I owe on the $330 of income that I received. That gives me $205 extra in tax credits that I can use against taxes on income from other sources. I wish I would have bought a lot more of the stock in this company.

Right after the first of the year, when I actually got into this 1041, I purchased several thousand more shares of stock in these companies, and in all my different corporate accounts, and I'm going to continue to do so. Every time they take a little bit of a dip I'm going to buy some more.

In buying these kinds of credits, I am not getting 20 and 30% returns a month. The equivalent yield, when the stock gets down around $16 or $17, is about 22, 23, and 24%. Not bad for a New York Stock Exchange company—nice safe company, and bam, you get income, you get credits, and you also get some depletion allowances, which I haven't really even covered here. Think about investing for tax credits. Go out looking for these Section 29 or Section 42 tax credits, where you can take the credits directly against the taxes that you owe on your investment income. Boy, what a great way to go.

52

Diversified Investment Strategy

You can blend strategies and get a diversified investment strategy custom tailored for you, and this is based on where you are. I've read a lot of these life insurance type, annuity type reports that are trying to sell people different kinds of investments. They talk about the accumulation stage—ages 20 to 40; the maintenance stage—ages 45 to 60 or 65; and then the retirement stage which is 65 and on. They then ask, "Where are you? Are you in the accumulating stage, are you in the maintaining stage, or are you retiring or getting ready to retire?" Then they try to sell people different kinds of products for different stages of their lives.

My apologies to all life insurance agents and annuity agents out there, but I come from the real world. Thousands of people come to my seminars every month. I travel all around the country, and I get to talk to people who are facing real problems in the real world. I see 70 year old people starting all over in life with nothing. I see a 55 year old husband and a 52 year old wife getting a divorce after going through a disastrous bankruptcy, and not having anything. I see people who are 28 years old making $200,000 with their businesses, that should be made by people who are older.

Nothing makes sense anymore, because no age group fits, whether you're in accumulation, maintenance or retirement stage. Now, I will make one case for this—of all of the people I've met, everyone needs more cash flow. Everybody needs more monthly income. J. Paul Getty, the richest man in the world when he died, had a pay telephone in his home for his guests to use. We all need more cash flow.

By the way, don't tell your stockbrokers that you have disposable income, because they usually have a tendency to dispose of it, and then you have nothing. You can take your company's profits, your career profits, and do this: invest for cash flow. Now, if you invest for cash flow you will always be able to buy more investments.

The principle of an investment that produces income is that income can produce more investments, which, hopefully, will produce more income. Keep the spiral going, and at some point in the future you'll have lots more investments. If you're just investing for growth, yes, you could do a good job with that if the returns are really excellent, but usually they are not that good. You'll always have a need for cash flow.

Remember: cash flow, tax write offs and growth. Ask yourself this question: will your need for tax write offs change from year to year? Yes, your need for tax write offs will go up, and it will go down, from year to year. Will your need for growth change from year to year? Yes, some years you need a lot of growth, and some years you don't need very much because you're doing okay. Will your need for cash flow change? The answer is "yes," you will always need more. Almost every person, in every situation, needs more monthly income. So, my type of diversified blended investments are those investments that primarily put the emphasis on building up monthly income. I like monthly income type investments.

However, most investments are not. For example, you can get involved in blue chip stocks, which usually produce dividends on an annual or semiannual basis, sometimes even on a quarterly basis. You can invest in utility stocks that pay monthly and/or quarterly payouts, and you can get some nice steady income. You can invest in all the different products we talked about, and get some nice income that way. No matter what the investment that you're looking at, you should get involved in each one of them and measure them, rate them, and judge them by their ability to produce monthly checks.

We live in a monthly income society. We live in a monthly debt society. Your phone bill, your cable TV bill, your rent, your house payments, your everything, comes in on a monthly basis. So why not create an investment that is secondary to you.

For most of you reading this right now *you* are your only income producing asset. Whether you run your own business or you are going to work, if your assets, meaning you, do not show up to work, there's no income. What I try to stress in all of my seminars, is to build up a grouping of assets that produces income.

If they produce tax write offs, great. If they'll give you some growth for the future, wonderful. But produce more cash flow, so that you can replace the income that you are making right now by working at your job or by running your own business, and then have excess cash flow so you can truly live the life-style that you want to live.

This strategy has to do with seeking out information, getting an over abundance of information, having a treasure chest full of knowledge, especially when it comes to investing in these stock market type investments. There's just no substitute for pure un-adulterated knowledge. I've said this so many times before—you pay for education once, and you continually pay for ignorance. It is so true.

53

Treasure Chest Of Knowledge

Derrick Bock was Dean of the Harvard Law School, then he later became the Dean of Harvard, and now he's retired. When he was Dean of Harvard Law School, he said, "If you think education is expensive, try ignorance." Now, it's really tough to absorb the plethora of information that is available out there.

Again, give us a call at 1-800-872-7411 to get more information on WIN—Wealth Information Network. Our internet subscription service and IQ Pager, our paging system, which sends a message to you as events and announcements are made on Wall Street and keeps you up to date and informed.

I know this may sound weird, because nobody ever does it; however, I once read a statement by a very wise man who said that we should invest 10% of what we make in education. If you're making $80,000 annually, that means that you would be spending $8,000 annually in seminars and books and educational tools.

I didn't think very many people did that, until one time I was teaching a seminar in Miami, and a lady came up to me and said that she had purchased over $5,000 worth of books by all these different authors. She purchased about $1,000 worth of mine at that time, and I was very flattered. But she had purchased $4,000 of other people's books, too. I said, "That's amazing, the amount of money that you spent on these books."

She replied, "You know what, I've gained something from each one of them." She continued, "Every book I've read, whether I spent $100 on it, or whether it was a waste of my time to read the majority of it, if I got one good idea that saved me $10,000 on a property I was purchasing, it was well worth it. So, what is the value of knowledge, and where are you going to go to get it? What is the value of one idea? You can literally take your car and turn it into a college on wheels, just by listening to tapes while you're driving.

I hope that I'm one of those key educators in your life, and I know that as you get a feel for this book you are going to see it is really like a huge, gigantic table of contents. I will give you as much information as I can on each one of these; however, please refer to the Available Resources for a complete listing of our products, where you will find more information on the specific topics or strategies you are interested in.

Let's just do a little thinking here on where you are. Here's what I've found. I do a lot of consulting with people on where they're going to be, because a lot of people come to my seminars, they come to our Wealth Academy and get really excited about a certain way of making money that's going to require them to do a lot of work.

54

You

If your company really requires a lot of your time, then you may not have the time and the energy to be working your stock market investments or your real estate investments, particularly if you have a SEP-IRA, or a corporate Pension Plan. If you're really busy working your company, you may want to choose, within that retirement account, certain investments that require no work, almost no-brainer type investments like some of those high grade mutual funds, or stocks that are just blue chip stocks that you don't work that much at all.

Later on, when you're going to sell your company, or it gets a little more stable and you don't have to work quite as hard, or you have some really good key employees in place and it gives you some free time. At that point in time you can take more of an aggressive stance on your investments. I've rarely met anyone who could go at the energy level necessary to make huge rates of returns in their brokerage accounts while they were busy running their companies. They just don't really go hand in hand. It takes a lot of intensive work to call your stockbroker, to place your orders, or to go out and buy real estate. Pick and choose which areas you are going to get aggressive with.

So, at first you get aggressive with your company—you build up, and you pour money back in your company. The best investment you can make is in your own gray matter, your own brain. The next best investment you can make is in your own company. Very seldom do I see a business owner who has a nice company and would take $10,000 and invest it in the stock market. Who would do as well with that money in the stock market as they would by putting the money back in their own company, paying for some more advertising, or expanding their business if that's what they choose to do? Where are you, and where do you want to be? You've got to decide which entity you're going to be the most aggressive with. If you choose other areas to spend your energy in, then you need to choose low maintenance stock market investments.

SECTION FIVE

This section contains information on several different ways to make money with your business. If you decide that you do not want to own a business, or if you're you've been here before and have moved on, then think about some of these ideas in regard to the companies that you'll be investing in. Because these are tried and proven strategies from coast to coast, I'm sure that it would do us all well to make sure that the companies that we're investing our hard earned dollars in are taking an aggressive stance, and applying some of the principles that I'll be talking about here.

We talked about gold before, from the hedging-your-bet standpoint, and about possibly investing in gold or gold stocks, but what I'm talking about now is investing in gold coins—the hard asset itself. I, particularly, don't buy gold nuggets or gold powder. First of all, I don't know where to find them. Secondly, I don't want to have

to have them assayed and checked out each time. So I invest in gold coins. More particularly, I invest in American Eagle Gold Bullion coins. I like them. Before we get into these coins, let's go back and give you a brief history of this, and talk about why gold is such a hedge.

Back in early 1920, gold was trading for around $16 an ounce. You could take a gold coin into a men's clothing store at that point in time and buy a nice men's suit. You could also take $16 cash in and buy the same men's suit. Today, if you were to have that same gold coin, which is trading for $380, $400, or $420 an ounce, and you walked into a men's clothing store, you could buy a nice men's suit. Also you could take $420 or $380 cash, or whatever, and you could buy a nice men's suit with it. You see, it's not that gold has gone up in value, so much as it is that the dollar has gone so far down in value.

Picture yourself in Southern California in the early 1960s. Around that time, you could go out and buy a house for as little as $12,000. Today, you see those houses selling for $160,000, $180,000, and $200,000. Now, if you had the amount of gold necessary to buy that house for $12,000 back then, and you moved ahead 30 plus years into the future, that same amount of gold would still buy that house, even though that same house is now worth $160,000 to $200,000. But, if you had $12,000 cash, what would that buy today in Southern California? It would barely make a down payment. Once again, it's not that gold has gone up in value; it's that the dollar has gone so far down in value.

Let me give you a little bit more of the history. Our government minted gold coins for many, many years and stored them in Fort Knox. Then, in 1929, the government called in all the gold. Everyone had to bring in their gold, although they were allowed to keep some jewelry. The government basically recaptured all of the gold coins the people brought in. Everyone thought they were really getting a good deal, because the government was paying $20 an ounce for the gold when it was trading for $16 an ounce. But then, after the government had gotten all the money back, in 1931 and 1932 they arbitrarily set the price of gold at $35 an ounce. So, the value of the gold that was taken in at $16 was half the amount of what you could have gotten for the gold at $35.

I imagine a lot of people reading this remember gold at $35 an ounce. For many, many years it was $35 an ounce. America, for many years, was on a gold standard. Which means that our dollar, our currency, was backed by gold. Starting back then, in 1929 and 1931 we went partially off the gold standard. In 1969, under Richard Nixon, we went a huge percentage—75%—off the gold standard. Actually it started with Lyndon Johnson in 1969, and then with Richard Nixon in 1971 and 1972, we completely went off the gold standard, to a totally monetary policy.

We've not been on the gold standard since that time. By the way, look at what has happened to the currencies around the world with all the fluctuations. We really should get back on the gold standard, and I don't see that happening. I hear talk about it every now and then. I see currencies around the world that are still on the gold or silver standard that are much more stable than ours. I've made this point before— just because we as a country are off the gold standard does not mean that you need to be off the gold standard.

You can still have a certain part of your portfolio in gold. Let me tell you what I think that portion should be: I believe that perhaps 10% of your portfolio, should be in gold. Now, that may not appeal to some of you because you are saying, "Hold it. It's not earning any rents. It's not paying any dividends. It just sits there." But remember, gold paces inflation, and is a hedge against inflation. So, as inflation goes up, the value of your gold is being held. At least your buying power is steady.

Let me give you another comparison. Let's say that you're 35 years old and you put $2,000 in an IRA account today. The $2,000 is invested in a savings account, a CD, a mutual fund, or whatever, and it's earning 3, 4, or perhaps 5%. Now, 30 years from now, at the age of 65 you want to start withdrawing that money. Even though it's earned a little bit of money in the meantime, the buying power of that money over 30 years could be around $600 or $700.

Now, however, if you had $2,000 held in gold, at the age of 65 you would still have $2,000 of buying power, or close to it. See, gold is a hedge against inflation. The United States did not mint coins for many years, but a lot of other countries did—South Africa with their Krugerrands, Australia with their nuggets, and Canada with their maple leaves. Many, many countries have gold coins.

In 1986 the United States Government and the United States Mint got back into the minting process. They mint four gold coins now—a one ounce coin, a one-half ounce coin, a quarter ounce coin, and a tenth ounce coin. These coins are circulating with "$50" written on them. They used a lot of the same artwork that was on the old St. Gaudins coin back in the early part of the century. However, they did change the eagle on the back from one large eagle to a family—a mother and father flying into the nest—the artwork is quite beautiful.

If a coin was made of pure gold, 24 carat gold, it would really be quite soft. You talk about biting gold, I've done that, by the way, and it hurts your teeth. You don't want to do that, especially because it gets scratched quite easily. The United States Mint mixed in something that toughens it up, to make the gold a little bit harder. Because of that, it is 22 carat gold. It's still considered fine gold, but it's 22 carat; therefore, now we have the bullion.

With the American gold coin, when I say one ounce, it obviously is one troy ounce, which means it is 1.1% of our regular ounces. How do you buy these coins, and why would you buy them? One reason to buy them is that they're easy to store, because you can put them in a safety deposit box or a safe at home. How do you buy them? That's not a problem either, because any coin dealer will have gold coins available. Some dealers don't have very many, so you may want to shop around to find a coin dealer that has a substantial inventory of gold coins.

Now let me tell you how you buy them. Let's say that gold is trading at $380 an ounce. You go into a coin dealer, and ask what the spot price of gold is. It changes twice a day. It starts off in Hong Kong and other various places in the world, and it ends up in London, and then comes into New York. On the London Stock Exchange it's set twice a day. So any coin dealer or any gold broker can find out within a matter of hours the price of gold—there's no jimmying of the gold price. Nobody can really pull any shenanigans here.

A few years ago, when Russia decided to dump several billion dollars worth of gold on the market, obviously, the price went down. It's the law of supply and demand. And then, the price kind of crept back up. Then Indonesia dumped a bunch of gold on the market and the price went down again, and then it crept back up. There is a tendency, obviously, for gold to continue to go up, because inflation continues to go up.

The coin dealer will charge you the spot price of gold, the $380, plus $10, $15 or $20. Most of them charge around $20—they charge spot plus $20. So, you walk in and for $400 you can buy a gold coin. If you turn around and walk out the door, and you walk back in just a couple minutes later and say, "I'm sorry, I made a mistake. I should not have bought this today. Can I sell it back to you?" They'll then give you gold spot minus about $10—$370.

This is how coin dealers make their money. When dealing in gold, they are buying at one price and selling at another price. I really don't get involved in gold from a numismatic point of view. I'm not buying the rarity, though I have purchased a 1921 coin and a 1923 coin just for seminar purposes, where I could show them to the attendees and compare them to the current coins. I'm not really doing it for that, I'm doing it for gold content only, to have in my own little gold reserve account.

I buy gold coins with my IRAs and my Pension Plans, which is tough to do, by the way, to find a Pension Plan administrator or trustee that allows you to buy gold. When you do buy gold, they usually give you a receipt showing the type of account that made the purchase.

By the way, in some states, like California, if you're buying under $1,000 worth of gold, they make you fill out all kinds of forms. They want names, addresses, and all that, and they want you to pay a state income or sales tax on the gold purchase. Obviously, a lot of California people buy their gold out of state, and then they don't have to list themselves on these forms as owning gold.

Who'd want to do that? Who would want to create a flag that's saying, "I own a bunch of gold, come on over." I remember a few years ago when Ted Turner bought about $23 million worth of gold, and somebody asked him, "Where are you going to keep it?"

He replied, "Like I'm going to tell you?"

Then they asked, "Do you keep it in a bank?"

His reply was, "No, but I keep it in a building next to a bank."

You know, nobody even needs to know that you own gold. So, you just buy it over a period of time.

That way, if there's an emergency, or if the whole economy goes down, or whatever, I will have gold coins available to purchase with. I'm also buying it as a hedge against inflation, and, I just personally like the look and the feel of the gold coins. I have purchased gold now from many, different countries. It's kind of my hobby, though I don't like to pay much more than the spot price for it. I have purchased gold from many different countries, but my primary portfolio gold is in American Eagles.

Let me tell you my little personal game with gold. I've set gold up as a reward system for myself. After I go out of town and teach a seminar, and come back with the profits that I made at that seminar, I always go buy a gold coin. I don't always do that, but most weeks I do, and let me tell you what's happened. If you're making several thousand dollars, you don't miss it. And then, all of a sudden you end up with a whole box, or a whole envelope full of gold coins. I'm not really big into selling them, because I'm holding them for the long term. I have sold them in the past, so let me tell you what I do when I sell them. If I go in to sell a gold coin for $380, I always buy one or two American Eagle silver coins. Now, they're only $6 or $7, but I've got this little rule that I always go out of a coin dealership weighing more than when I went in. So, if I sell one ounce of gold, I buy two or three ounces of silver—I weigh more, and I've got more coins clinking in my pocket than when I went in.

That's just my own little game, and it has worked very well. So, when I do something really well, I go buy a gold coin as a reward, and I've ended up now with a good number of coins as my own portfolio.

This strategy is about getting wealthy very, very rapidly. I've hinted at this many times, but if you really want to build up wealth substantially, wherein you can get cash flow, tax write offs, and growth all at the same time and with a small amount of money, you either have to deal with real estate, and/or do it by owning your own business. The benefits of ownership—being able to get the cash flow, tax write offs, and growth, faster and better.

56

Getting Wealthy— Rapidly

A lot of people can start a business with very little money. I really encourage people to get a chunk of money to get started. The number one cause for business failure in this country is lack of start up money. Ninety-two percent of all businesses fail because they don't have enough capital to get up and going, and to keep going long enough to eventually be successful.

You need to start up a business. Now, that business can be run out of your back bedroom. I'm not saying that you have to have a lot of inventory, or a lot of exposure to risk. If you want to stockpile wealth very rapidly, that comes from buying and selling something, from manufacturing something, from creating wealth where wealth did not exist before. Virtually nothing works faster than that. You can hardly find any investment around that will make you money more rapidly than owning your own business—if you do it and run it well.

A lot of people reading this are not cut out to be businessmen or businesswomen; and, therefore, this is not go-

ing to work for them. If that's the case with you, that's fine—
you need to be investing in companies, though, that are entrepreneurial in nature. You need to either be an entrepre-
neur or invest in companies that have that money at the beginning, where they are expanding quite rapidly. That goes
back to our stock market type investments, where you can
accumulate your wealth very quickly, but you have to find
somebody who's growing rapidly.

Let me tell you what I've learned about this: for those of
you who don't want to own your own business, but want to
tap into the same energy and the same potential, I learned
from a very wise man long ago that if you are not going to be
a star yourself, latch on to somebody who is going to be
one. I think that's some good advice. So, you latch onto a
star, and you realize that every company needs a star.

For example, for many years, Michael Jordan *was* the
Chicago Bulls. If you said the "Chicago Bulls," it was syn-
onymous with Michael Jordan. Walter Payton with the Bears,
and Magic Johnson with the Lakers, every team had a star.
Now, some teams were lucky enough to have two stars, but
very seldom did you ever see a team go to the playoffs, and
win the playoffs, unless they had a real star. So, you look at
a company and ask, "What's the star here?" It could be either a person or a product, but they have to be famous for
something.

57

Learning the Jargon

You can play the business game and you can play the
investment game, but there's one underlying factor: with every business you need to learn the
jargon, the language. I learned this
from my friend John. He said, "Teach
me the rules and I'll play the game."

It's not that any business gets
easier, or that the rules change, it's
that your ability to do things gets better as you do it for awhile.
So, may I encourage you, if you are going to get involved in

any business endeavor, I mean even if you become a pro-duce manager at a Safeway store, to learn the rules. You need to learn the language, the jargon of it. You need to learn the game.

That's what I say about the IRS—I want to learn their rules better than they know them. I'll read and study every-thing I can get my hands on. I really believe that if you get to know the rules better than the IRS, then you can do wonder-ful things. But they keep changing the rules on us. Did you know that nobody in the United States has ever read the full tax code? If you got all the code, think of the rooms that it would fill up. It would take the average American reader about 15$^1/_2$ years, reading eight hours a day, to read the whole tax code book. So you see, nobody has ever read the whole thing.

I've read bits and pieces of it. I read all the codes regard-ing real estate, small businesses, corporations, and topics like that, but I haven't read about energy depletion allow-ances and such. I don't really care about those kinds of things. Now, I'm starting to get more involved. I'll start to study more about them, but up until now I've become an expert on read-ing the tax code on those certain topics that I enjoy, that I'm involved in myself. I want to learn the rules better than any-one else. It's when you know the rules that you can really amend them, change them, and work them.

Back to your business—teach me the rules, and I'll play the game. You've got to learn the rules and always get better at the language of your business.

The key to building up a business is to find a product or a service and sell it. You could do that by coming up with some little niche, or some little thing that you're going to manufacture, or some service that you could offer, but usually a business is made by making something bigger or better than what was previously there.

58

Finding A Niche

You could sell a car stereo. You go to the manufacturer of the car stereos, and you add to them different speakers. So you put together a speaker and a booster system, and all of a sudden, boom, you have a whole new market niche. And you have a product that you created that you can make a lot of money on.

For many years IBM and Apple had actual dealers that signed contracts with them, but a lot of other people wanted to market their computers. So these people signed VAR, or Value Added Retailer agreements, with Apple and IBM. These companies would not be allowed to sell the computers directly. They would, however, add some software programs, or a computer printer package, and sell it together with the computer. The value was made in the software programs that would go with the computer, and the computer was sold almost as an afterthought.

You see, you find a product or a service and you add value to it. The purpose of being in business is to get and keep customers. Well, to a lot of people it's to make a profit. Yes, you have to make a profit or you don't stay in business, but the underlying theme of any business should be to get and keep customers.

Let me tell you what this means to me. I'm really big into this. You know, I used to have one of those businesses, even when I was doing my real estate, where you receive an envelope full of coupons in the mail. In the envelope you might get one for windshield repair, one for a chiropractor examination, or whatever. You've probably all received those— Val-Pak, American Advertising, there are other companies around like that. Well, I started up a company like that in Washington, and I was very, very good.

I loved that business, because I love designing ads and coming up with marketing ideas. We would go to a spaghetti company and negotiate a coupon where you would buy one spaghetti meal and get one free. We had deals with

Dairy Queen, Burger King and all kinds of companies. I sold that business because I could make more money elsewhere. I sold that business, but I still love that business.

Let me tell you what happened in Scottsdale when I was living there a few years ago. I got an envelope in the mail, and it was full of coupons, and one in there was for a pizza. You could get a large pizza and 50 Buffalo style chicken wings—those spicy chicken wings like the ones at the Anchor Bar in Buffalo, New York. I really got excited about this, because I like Buffalo wings and I like pizza.

So, I called to order the pizza, and I also asked for several extra toppings, and I got some drinks, all of which came to $22, instead of $10.95 like the coupon stated.

When I went to pay for it, the cashier said, "We need your coupon."

I asked, "Why?"

"Because we need to staple the coupon to the back of the receipt," she replied, "that's how we keep track of you receiving the special price."

And I asked, "Why would you take this coupon away from me? I used to have a business like this, I'm really into marketing, and it worked. It got me here." Now, she thought I was a trouble maker so she called the manager of the store over.

When she came over she asked, "What's the problem?"

I said, "My name is Wade Cook, and I'm really into marketing, and I don't understand why you're taking this coupon away from me."

She asked, "What are you talking about? We have to staple the coupon to the receipt."

I said, "I know, I know. I've heard what you do here. I heard about your little system here. I don't understand why you would take this coupon away from me."

"What are you talking about?" she continued.

I replied, "Look, it worked. Mary, I used to have a business like this, and I would venture to say that you probably paid for a 10,000 piece mailing. I bet you paid around $550 to $575, because I used to charge $450 to $475 when I was doing it several years ago." I guessed it right on. She paid $575 for a 10,000 piece mailing.

"It worked," I said, "I would venture to say, because I'm looking at this coupon and it's an okay coupon, that out of the 10,000 pieces you got about 125 to 175 responses."

"Yes, that's about how many we've had," she replied.

"Well," I said, "I don't get why you would take this coupon away from me. I mean, about 150 or so people have responded with this coupon. Why would you take away from them the very thing that got them here? It seems to me that if they're a good customer, you should give them about ten coupons and have them give them to all their family members and friends."

You see, it worked. Remember, the purpose of being in business is to get and keep customers, and, by the way, the purpose of being in business is to get and keep solvent customers. I hope, for example, that you become customers of mine on a long term basis, and become clients of our companies.

There are a lot of companies out there that do estate planning. You've all heard of estate planning. You know, people will talk about estate planning and buying enough investments or insurance to cover you upon your death, and possibly a Living Trust. Those estate planning type people are usually life insurance agents trying to sell you a life insurance product; and they do a good job at it. You've all heard of financial planning where somebody will get you to have a balanced portfolio, and they'll tell you all sorts of stuff on how much stock you should own and how many bonds you should own. It's almost like paper mills. They're trying to get you to buy something so that they can get a commission.

Well, what I saw in all this many, many years ago was a group of professionals selling people products and getting commissions for doing so. What these people really needed, though, was to structure themselves better. I learned by hard and sad experience of my own that you don't want to have all your things owned in one legal structure. Out of necessity, I set up my own Nevada Corporation. Then I got tired of my attorney charging me so much money when I did my second one, that I went over there and learned how to do it myself.

Well, at my seminars I started mentioning to people that I could set up a Nevada Corporation for them. Then we added Pension Plans to that, and we got a really good pension administrator. We'd set up people's Pension Plans because people got tired of being ripped off by these companies who would get them in at a low price, but then just nick them and ding them to death on all the annual fees.

We then started setting up Living Trusts for people. A lot of attorneys that teach Living Trust seminars don't have the foggiest idea of how good Living Trusts are, and how limited they are, because Living Trusts don't protect people against losses. And then we went with Family Limited Partnerships and Charitable Remainder Trusts. Now there are five of those products which we'll talk about in more detail later on.

You, the person reading this book, may be able to go out and find someone who sets up Nevada Corporations. I do have a couple of competitors, even though they don't do anything close to what we do in the quality of Nevada Corporations, the amount of stock, the redeemable rights and all the things we set up in a Nevada Corporation. And there are several companies that set up Pension Plans, but nobody sets up a Pension Plan like we do. We allow you to be the trustee and handle all the money, and charge no annual asset maintenance fees like everybody else charges.

I've now reviewed over 300 Living Trusts by different attorneys. I've only seen one done properly, by an attorney in Orlando, Florida who does a good job. I've seen one of his Living Trusts and I was very impressed. I've not seen one done properly by all the attorneys in California, Washington, Arizona, et cetera. I've looked at Living Trusts from all over, and they're embarrassing.

I established a company, which, by the way, I didn't particularly want to do. It's almost like filling a market niche. I've even been kind of forced into that because people say, "Will you set up my Nevada Corporation for me? Will you set up my Pension Plan?" So, I set up this company to do all that, and we charge really reasonable rates to provide that service, so people can keep their profits working for their companies.

The reason that I'm bringing it up here, again, is because I fell into a market niche. Nobody does what we do. Now, you may find one company that will set up a Nevada Corporation, maybe another company that will set up Pension Plans, and there are several attorneys that set up Living Trusts, but you won't find one company that does it all. I challenge you to find one company, not only that does them, but that knows them, and can integrate them together and show you how they all work together.

Wade Cook Seminars, Inc. is the only company in the country that does that. We have no competitors. I'd like to say that we're kind of like this company and we're kind of like that one, but we have no competitors. Nobody comes close, they're not even trying. We've got a really, really neat business, and it has grown into a multimillion dollar business, because we provide a service so well and we have so many repeat customers.

The key to wealth is repetition and duplication. For example, when I do the Money Machine, part of the reason it works so well is that you get good at doing the same kind of properties over and over again. When you do Rolling Stock, you do it over and over and over again and you get very, very good at it.

59

Duplication

Now, I know I'm going to step on a few toes here, but we're talking about being in business. If you have a business where you're fixing people's refrigerators, or your business is installing air conditioning units, you are probably never going to get wealthy. I hate to say that to you, but you're probably never going to get wealthy because what you have with your little business is a glorified job. It's the same thing that every other repairman does. Unless you can make it unique and duplicatable, you're just doing your time. If you have to trade your time for money, that's almost the same as if you're working for someone else. You can do the same thing over and over and over again, but that's not what we're talking about.

We're talking about manufacturing hamburgers, or, as in my case, manufacturing books. I can sell the same book, we can print 50,000 or 200,000 copies and sell them to the book stores, and we can make a lot of money. Remember, it's the meter drop again. It's the same concept. So, if you're going to get into business, or if you're going to buy something that you're going to sell in your business, then you want to be able to duplicate it over and over again.

I'm going to finish this by saying something very strong. My recommendation is don't ever do anything—in a business sense—unless it can be duplicated. Why? Why do something that you cannot duplicate and maximize the profits? You need to get better at maximizing your time to find these things, you need to get better at delegating, setting up the system so it will do that, even at setting up the entities.

Let me tell you what I mean by that. We duplicate entities. We've now set up thousands upon thousands of Nevada Corporations. I take this so very seriously. I work with
and train my staff for months before I'll allow them to be
with a customer.

They sit with more experienced staff consultants learning how to structure people, how to set up a Living Trust
with two or three different corporations from their different
businesses, how to have one as a parent company, and move
money over into a Pension Plan, how to have their rental
properties in limited partnerships, and how to have the Nevada Corporations be the general partners. They learn how
to integrate these entities.

I want to grow and expand my companies so we can be
of greater service to more people. It comes back to the same
thing—the key to wealth is duplication. Most people have
more things in common than they have different from each
other. We still want to be responsive to their needs, so we
work really hard at training our staff. We have people flying
in from all over the country to Washington State so they can
meet with my staff in order to get set up and structured, so
they can make themselves invisible and not have to worry
about all the risks and the worries. People come to our Wealth
Academy, and our staff meets with them there and sets them
up there.

60

Ownership

If you want to get very, very wealthy you need to own
more. That's simple, because you do an asset balance and
asset liability statement to look at
what you own. If you want to get rich
in real estate you've got to buy more
properties. If you want to get rich in
business you've got to own items.
What can you own?

First of all, you can buy the rights to something. There
could be, for example, an old product or an old idea that

you could buy the rights to and revive, or you could buy the rights to a product and change it; just make sure you secure the rights.

In the book business it's securing the actual copyright, or the publishing rights to a book. In the computer business it's the copyright or the publishing rights to different materials, or the rights to manufacture something.

Rights, ownership and products go hand in hand. If you want to build up your net worth, you need to build up what you own. If you can buy those things with leverage, or if you can buy those things at a super bargain price, that just makes it all the better.

What wealth comes down to is owning and controlling more items. So, the tools of leverage and the tools of ownership can be enhanced, but don't think that you're going to be able to get wealthy without owning things. Ownership sometimes involves taking a little bit of risk. Sometimes it involves putting up money; sometimes it involves taking an idea and making it better, adding something to it, changing an old idea to a new idea. But ownership is where it's all at.

Once you have ownership and business enterprise, next is positioning. Now, positioning to me means that you need to be the "firstest with the mostest." There is a book, by the way, called *Positioning*. I recommend that you buy and read it. In there, the author talks about being the "firstest with the mostest." Hertz Rent A Car

61

Positioning

will always be number one because they were the first rental car company in America. They'll always be the "firstest." As far as first national rental car companies, they'll always be the "firstest," and because they were the "firstest" they'll always be the "mostest." Avis will always be number two.

In the United States, Coca-Cola will always be number one and Pepsi will always be number two. Conversely, in

Russia, Pepsi will always be number one because it was there first, and Coca-Cola will always be number two. You see, it's a matter of positioning. Now, if you cannot position yourself to be somewhere with your business, or your thing that you own or whatever, if you cannot position yourself to be there the "firstest with the mostest," then one way to succeed is to reposition everything else.

When I used to teach my real estate seminars, I'd stand up in front of the audience—a group of people who had just gone to a $400 to $500 seminar to learn about rental properties and I'd say, "For many, many years there have been two ways of doing real estate—one way was to buy real estate and hold on to it forever; the other way was to buy a house and sell it. You've heard me do this before—buy it, fix it up, and sell it; then do it with a duplex, and then a fourplex, et cetera. Those are the old ways of doing business. Let me show you a new way." Then I'd go through and show them the Money Machine, that there was a different and better way of making a lot of money in real estate.

62

Dramatize Your Advertising

Dramatize your advertising. I wasn't the first one there talking about real estate, but I was the first one there talking about my style of real estate. If you're going to make a lot of money you've got to get maximum dollar out of your advertising. First of all, we need to get big results from small dollar amounts, and the only way to do that is to make sure that you monitor what you are doing. I particularly don't like advertisements that are called information advertisements—the ones talking about a new car coming out, or whatever. Why not give $1,000 off, or a coupon, or a special? We have information advertising and we have action advertising.

I'm big into the action advertising—move *now* and take advantage of this *now*; you can save this *now*. The fear of losing out is one of the greatest fears in the world. People want to have all the different benefits of owning something, of buying something. That's what you need to be selling, by the way, is the benefits of owning your service or product.

A benefit can only be derived if somebody buys and uses your product. A feature of the product stays with the product whether somebody buys it or not. So if I'm trying to sell a house and it's got a big fenced yard I can say, "This house has a big fenced yard and your wife won't have to worry about the kids running out in the street." See, that's a benefit of ownership. The fact that it has a fenced yard is a feature. They'll only be able to take advantage of that feature if they buy the property and use it. So the benefit comes from buying and using the product.

The fact that this car you're trying to sell has the best engine on the market means nothing to some people, unless you say the car will save them an average of $615 a year in gas because it has the best engine on the market. You see, the benefit is the savings. So you need to be selling benefits and not features.

I used to have a print shop and I love the printing business. I've determined that the reason most print shops are in business is because most advertisements fail. Somebody with a business will continually return with idea after idea hoping one of them will work. So, my recommendation is that when it comes down to advertising, if you're not a professional yourself, you need to trust the professionals. Get someone to design your ad, design your brochures, design your radio and TV programs—hire professionals. The owner can come up with the idea, and then he needs to hire professionals to handle the technicalities of making it happen.

The last thing I'm going to say on this topic about your advertising is that not only do you need to dramatize it, but you need to get famous for something. That can be the star in that company or it can be a product.

When I was doing advertising, I went to this restaurant one time that had a great hamburger and said, "Let's try something. What are you trying to get famous for?"

"I don't know," he replied. "I'm not trying to get famous for anything." Well, that wasn't the answer. What are you getting famous for?

I went in and asked, "What are you getting famous for?"

He said, "I don't know."

"Let's go back in the kitchen," I told him.

We went back there, where he had a pretty good pastrami sandwich and a pretty good hamburger, and I put them together. I put some really good pastrami on a hamburger and said, "Here take a bite of this."

He liked it, I liked it, and we called it the Murkle Burger—it was Murkle's Hamburger Stand. We started doing all kinds of advertising—"Buy one Murkle Burger, get one free." He got famous for them. He started out making about 50 a day, and pretty soon was selling 300 to 400 Murkle Burgers a day. He got famous for that. The people would come in to buy the Murkle Burger—he had a pretty good profit margin on that—but he made his money on the french fries, the drinks, the milkshakes, and all that he would sell in addition to them.

You need to look at what you're getting famous for, and base a lot of what you're doing around that. So, whatever you're getting famous for, just push it and push it. All the other sales will come because of that.

You are really only as good as the people around you. When you get into business, those around you are the ambassadors to the business. They asked Marriott, "Who is the most important person in your business?" They asked Disney the same question. "Who is the most important person in your business?" You'd be surprised at their answers. You may say, "Well, the ambassador of the business would be at the hotel check-in counter, or the bellman, or the person greeting you at the door. Everyone responded, "Our most important person is the operator." The person on the phone line with potential customers—the operator—that was the most important person in their business.

63

Ambassadors To The Business

When Disney was asked the same question, the most important person in the Disney company was the street sweeper at Disneyland. Now, I know that sounds really funny, but all these street sweepers, by the way, would go through two and three weeks of training. Why? Because the vendor operators at Disneyland or Disneyworld are very, very busy. The street sweeper, while keeping this place clean, is constantly being asked questions. Where is this and where is this and where's the bathroom? They're constantly in contact with the people. So, you wouldn't think that they'd have to train them much more than an hour to sweep the street, but they train them for a long time.

You have to make sure the people around you are well trained. When my employees say, "Wade, there is going to be a seminar in San Francisco on this topic and it's going to cost $300," I'll do anything I can to get them there. We pay for education all the time. They liked the trip to San Francisco, too. And I usually have them take their spouse so they can make a nice little business trip out of it. It is vital to train and work with those people.

I think knowledge unlocks doors of opportunity. I want the people around me to be really well trained. I would like a lot of people, and I have a few, that are just as smart or smarter than I am when it comes to entity structuring. That's exactly what I want. I want the customers to know and feel confident with my people.

You are limited in your own business because if the people around you are mediocre, then your results are going to be mediocre. So you need to surround yourself and hire good people, and even better people than what you're used to, so they can pull up your business. There are so many people out there pulling businesses down.

64

Keep Your Conquered Territory

Keep the territory that you conquered. Now, I bet a lot of you have never heard this before, but maybe if I can relate my personal experience, some of you can relate to this. I was out buying and selling properties, starting up an advertising business, had other investments, was doing all kinds of things, then all of a sudden a lot of things started to come unraveled.

Because I was so busy with some of my other entities, my real estate business started to suffer. I went to my attorney and he said, "Wade, you know what? You're like Genghis Kahn." He was a really good friend, by the way, and he was one of those few attorneys that doesn't act like an attorney.

For those of you who don't know, Genghis Kahn was incredible at capturing territory. He went all over Asia and just captured territory after territory. Then he left his brother-in-law behind to run Mongolia, and a prince that swore allegiance to him to run Tibet. Then he'd go conquer another territory and leave somebody else there to run that territory. As soon as he left each territory; guess what happened? Everything came unraveled. They would defect on him and take over the country. See, he was very, very good at capturing territory but he was not very good at keeping the territory. It's really what we keep that makes a difference.

May I recommend to you that you get to be an expert at your business, at whatever product or service that you're marketing. Another good friend of mine said, "I would rather want what I don't have than have what I don't want." So, you need to make sure that you can keep the good parts of that business.

The Chamber of Commerce came out with statistics that said that out of 100 businesses that start up today, one year from right now only 20 of those will still be in business. Out of those 20 that make it, the year after that, only 20% will be in business. In effect, if 100 businesses start today, in about two years we have a net of four or five businesses that are still in business. Why? I mean, 80% of businesses fail in the first year, and you know what? Do you know that people who get involved in franchises as a franchisee—they buy a sandwich shop or a barber shop or whatever—that 85% of all franchisees make it their first year?

Now think about that—80% of people try and reinvent the wheel; 80% of people trying to do it on their own are failing. But 85% of the people that are getting involved in a proven entity are making it. Why? Because they have the camaraderie, they have the manuals, they've got the tried and proven formulas; they've got all that.

By the way, that's what I've tried to do at our Cook University. Even though we don't sell any franchises as such, we try to get people the support, the track to run on, the manuals, forms and documents. That way if they want to go home and start a business, or do the Money Machine or Rolling Stock, they have the training in detailed, step-by-step, question and answer format.

There's a lot that people can learn on tapes, but there's really a lot more they can learn by being there and seeing someone in person. So, I invite you to come—this is my little pitch, if you'll allow me—to Cook University. Call 1-800-872-7411 to get more information.

65

Network Marketing

Now don't hate me for doing this. Don't hate me, but I've got to mention it here, and I'll tell you why I'm going to mention it. If you want to be in business, but you don't know how to start up a business and you don't have $50,000, up to $100,000 to start a business, one of the things that you can do is to get involved in one of the network marketing companies. A lot of you are going to stop reading right now. Please don't. Just hear me out on this. I know that multilevel companies have a black eye in the business. I've been involved in a couple myself, and I've been in one of the best ever, and they've both gone out of business on me.

From a personal point of view, I really don't like them very much. But you know what, every time I get up and tell my jokes about these multilevel companies, and the downsides and all that kind of stuff, every time I do that I have somebody who calls me up and says, "Mr. Cook, I really need to meet with you. I've got a really severe tax problem." When they come and show me all of their stuff, they're making $200,000 a month. Almost every time somebody does that, they're from a multilevel company.

I know it's like a revolving door. For every 2,000 or 5,000 or 10,000 people that get involved, only one, two or three make that kind of money, but I see it all the time. I see people making hundreds of thousands of dollars a year in these multilevel companies. So much so that they need tax write offs. They need to learn other things to do with their businesses.

I teach seminars about Nevada Corporations and Pension Plans at some of these companies, where I can go in and show them how to structure themselves and how to run their multilevel business as a company. I'm not interested in their shampoo, I'm not interested in their carburetor cleaner, what I'm interested in is helping them get structured.

So, I'm not interested in multilevel from that point of view. But a lot of people getting started don't want any risk. Well, you have hardly any risk at all. And, by the way, I don't like any of those multilevel companies that make you buy $2,000 or $3,000 worth of stuff. The most I ever want to spend on products is $50 or $100—that's what I advise you.

Multilevel companies are easy to start up. You can operate them out of your back bedroom. I don't believe you have to go out and hit up all your friends. There are all kinds of advertising, marketing, and other ways to get involved.

A lot of money can be made with very little exposure and very little risk. That's the only reason I'm bringing it up here. If a lot of people want to break off on their own, then why not do so gradually? Instead of quitting their job and starting up their own company, why not start up their own company part time to see if they really like having their own business? To see if they like keeping the records, the bookkeeping, the advertising and all that, so they can get their feet wet without a lot of exposure and commitment. That's what these network marketing companies can bring to the table.

SECTION SIX

Now the plot thickens. We are moving from investment strategies to talking about how to keep more of what you're making, how to lessen your risk, and how to seriously reduce your taxes. All this can be done legally and lawfully. I will be showing you how to use and integrate all of these different entities: Corporations, Living Trusts, Pension Plans, Charitable Remainder Trusts, and Limited Partnerships. I will show you what they do and how to put them all together.

Legal Structures

The whole thrust here is to divide and conquer. Make sure that you do not make all of your money in one legal entity, and that you do not hold all your assets or have your income made by one entity. Basically, there are three different Goliaths out there. One of the things that can jump up and bite you in the fanny is a lawsuit. The second one is income taxes, which can seriously curtail what you're trying to do. The third one is death taxes.

66
Divide And Conquer

Now, think about these three again: lawsuits, income taxes, and death taxes. If you make all the money that you're going to make under your own name, and if all the assets that you hold are held under your own name, then you stand pretty vulnerable. Think about that. Can one lawsuit then wipe out everything? Can having just one income tax bracket for everything minimize your money?

The answer to all three financial problems is to split up your assets to make sure that you do not own all of your things in one legal entity. Let's go through all of these in detail. As we go through them, you'll hear a lot about these different entities. If you need more information or forms and documents, once again I'll refer you to the available resources of this book, which list all of the ways we can furnish that information to you.

What we're trying to do is to make sure that you have a lot of money set aside for your retirement, and that as you're growing, you grow as rapidly as possible by keeping the chips on your side of the table. If you have a business that could bring about different risks and exposure levels, you protect the other business enterprises that you have.

If I were to own three rental properties, I wouldn't want to own those in one corporation or one limited partnership. If I bought a Chinese restaurant I would want that in a separate, distinct corporation. If I had a 20 unit apartment building I'd want that in a limited partnership.

I have different tax vehicles. I have them isolated away from each other. Somebody coming into my Chinese restaurant corporation and suing would affect that corporation. That corporation may even have to go bankrupt, but it would not affect the other corporations and it would not affect me personally. So the thrust behind this whole thing is to divide and conquer.

67

A Corporation

This strategy is about the importance of having a corporation. We're not talking about a Nevada Corporation yet. We're just talking about a regular corporation. I'm going to give you a list of reasons why I think corporations are good.

The number one reason why corporations are so powerful, and the workhorse of this whole business enterprise is simply because the alternatives are not very good. Sole proprietorships, in particular, should be outlawed.

Let me tell you what I do on a day-to-day basis. We have a staff of 30 to 45 people that consult with people all over the country. We help people set up their corporations and their limited partnerships. We help people decide on real estate transactions, on which ones they're going to do and not going to do, and how much money they are going to make, et cetera. That's what we do.

Now, every day we get incredibly great phone calls from people who are making money. But most of the phone calls coming in aren't about the good stuff. They are about the bad stuff. By the way, we only do consulting three or four hours a day because that's about all our staff can handle. We don't like all these negative things, and almost all the negative things happen because people did not take time to set themselves up legally and structure themselves.

People call on the phone and they say, "I went to your seminar eight years ago. It was wonderful. I loved it. I went out and made all this money, and now I'm getting sued," or, "Wade, I should have listened to you a long time ago. I went out and did it. I made a whole bunch of money, but now I'm getting killed on taxes, 40% of what I make is going to the government."

Had people taken time out to do it right, to get financially fit for the opportunity, then they wouldn't be having all these problems. And again, the number one entity, the one that everybody needs is a corporation. Of all the people I've met—the tens of thousands of people I've met—every one has needed a corporation. Most people need two or three corporations, or perhaps four or five to handle their different investments. They at least need one or two corporations for moving money from one state to another. They need corporations to have different tax brackets. They need to have corporations to protect their riches for their children to use for college, and to retire on later. There's so much that can be done with a corporation, and in a lot of ways corporations are light years ahead of a Living Trust for estate planning purposes. A Living Trust avoids probate, but a corporation allows all kinds of things.

Now for my list of reasons why I think corporations are so great:

1. Sole proprietorships are so bad. You go to these attorneys and they tell you to go ahead and be a sole proprietorship because you're not big enough to be

a corporation. Well, now you have no tax planning vehicle at all. You have no lessening of your exposure to risk in liability. You have no ability to move money off from one year to another. You just minimized everything that you could do by doing it as a sole proprietorship.

2. If you're ever going to do personal investments or run a business, the corporation helps you divide up your income and your assets into different legal entities, thereby lessening the risk of loss.

3. The risk or the exposure to liability by the officers, directors, and the shareholders, in most instances, is seriously reduced or eliminated by a corporation. You, as shareholder of your own little family corporation, are not liable for the activities of the corporation. As an officer, if you do something illegal then you may be held liable.

   If you run a corporation right, you set it up and you do it right, it takes title to businesses, it takes title to real estate or whatever, and if it's running and operating the right way and the books are accurate, then there's no way that somebody can go through the corporation and sue you. I know these attorneys talk about piercing the corporate veil, and I challenge them all the time to find me one case where it's happened. So far, no one has done it; that's just attorney talk. And, by the way, what's the alternative?

4. Corporations are eternal, they're perpetual in nature. Some of you right now are going to be setting up corporations that will be around 200 and 300 years from now. They'll support your kids, your grandkids, and your great grandkids in these businesses and enterprises that you're getting into. The corporation will outlive you.

5. From an estate planning point of view, corporations are phenomenal. They allow you to divide the stock in any way you choose to your kids and grandkids. You can have voting stock and nonvoting stock, and you as the parents keep the voting stock. You can have preferred stock and common stock.

You can divide small amounts to the parents in a corporation that's just getting started, and give huge amounts of stock to the kids. There's no tax consequence, because the stock is not really worth anything at the very beginning. When you put money into the corporation, you can loan it to the corporation, so that you can get the money back in a year or two as a loan repayment and have no tax consequences. I could go on and on, but I think you get the point. If you need more corporate information, give us a call at 1-800-872-7411.

Choose a Nevada Corporation—I just cannot stress the importance of this. It doesn't matter what state you are in, you should set up a Nevada Corporation. Why Nevada? Because in Nevada there's no corporate income tax, no stock transfer tax, no franchise tax, and no succession tax.

68

Choose A Nevada Corporation

Don't get me wrong here. If you do business in one state and you make a profit in that state, you will have to pay some business taxes on the profits there, but you will not have to pay taxes on money you make in other states. You will not have to pay taxes on money that you make on a national basis, like your investments.

For example, you could have a California company, but do that as a Nevada Corporation. Now, that Nevada Corporation could also have a brokerage account at Charles

Schwab, or whatever, in Las Vegas so that none of those dividends or capital gains are being taxed in the State of California.

If you do business in California they tax you on any money you make in that state, any other state, in any other country in the world. California acts like a state in and of itself and not as a part of the United States of America. Several other states are moving in that direction. Taxes are a big reason, but everybody wants to make them the only reason. I think it's about 20% of the reason why you should be a Nevada Corporation.

In Nevada, the officers of a corporation cannot be sued for the activities of the corporation. These officers could be you and your wife, or you and a couple of friends that have set up a corporation. In Nevada, they simply legislated it out of existence—the officers cannot be sued for the activities of the corporation.

Also, Nevada is a total secrecy state—no one can find out who owns the stock in your company. Nevada is the only state that has not signed an information sharing agreement with the IRS.

In Nevada, anybody can own stock in the company, which means foreigners can own stock in the company. To make a long story short, Nevada is the number one place.

Delaware used to be the number one state. By the way, in some of my books I do a side-by-side comparison of Nevada and Delaware. Delaware was the best for many, many years and it's now second best. Even if you were to compare the top two states in this country, Nevada and Delaware, Nevada would win hands down, but there really is no comparison. The list reads Nevada, Delaware, New Hampshire, Idaho, and then on down—with number 50 being California.

So no matter what state you are doing business in, you need to set up your legal structure in Nevada. If you domicile it there, you can do business in a myriad of states and you lessen a lot of exposure to risk.

We have the best company ever for setting up these Nevada Corporations. We set up a corporation with 25 million shares of stock. That's the authorized stock. We encourage you to issue a million shares. We set up the corporation in Nevada with redeemable stock so the company can buy back the stock.

Let's say, for example, one of your kids marries somebody that you don't like. You can buy back the stock at par value. So, if you've issued 200,000 shares of stock to that child, you can buy that stock back at $200 because the par value is at .001. We set it up with preferred stock and common stock, which nobody else, that I know of, does.

Right now I'm the second largest producer of Nevada Corporations in the whole country, and I'm fast approaching number one. My competitor, the one who's in first position, has been in business 13 years longer than I have. (We'll catch them this year or next and have as many corporations set up as they do because we are the very, very best.) If you want to set up a Nevada Corporation, call us at 1-800-872-7411 and we'll start all the processing there, and then send it down to our Las Vegas address where it's all handled appropriately in an efficient manner. Make sure that your corporation does for you what you really want it to do. For a free seminar on cassette, call 1-800-872-7411 and ask for the "Power of Nevada Corporations."

69

Corporate Tax Strategies

I'm just going to give you a list of my favorite corporate tax strategies, and hope that you are able to make them work for you.

1. You can have different tax brackets. You need to avoid this control group situation where the same owners own the same corporations and the same percentages, or you have control of them, because then they can be taxed as one corporation. So you have a corporation set up that is owned by a limited partnership. You have a corporation that controls another limited partnership. You have a corporation that is owned by your parents, for example. They own all the stock in it. You have another corporation that's owned a little bit by you and a lot by your children. So there's no centralized control, and they're all taxed in their own different tax brackets.

2. A corporation can be set up in different jurisdictions. For example, Nevada—you can also have a company in California, Utah, Texas, Tennessee or New York, and that company is doing business in that state, and it hires a consulting company, your company by the way, from Nevada to come in and manage it's affairs, or to do consulting services. If you have a company making $80,000 in net profits, it could pay off $60,000 of that a year to the Nevada Corporation, and thereby lessen the taxes due in your state. Now, we're not trying to say Federal taxes here, because now you have a company netting $20,000 and another company netting $60,000, but the $60,000 is being netted by a company that's in a state that has no taxes. So you can have different jurisdictions.

3. A corporation can have a different year end. You can set up a January 31st year end, for example, or a March 31st. If your company starts into business in February

and makes a lot of money, and gets that money past December 31st of that year, it has moved the money from one year to the next.

If you pull the money out in December, you're going to have to pay taxes on that money right away. But if the corporation could move that money into January of next year, and pay you a rather large chunk of money as a reenlistment bonus, or pay it out to two, three, four, or five different people, like you, your wife, and your children, then you could avoid estimated quarterly taxes. Now on January 31st, when the corporation does it's year end tax return, it has no income or very little income. And it has seriously lowered its tax liability.

Now, think this one through. (By the way, you got the money in January.) Do you remember that the best time of the year to buy tax shelter type investments is in January? In January you get a full year of the write offs, in February you get eleven months, and so on.

If you buy rental real estate, a limited partnership or a tax shelter in December, you get one month of the write offs for the year. So the best time to buy real estate or tax shelter type investments is in January. Well, you got a big chunk of the money in January, so you keep some of it to live on, and you take the rest of it and put it into tax shelter investments. That way you get all the write offs for the whole year so that the next April 15th, 15 months later, when it's time to pay taxes on the money you pulled out that year, you may not have to pay taxes, because you've got all the write offs to offset it. Having an off year end is quite phenomenal.

Another quick point: just to keep everything simple, you may want to set your corporation up as a March 31st year end, so that you're on a calendar quarter. You know, January, February, March. January 31st is really the best, but from a bookkeeping point of view it's a nightmare, because all of your 940s and 941s come due on a calendar quarter. You almost need to have two sets of books, and it's quite a mess. To keep it simple, you could have a March 31st year end just so your books match up.

4. From an estate planning point of view, a corporation lets you gift stock to children so that it's not in your name, while building and growing a multimillion dollar company. Having very little of that in your own personal name is quite effective.

5. A corporation can pay for different expenses that you can pay for, but you cannot deduct. Your corporation can buy tickets for two or three employees to the hot sports team in town, or be a football season ticket holder. Take advantage of your corporation. It can buy cars and trucks. It can pay for medical insurance. It can do all kinds of things.

6. I'm really not big into "S" corporations. I really like a regular, ordinary or a "C" corporation. C corporations can deduct all kinds of things that S corporations cannot. C corporations can take advantage of that 70% exclusion rule, which allows the corporation to claim only 70% of a dividend that you received from a company; S corporations do not qualify.

The whole crux of this thing is that you create different legal entities that pay taxes on their own. Again, I've got hours upon hours worth of corporation strategies that I've condensed into a brief overview.

Once people start understanding what corporations are they ask, "How do I get my existing rental properties and my business into the corporation?" Take a little rental house that you bought many years ago for $60,000 that's now worth $160,000. If you put it into a corporation, the IRS may consider that a sale, and you may have to pay taxes on the capital gain, so you don't want that.

70

Getting Your Business Into A Corporation

Under Internal Revenue Code 351, if you own 80% or more of a corporation, you can start gifting away stock in the corporation to make sure that it gets down to the 5/5/30/30/30 strategy—Mom and Dad each own 5% and each of the three kids owns 30%—over the next five, 10, or 15 years. For example, if a husband and wife own a house in joint tenancy, and they own 80% or more of the corporation in joint tenancy, the transfer is not considered a sale. (By the way, we just shot down our 5/5/30/30/30 strategy, because in this example the parents have to own 80% on the day that the asset was transferred into the corporation.)

Let's go back to the example, though. You deed the house, transfer or assign the businesses into the corporation. If the same owners of the investment own 80% of the corporation, then it triggers no sale. It's just the law. It's Rule 351 and that's just the way it is. It triggers no sale.

Also, if you've had this property as a depreciable item, the corporation gets to pick up on the existing basis of the property and continue the depreciation schedule. Those of you who don't have rental properties don't need to worry about what I just said. Those of you who do have rental properties and understand depreciation schedules will know what I'm talking about. You transfer the property and the corporation now picks up on the existing basis of the property.

If you bought a property for $60,000 and you've depreciated it to $40,000, you put that property into the corporation and sell it for $160,000 or $180,000 in a few years. You've got $120,000 capital gain in the corporation. Why is this so exciting? Well, why would you want to have a $120,000 capital gain in your own personal name?

In a corporation, the corporation that received the money can now pay off some of that money to you the next year. Move the money from one year to the next. It could pay some of that money to another corporation you have for consulting. It can put a big chunk of that money into a Pension Plan. You have a whole variety of things that you can do to shelter that money, to pay it out. You have all kinds of tax tools available that you don't have as an individual. As an individual all you can do, basically, is pay taxes on it. So a corporation gives you so much more flexibility.

A corporation allows you to get your family involved. Now, I've talked about ownership where you could have 5% of the ownership. For example, when you're 85 years old and your boy, Johnny, is 60 you can say, "Well, it's about time for Johnny to start taking some responsibility here." You could give him more stock and more control at that point in time. So, from an ownership point of view you can involve your kids to whichever level you want. By the way, you can involve them and not really have them know about it. You can have stock held in the corporate books that they don't even know about.

71

Family Involvement

Another thing you can do, obviously, is to get your family involved in the work part of the corporation, not just the ownership. You can have different tasks, responsibilities and assignments that your family and/or your children can do. Think about this: if you're going to be wealthy then your kids are going to be wealthy. So why not let them have some of the responsibilities of helping you build up the wealth? It's pretty exciting, because your family can learn some really strong work ethics from what you as Mom and Dad did to build up your family estate.

We're going to switch off the corporation. From time to time we'll come back to corporations and how they work in regard to these other legal entities and how they are integrated together. However, for this one it's just the basics of a Living Trust and what this is all about.

72

Living Trusts

Has anybody noticed that Living Trust seminars are kind of a phenomena the last few years? You didn't see them seven, eight, nine, or ten years ago. It's kind of a recent phenomena. I've been teaching Living Trust seminars for over a decade. What I see is a lot of these ambulance chasing attorneys out there teaching right now. They don't get it. They understand the basics of a Living Trust, but they don't understand how limited they are and yet how wonderful they can be.

The reason that Living Trusts have really gotten popular is because of the problems of probate. Even though some states have streamlined the probate process, it is still a horrible, ugly process.

When someone dies, if they own things, in order to transfer those things from one person to another it has to go before a court. Now, I believe that a will is the most dangerous document in this country, because it lulls people into a state of complacency. People think that because they have a will everything is going to be taken care of. Nothing could be further from the truth.

All wills, 100% of them, have to go through the probate process. So having a will is just slightly better than not having a will. By the way, why do you think attorneys will write up a will for you for $50 and keep it in their safe deposit box for the next 40 years waiting for you to die? Because they want to get their claws into everything that you're about. I mean, your estate is their retirement vehicle—and you want to keep your estate and your affairs out of the hands of attorneys upon your death.

The only way to avoid probate is to not die. If you do die there's another really, really good way that almost assures that you'll avoid the probate process—die as a pauper, then you have nothing to transfer from you or your estate to anybody else. Think that one through: you die as a pauper; you don't have anything.

You could work for and control $10 million or $100 million in assets, but none of that is in your own personal name. How do you set it up so you can do that? Well, you put everything that you own—remember that 5% of the stock in one of those corporation and 2% in another corporation that you and your wife own—you put that into a Living Trust. The trust now owns that stock.

Upon your death the trustee, whoever you choose to handle your affairs when you're not here, steps in and takes control of your company. You don't have anything in your estate, and there's no cause for probate because everything has been transferred before you die.

Well, while you're alive, we're going to set this trust up as a Living Trust, an inter vivos trust. You may want to make changes to it from time to time, so we'll set it up as a revocable trust. That is really two different trusts, which today is actually a hybrid trust of those two. Sometimes, it's referred to as a family trust, which is pretty much the same thing.

A Living Trust has two functions upon your death. One function is that it keeps everything together, those things that you want to keep together those things that will support your family and pay for your kids to go to college. The other thing that it does is to give things away, just like a will. "I give to my son the '57 Chevy, I give to my daughter the jewelry"— it gives things away.

It gives certain things away and it keeps certain things together for your family. Eventually, the Living Trust is going to end; it will disburse everything when your children get older, but a Living Trust is remarkable because it avoids probate.

Now remember the three reasons for estate planning: the first is to avoid probate, the second is to avoid or reduce estate taxes, and the third is to provide for the continuity of your assets. That's what this does. Living Trusts are great. Now let me just give you a few other items that you need to make sure of. (This is where a lot of these attorneys go wrong.)

1. A Living Trust needs to be fully funded. You need to have everything put into the Living Trust, everything you own. From now on you cease to exist. You don't have anything in your own name. When you go to the movies you're going with Living Trust money. When you buy groceries you're buying groceries with Living Trust money. Everything you do, you do as a Living Trust—this is you. The Living Trust is really you while you're alive. Now, you, as the husband and wife, are the co-trustees of this trust and you just handle your everyday affairs; just remember, it needs to be fully funded.

2. In case you forgot to put something in the Living Trust before you died, there is a document called a Joint Pour-Over Will, or a Pour-Over Will, which pours over, into the Living Trust upon your death, anything you forgot to put in the Living Trust. Is this the answer? You need this Joint Pour-Over Will, but you should never have to use it, because your Living Trust truly needs to be fully funded.

3. This is where another big gap exists in the Living Trusts prepared by most attorneys. If you use us to set up your Living Trust, we will set it up with what is called a catastrophic illness clause in case, for example, you were to get seriously ill, and have $300,000 or $400,000 in doctor bills.

If you apply for Medicaid and your financial statements show you're worth quite a bit of money they'll say, "Just sell off your assets to pay the bills." Now watch what happens: if you or your wife were to get sick, you and your wife could decide to execute this catastrophic clause. At that point in time the husband's or the wife's half of the trust becomes irrevocable; it becomes a grantor trust. Everything in that trust is now held by the trust, and it has nothing to do with the ownership of the husband or the wife at that point in time.

Let's say it's the husband that is sick. Now, his half of the Living Trust is irrevocable, and the wife's half is still a revocable Living Trust. When he goes in to apply for Medicaid and they ask him how much his house is worth, he can reply, "Zero." Again, when they ask him how much his investments are worth—zero. You see, you don't have anything. Everything is out of your name and you now qualify for full Medicaid. So, Living Trusts are really great because they can trigger certain events in the future that will still protect your assets.

4. This last one is really, really important. If you own a house in a joint tenancy as a husband and wife, which, by the way, is not quite as good as owning as tenants in common, which is nowhere near as good as owning it as a Living Trust. If you live in a community property state, a lot of the things that I'm going to show you right now are available to you. But let's talk about joint tenancy.

You own a house in joint tenancy; you bought it many, many years ago for $100,000. The house today is worth $500,000. Upon the death of the husband, the wife goes to sell the house because she doesn't want to live there anymore. She sells it for $500,000, and the IRS steps in and says they need to determine what taxes are due on the deal. They will want to know how she owned the house. It was owned in joint tenancy.

Well, we just divide the house in half. What is her basis? Her basis in the property is $50,000, or half of the $100,000 original purchase price. Then they allow her to receive basis at the time of his death. The house is worth $500,000 when he died. His basis then would have been $250,000. She sells the house for $500,000, her basis is $50,000, her husband's basis is $250,000, add those two together and you have a $300,000 basis in the property, which generates a $200,000 capital gain.

If she's older than 55 she has the $125,000 one time exclusion, but she'd still have to pay capital gains on $75,000; if she's younger than 55, she would have to pay capital gains on the whole $200,000. I know a lot of women out there that dislike the IRS more than men. They'll stay living in that house for 18 or 20 years just to spite the IRS, and not have to pay them any money. And they don't really even want to live there.

Let's do it a second way—don't own the house in joint tenancy. (By the way, I dislike joint tenancy immensely.) You own the house between the husband and wife in a Living Trust. Upon the death of the husband, the wife sells the house for $500,000 as co-trustee of the Living Trust.

In steps the IRS. They need to determine what the capital gains are. Again, they want to know how the house was owned. It was assigned in a Living Trust; the wife receives the house. How much was it worth when her husband died? It was worth $500,000. All right, she gets to receive it at the full stepped up basis, not half. The wife sells it for $500,000. The full stepped up, or new basis is $500,000, and she has zero capital gains and no taxes to pay.

These Living Trusts are really sharp. They really function well. Most of the attorneys that teach Living Trust seminars have no idea of the consequences or the tax liabilities and the tax savings afforded by a Living Trust. They're really quite remarkable. You need to have one. By the way, if the wife stays living in the house, and sells it later for $600,000, she has now established a new basis of $500,000 at the time of her husband's death. In that scenario she'd have a $100,000 capital gain.

73

Living Trust Tax Angles

Living trust tax angles. Now, if you got excited about the stepped up basis in number 72, let me finish it up here. Not only does your personal residence go to the stepped up basis, any investments or assets that you own as husband and wife, if owned in the Living Trust, go to the stepped up basis, too. For example, if you have a stock market account, mutual funds, a couple of rental properties, and a business enterprise all owned in the Living Trust, upon the death of one of the spouses, say the husband, the wife can sell off anything and everything and pay no capital gains at all.

We're not just talking about saving on inheritance taxes here because everything can go to the wife with no tax on inheritance; but, when she sells anything the IRS goes back to the basis of the item. The IRS would have to figure out her half of the basis if it's held in joint tenancy, but in a Living Trust everything goes to the stepped up basis. So she can sell off anything and everything and pay no capital gains at all.

While you're alive and you own your house and you have a mortgage on the house, how does this work? Well, you make the payments to the bank on the mortgage, so you still get to deduct the interest on the mortgage. While you're alive, the Living Trust functions under your own Social Security number. It's as if it doesn't exist, in a way, so it's kind of neat how the IRS treats it. It's there, it kicks into gear upon your death or incapacitation, but while you're alive it operates under your Social Security number so you still get all the same deductions.

This one is about getting ready for a great retirement and setting up a retirement entity. You've all heard of tax free investments, like municipal bonds and some other investments that produce cash flow, tax write offs, and growth, but how would you like to have an entity set up that takes everything that you would ever get involved in—everything—and turns it all into a tax free investment?

74

A Great Retirement

You have a few choices. One choice is to set up an IRA. I believe that everybody should have an IRA, even if you cannot deduct the standard $2,000. You should also set up IRAs for your children, and if you have a company pay your children each $2,000 to work for your company, then put that whole $2,000 into an IRA. Think about what you just did—you got rid of $2,000 out of your company, so that's less taxes, but now the $2,000 is going into an IRA for one of your children.

The second choice is a SEP-IRA—Simplified Employee Pension IRA. If you're self employed or a sole proprietorship, you can sock aside up to $30,000 into a SEP-IRA. If you're self employed you can also set up a more elaborate Keogh plan. I like a Keogh plan for a sole proprietorship, and/or a corporate Pension Plan if you are a corporation.

The plan that gives you the maximum strength, maximum protection, and maximum power is a corporate pension, and there are many, many reasons for doing that. I love corporations because they can take advantage of having this great Pension Plan. You can put away up to $30,000.

Don't let your CPAs tell you it's $22,500, because they've lowered the limits on Pension Plans. Don't fall into all the garbage that's being taught out there. You have different types of plans—money purchase plans and profit sharing plans. You can put 5% in your money purchase plan and 15% in your profit sharing, that's 20%. The limits have been lowered to $150,000. Well, 20% of $150,000 is $30,000. So you still put aside your $30,000, and, by the way, if somebody is telling you $22,500, you hang up the phone on them and you call my company. We'll help you set up your Pension Plan.

In a corporation you can set aside huge amounts of money. Based on the compensation that you're paying yourself, your wife, or any of your employees, you can put aside up to $30,000 per year per person. That's $30,000 for the husband and $30,000 for the wife. That becomes a tax write off right now; it's a donation. Because it's a sponsored plan, you get to have that as a contribution to the plan, and you get to deduct the money right now. You have a big, huge tax savings right now.

You also get to be the trustee of this plan. What does that mean? It means that you've got the checkbook. It's in your glove box, it's in your purse, it's in your pocket, and you're out writing checks.

So you set up this tax free entity, you get the tax deductions, and now you've got the checkbook. If you have a Pension Plan set up at Charles Schwab or Dean Witter or Merrill Lynch, as I've said before you're limited on what you can do. You can do their types of investments. Now, you may still be able to make a lot of money with that, especially if you do the Rolling Stock plan, but why not have the checkbook?

If you're driving down the street and you see a house that you can buy and fix up using my Money Machine style, then buy and sell the house. Make a huge amount of money, with multiple checks coming in for 25 or 30 years. You've got the checkbook. You're in control of the investments of this Pension Plan.

What I'm talking about is called a self trusteed plan, where nobody else touches your money. You keep control of your money and put your whole financial destiny into your own hands. Think about this: a lot of people ask me what a trust is, as if a trust were a thing. A trust is not a thing.

A trust is a relationship between three people. There is a trustor, that's the person that sets it up and funds it; there's the trustee, that's the person that takes care of the money; and there's the beneficiary. In most trust situations those three people are different. For example, if you want to give money to your kids, you set up a trust, you put the money into a bank, the bank takes care of the money as the trustee, and your kids get it later on. But think about this one.

In the Pension Plan I'm talking about here, who's the trustor? You are. You're the corporation that sets up the Pension Plan. Who's the trustee? You are, you've got the checkbook. And who's the beneficiary? You are. You're the trustor, the trustee and the beneficiary of the same money. It doesn't get more exciting than this, because you control all the money going in, how much you're going to put in, you control the money once it's in, and you can control the money coming out. That's pretty exciting!

A couple of quick points about this Pension Plan. Again, I've got all day seminars on Pension Plans that give you a lot more detailed information. You need to get better at the law of leverage. We set up a Pension Plan that can have a margin account. We're the only one that I know of in the whole country that sets up Pension Plans that have the availability of having a margin account, and we charge a fair amount for that. Remember, you have the checkbook, so you can put some money in this brokerage account, you could put some money over here, you could have some in CDs, whatever you want to do. You're in control of the money.

Another quick point: the money is liquid in there, which means that you can borrow against the money. Remember, you're the trustee, so you're on the loan committee and you can borrow the money. You have to borrow it for serious reasons, like medical expenses or buying a house or something like that, and you have to pay it back within five years at a fair interest rate. But you can borrow the money if you need to get at the money in the future. In your Pension Plan, it's easy to set up. It's easy to operate because we do a lot of it for you.

If you get involved with other companies that set up Pension Plans, they may get you in at dirt cheap prices. However, then you have to buy all of your investments through them, and they not only charge you their normal commissions, but sometimes they charge you pension fees on top of that. Also, if they're managing your money, they definitely charge you annual fees at the end of the year, sometimes up to 3% of your assets in the Pension Plan. We have no such fees if you use us. So be very careful on who you choose to help you with the administration of your Pension Plan. They're one of the neatest entities around, but they're also highly regulated. So you need to be very, very careful.

Now you control it, you can diversify your investments, you can put in huge amounts of money, get tax deductions right now, and the money sits there and grows tax free. When you sell your properties, all the capital gains have no consequences. All the income, investment income, interest income, dividend income—no consequences.

The entity that you should be using to get wealthy is a retirement entity. Most people have never thought about that. They're always trying to build up their company and get their company rich, or to build up their own personal net worth and get themselves rich. But why not sock aside money into a pension account and have the pension account get rich.

A lot of the strategies that I told you about in the stock market are incredible strategies, but why not do them in a Pension Plan? Why not buy and sell, do the Range Riders, do the Rolling Stock, invest for dividends, do all those incredible strategies that help you get 80, 100, or 200% returns on your money? Do all of these strategies in a Pension Plan, so that you don't get killed on taxes.

U se a variety of these different entities. For example, you can have a Keogh plan, but if you have a Keogh plan then you do not qualify for a SEP-IRA. You can have an IRA and you can put aside the $2,000 into an IRA. I've helped people, for example, set up a corporate Pension Plan for one of their businesses, but they had another business that was a partnership

75

Use A Variety Of Entities

with their children. They set up a plan there, and they're putting aside money for their children in the partnership plan. Use these different types of retirement accounts to have your investments in—that's diversity.

The next thing is that you need to diversify your investments. You need to get involved in a variety of different things. Now, please understand that I really believe that the Pension Plan should have a mission, it should have a theme, it should have a central area that it focuses on.

For example, if you're going to get good at Rolling Stock, then have your Pension Plan buy and sell those three or four stocks that you're really good at. If you're going to do mutual funds, get really good at mutual funds. Study them. A Pension Plan should have a theme, but while it has a lot of its money tied up in one central type of investment, it can also get involved in things like limited partnership units in some real estate investments or other kinds of debt. It can buy bonds. By the way, a perfect type of investment would be the zero coupon bond. Remember that one with the phantom income? Well, you don't have to worry about phantom income in the Pension Plan, because it pays no taxes. Why not then in an IRA or in a corporate Pension Plan, buy that zero coupon bond that will mature when you're 65, and a big one to mature when you're 70? Hey, you want to have a huge good time and travel the world when you're 70. So buy a bunch of bonds today that will mature when you're 70, and then you pull them out of the Pension Plan at that point in time.

I could just spend whole days talking about the flexibility, the freedom and the power it brings you when you understand about investing in an entity that pays no taxes. Everything else you're doing, if you get rich under your name, every April 15th you have to pay taxes to the IRS. If you get rich under a corporation, it has to pay taxes. The Pension Plan just sits there and waves at the IRS on April 15th. So, that's the entity that you should use.

76

Gifting

I'm sure everyone probably knows that you can gift away $10,000 per child per parent every year without any tax consequences. Now, what does this mean? Why am I even bringing it up here? Well, if you're worth quite a bit of money right now, and if you realize that when you die your estate and your family is going to get killed on taxes, before you die you can start gifting your assets away. The problem is that most people don't have a nice neat little grouping of $10,000 worth of assets lying around the house. Another problem is after you gift everything away, when it's time to retire and live the good life, you don't have anything.

How do you solve this problem? How do you take advantage of gifting? If you've got $80,000 equity in a house how do you gift it away? How do you do that? I mean, I'm pretty good at this stuff and I don't know how to do that. If you have a $10,000 CD, that's easy to gift away. I really like gifting, but I see some problems with it. Most people know about it and they don't do anything about it because it's too tough to do.

My encouragement to people in my seminars is that if you want to get wealthy you've got to do more, you've got to be more, and you've got to work out your problems. A lot of times I see people with tax problems, then they go buy real estate or other investments that will solve the tax problems, and those other investments get them wealthier. See, it's like a really neat cycle that you get into, but a lot of people don't realize that.

A lot of people say, "I'm getting killed on taxes. I'm just going to quit working overtime. I'm not going to make any more money. I'm not going to expand my business."

I say, "Hogwash! Let's grow! Let's be true to our personalities, and if that's what your true personality is—grow and build a big business!"

Let me talk about gifting from a whole different angle. Be more. Do more. If you know that you can gift away $10,000, let me give you several recommendations. Why not then gift away $10,000, and buy a $100,000 rental property with it for your kid? You take the $10,000 as a gift and you're buying a huge investment that will make them more money in the long run.

Why not buy a zero coupon bond for your kids or your grand kids? You could buy close to a $80,000 or $100,000 bond with the $10,000. Why not take the $10,000 and buy, depending upon your age and your health, a $250,000 paid up life insurance policy where you never have to put any more in? It's paid up, you don't have to put any more money in. So, you create an estate for one of your kids or your grand kids with the $10,000. You get the point? Take the $10,000 and leverage it. Buy more with it.

Let me show you how to gift away assets. If you have stock in a corporation, you can just start gifting away the stock. If you have units or stock in a trust, you can start gifting that away also. But the entity that I'd like to share with you right now is a limited partnership. We're going to call it a Family Limited Partnership, because a lot of times people only involve their families in it.

77

Limited Partnerships

The word limited means limited liability—if ten investors put in $10,000 to form a partnership to buy an apartment complex, they have $100,000. Let's say I'm the general partner and I take the investors' $100,000 and invest it. Now, let's say I forget to get insurance on it, the place burns down and we lose everything. What could you lose? You're limited in your liability; you can lose your $10,000. What about me? I can lose everything, I'm the general partner. I have general liability. They could put liens on my house, I could lose my business, I could lose everything.

When I see a man setting up a limited partnership my hat goes off to him. By the way, I'm the least chauvinistic guy you'll ever meet. Why did I say "man" there? I've been reviewing limited partnerships for over 17 years now. I've reviewed over 300 limited partnerships, and to this day not one time have I seen a woman be the general partner. Not one time. Now why is that? Well, I think they're too smart. I think that women realize that if they're going to put their necks on the line and risk losing everything, they're not going to get involved.

Well, I just bad mouthed being the general partner, but you still need to be the general partner. Male or female, you need to be the general partner. Simply put, you control the checkbook. You need to have the checkbook for this partnership, so you can control the direction of the investments and the direction of the company.

Limited partnerships can run businesses, they can have investments, they have their own federal ID number, they can have a brokerage account—they are separate legal entities. I like limited partnerships; I like them almost as much as corporations. A limited partnership can't have an off year-end like a corporation can have, but they're still limited in liability, just like a corporation is. The tax consequences of limited partnerships are really exciting—a limited partnership pays no taxes in and of itself.

Say that at the end of the year you own 5% of a partnership, your wife owns 5%, one of your kids owns 17%, another one owns 33%, and you have even given 20% to your mother and your father who are in their 60s or 70s. You gift out all these units. At the end of the year, if this partnership has made $100,000 in profits, the money is taxed down to the limited partners by their respective share of ownership. There are no taxes at the partnership level. (By the way, when we set up a limited partnership for people, we set it up with 100,000 units, and the units are then divvied up among the different people by percentages.)

Don't get me wrong, you don't have to actually give your money to the kids; your kids never see a dime of this money. It's just allocated to them in their tax brackets, and the money just goes into your own household checking account. You're buying groceries with it; you're going to the movies with it— the partnership is not taxed. It fills out an information return, a Form 1065, but the money is taxed down to the individual partners.

Let's say that you currently are worth a lot of money. You could set up a limited partnership for running a business; it has no assets of its own. It's a cash flow entity. It runs a business, it has a business, or it manages another business, and it just receives money and distributes money. That's one way of getting money into different tax brackets. But, let's say that you do have some existing assets: $600,000, $1 million, maybe even $2 million.

First of all, I really believe that if you're worth $2 to $3 million you should have multiple corporations. I don't think any one entity should own over 20% of all of your investments. So you should have at least five different legal entities.

For example, if you are worth $1 million, you should have three corporations and two limited partnerships that have about $200,000 equity in each of them. You could also set up a fourth corporation. If you have a lot of equity in another corporation or a lot of equity in your personal residence, with a corporation or a limited partnership you could put a deed of trust or a mortgage against your own personal residence. You could encumber all of the equity in your house, so if anybody ever sues you, they can never get at any of the equity. You do that as a trade.

You trade stock in a corporation and you give it to your kids or your grandkids. Then you put a lien against the property in the name of the corporation and you record the deed so that you can never ever lose the equity in your property.

Let's take a little time out here, we'll get back to the partnership in just a second. My job at the Wealth Academy, and my job as I go through this consulting series with a lot of people is to make them totally invincible. I literally set up a financial fortress around them so that they'll never lose anything. They could grow and become worth hundreds of thousands of dollars, but they'll never ever lose anything.

Now, let's get back to the partnership and I'll show you what that means from a couple of different angles. I'm going to use this example. You take your $2 million and put it into several partnerships. You deed, you assign, you transfer $2 million into the partnership. Now the units are divided. If you do it this way and you own everything, all the investments in the partnership, in this example the 100,000 units probably would have been 50,000 to Mom and 50,000 to Dad when the partnership was first set up. Now, think this one through, these are units. You have a ledger in the back of your partnership book and you have 100,000 units, 50,000 to Mom, 50,000 to Dad. Can Mom now give some of her units away? Figure out how much her units are worth and she can give them all away, but with no tax consequences.

She could give away $10,000 a year in these units. So she takes $10,000 and deeds them, assigns them to her children. Every year she gives away $10,000. You see what we've just done? We've now set up an entity that allows you to take control of your investments outside of your personal name, have the units owned by the mom and dad, and then gift them away to the kids. Mom and Dad are still the general partners.

They should keep 1% of the partnership units no matter what, but they could gift away 98 or 99% of all the units to their children, to their grandchildren, to their own mom and dad. They could give away everything, and still control the whole investment. They draw out all the salaries, they decide how much is going into Pension Plans, they have full control.

Now, let's see if we've solved the problem of gifting. The gifting problem was that you don't have a grouping of assets. Well, that problem is gone, because now you have nice, neat little groups of assets that you can give away.

When all the gifting is completed you still want to live that big happy life, you still control all the money in the partnership. See, the partnership now owns the investments, owns the rental properties, owns your businesses, et cetera. By the way, just to avoid personal liability, when you set it up make sure that your Nevada Corporation is the general partner. So your corporation, not you personally, is the general partner. This gives you another way of moving money out of your state to Nevada, and a bank account there to lessen your taxes, and you've avoided all personal liability.

Now, let me just mention another thing about limited partnerships: a lot of IRAs have had limited partnerships available to them, and sometimes these IRAs—the $2,000 that you put into a limited partnership—immediately goes down in value.

For example (and you'll be able to test me on this one because it's pretty wild), once I put $2,000 into my IRA, into a limited partnership that bought some movie production rights, video rights to movies. Now, it was making a fairly good return. I'd get my little $20 to $40 check every three months, and it was going into the account. I was getting a 6,

7, or 8% return on the money. I decided that I didn't want to have it anymore because it wasn't getting good returns; and I wanted to sell it.

I called up to sell it and the guy says, "Well, there's really no market place for them. We could put it on the computer and see if anybody wants to buy it."

"Are there a lot of other ones for sale right now?" I asked.

"We've got quite a few of them here," he said. "There are about 80 of them that are for sale right now."

"What are they going for?" I asked.

"Well, some people are willing to sell them for $680. Here's one who's willing to sell his for $620," he responded.

"Now hold it," I said. "You're telling me that the $2,000 I put into this IRA awhile ago, if I wanted to sell that right now I can get $620?"

"Yes," he said. He was really embarrassed to tell me that.

"Wow, this is great!" I said.

My wife said, "What?"

I said, "This is great!"

If the investment is $2,000, and I'm getting about an 8% return on my money, and if I could buy three of them …

"Are you telling me right now that I can buy three of these that other people want to sell at around $600? For under $2,000 I can buy another three of these partnerships?"

He says, "Sure, you could do that."

"I'm getting an 8% return on the $2,000, but I'm going to get it based on $800 or $600. That is a great return." So I put another $2,000 into them, and I'm getting about a 24% return on my money on these limited partnerships.

Now, if you get a little queasy here, I don't want you doing this. I mean, you've got to have a little bit of toughness to you, because those partnerships may continue to decrease in value even after that, and you could end up with nothing. I fared very well on these. All I'm saying is that I shouldn't have gotten involved in the first place, but I always try to make lemonade out of lemons, and this one worked out well for me.

I very seldom get excited about a legal entity like I have about the Charitable Remainder Trust. This is a phenomenal entity with a little twist to it that makes it really exciting. There are four kinds of trusts. Most of them don't work for what I'm going to show you.

78

Charitable Remainder Trusts

What I'm talking about is a Charitable Remainder Unitrust. Let's say you're making $50,000 a year, and you've got some investments, some rental properties, and all that. You can set up a trust, what is called a charitable remainder unitrust—technically, it's called a split interest trust.

The split interest in this trust is going to be this: you will be the income beneficiary and you'll choose a charity to get the investments that you place into the trust when you die. That will be the charity beneficiary. This charity beneficiary could be your church—I recommend that, because you have 30 and 50% charities. The government has an approved list of 50% charities, and churches fall into that category. You donate to this charity some appreciated stock or real estate. You're the trustee of this trust, you control all the investments held in trust, which could have been a rental property or anything else. You sell that property for cash.

The point is that you now get a $100,000 donation. You get a deduction. If it's a 50% charity that's eventually going to get the money, then you can deduct 50% of your current income. Well, if you're making $50,000 a year you get a $25,000 donation deduction, and now your income is only $25,000. If you're making $180,000 you could take $90,000 off and not pay taxes on that. Think about what I just said: you've been able to take something and give it to a charity that you really like, that you want to have the money later on, but you get a deduction right now, and an incredible savings off your income tax.

Now, if you take a $25,000 deduction this year, and you donated a $100,000 asset, you still have $75,000. So you take 50% of your income next year, then 50% the next year, and so on until that $100,000 is gone. Later on you could even donate something else. You can continue to make donations to this charity.

Now, each year, because you're the income beneficiary, you have to pull out 5%, even up to 15%, but you have to take out at least 5% of the assets. So, if you have $100,000 in there, you need to pull out $5,000. But hold it, we're going to show you a real neat angle to this.

If you use us to set up your CRT—Charitable Remainder Trust—we'll set it up with what is called "makeup provisions." What this means is that if you cannot pull out the money, if there's no income in the trust now, you'll be able to make that income when those assets eventually make money. So you have this makeup provision in the trust.

Now you take the $100,000 and buy stock with it, but you don't have that stock make dividends. So, year after year they're growing in value but they don't produce any dividends. Later on, when you're 65 years old, let's say that you have $400,000 in this trust. Your income is going to go down substantially. You know, you have a little Social Security, a Pension Plan, and your income will go down from $80,000 or $90,000 a year; to around $45,000 a year. But now, remember, you've got this $400,000 sitting there.

You have to pull out 5% of it, but here's what you do: at the age of 62 or 65 you start changing all the kinds of investments. Because it's time to retire, now you start buying high income investments, high yielding investments. You switch off the high growth to high yields. Well, it's easy to get 10% from them, a lot of mutual funds get 14 to 15%, but you get 10%. Well, 5% of $400,000 at that time is $20,000. You have to pull that out. But remember your return, 10% of the $400,000 is $40,000.

You've got $400,000 in investments in this account that you're the trustee of; 10% of that is $40,000. You pull out 5% of the $400,000, or $20,000. Remember all that money you didn't pull out for the last 20 to 30 years because there was no income in the trust? Well, with that makeup provision you start to pull out that money, or the balance of this $40,000, or another $20,000.

Let's say at the age of retirement you're making $60,000 a year. Your Pension Plan and Social Security takes your income down to $25,000; however, now you have $20,000 coming out and another $20,000, you're now at $65,000 a year and it's time to live the good life.

You've now lessened your estate. If you put all these donations into the charity, based on what they could have been worth in your own estate, your family would have to pay estate taxes on that. However, you've donated them to the Charitable Remainder Trust, and it's outside of your estate right now because this is a grantor trust, and you can't get the assets back out. By the way, the trust could also pay the premiums on a life insurance policy through an irrevocable life insurance trust. It could do that. It could pay all of the entities. You'll have to claim that premium as income, but now you ask, "What about my kids?"

First of all, this should not have been your only entity. You should still have a Living Trust and other entities to take care of your family. This one is for the excess things that you want to go to a charity upon your death. You buy a second life insurance policy on your husband or wife because the trust is going to stay in existence until the second person dies. Upon the death of the second spouse, husband or wife, the trust or the life insurance pays off $400,000 to your kids. They get everything that they were going to get anyway, and still the charity gets the other $400,000 in investments at that point in time. What a neat thing that you can do. You take deductions now, lessen your estate now, make sure your kids are taken care of, profit by incredible cash flow for yourself either now and/or in the future. This CRT is a phenomenal way to go.

79
Integrating Your Entities

This strategy is about the integration of all of these entities. There are three basic entities, and five total that I really think are important here in the United States. The three basic entities are the corporation, the Living Trust, and the Pension Plan. Those are the three basic entities that everybody needs. The other entities that you can pick and choose from are the Limited Partnership and the Charitable Remainder Trust. Now you understand these entities and how they work together.

For example, the corporation can be the general partner of the partnership. A partnership can own stock in a corporation. The stock that you also own in a corporation could and should be owned by your Living Trust, in order to make sure that none of the stock is in your own name.

You could take one corporation and put liens against your other corporation, or put liens against your personal residence to avoid any threat of lawsuits, and even if you do get sued you won't lose any of your equity. You can integrate these entities in so many ways that there's just no way that I can do justice to all of them in this book.

When you let us set up your entities we literally sit there with you and custom design them—have your corporation here, that moves money over here; that corporation does this and this; your Living Trust up here is an umbrella entity and owns the stock in this; you have your personal residence here, this is what you do here; you move money into a Pension Plan over here. It is really, really fun to show people how to integrate these entities.

I also have a good video tape of this, that is part of a bonus included with the Financial Fortress set of books and tapes. It's called the Entity Integration Video. It's about an hour and a half of me actually designing and diagramming these different entities, as you watch. I encourage you to sit down and take time to structure yourself, and to learn how these different entities interact with each other.

Take care of "You"—nobody is going to do this for you. You imagine tonight your CPA getting home, snuggling down into bed, pulling his covers up around his neck, and you tell me how much he's worried about your financial situation. You need to set these things up and do them yourself. You need to get going. You need to not only understand these different entities but you need to set them up. I have prototype Living Trust documents available to help you.

80

Taking Care Of You

I'm amazed at how many people buy our prototype Living Trust documents and go home and do nothing about it. Literally tens of thousands of dollars of information is in those documents, and some people don't even use them. Well, it's time to get going. It's time to quit making excuses and get these entities set up, so that you are financially fit for opportunity—if you don't do it nobody else will. So, you've got to get the information and you've got to get these entities set up. If my company can be of help in doing that, can help you get these things structured so that you are financially fit so you can sleep when the wind blows, then great. I'd love to help you do that.

SECTION SEVEN

This section is about saving money on taxes. Now, before we get into some of the details and specifics that we're going to cover in this section, let me just tell you my philosophy right up front.

My personal philosophy with regard to tax and wealth creation is this: cash, tax write offs, and growth are the benefits of owning anything. This is true whether you're buying a rental house, stocks, municipal bonds, or other tax shelter type vehicles. We're always looking for cash flow, tax write offs, and growth.

With most kinds of investments you get one or two benefits of ownership. We need all three if possible. The only two investments I've found that consistently give you all three at one time, and with only a small amount of money required to get started, are real estate and owning your own business. I hope you take this to heart, because this one tip will make you more money and help you keep more money than anything else that I'm going to teach. So, this is about you and keeping the money you make.

Tax Strategies

Saving Money On Taxes

Let's talk about real estate and other types of vehicles for saving money on taxes. A lot of people turn to real estate as a tax shelter. Or they turn to limited partnerships that do either real estate type investments or research and development, so they can get tax write offs. But the very investments that they are buying for tax write offs, hopefully, are also growing in value and cash flow. Now isn't that the best of all worlds? See, what I'm trying to get at is that I see that people are trying to get wealthy. As they get wealthy, they get there by buying things that save money on taxes. Now, that may be a little bit nebulous, so let's get more specific.

I'm a guest on radio shows all around the country. If they are live, almost every time before I get out of the studio, somebody will drive over there and meet me at the door. They want to talk about some wild idea that they've heard or that they are doing to get out of paying income taxes. Usually, I give them my time and I very seldom hear anything new. I've heard it all.

Don't get me wrong. I, like everyone else, am tired of the IRS, the intrusion, and the Gestapo-like tactics. I think we're all tired of that. I also think we're tired of a government that's just hell bent on getting at our wallets. It's almost like they're asking us to send them all our money, send them all our credit cards, send them all our hope and they'll finally be happy.

Every time that they push to take our money away from us, we have to push back to protect ourselves. We literally have to build a fort around ourselves. That is the whole idea behind all the entities that we've been talking about—building a financial fortress around ourselves so that we can keep our chips on our side of the table and not send an exorbitant amount of money to Washington, D. C.

Some of the things I've been told by the people that come to the radio stations to meet me are: become a patriot; get rid of your social security number; you are a sovereign citizen, therefore, you don't have to pay your income tax. I mean, I've heard them all.

I think that some of these ideas have a lot of value. The Constitution and the Internal Revenue Code pretty much say that we should be paying a voluntary income tax. I've heard all that as reason not to pay taxes. But I've decided that in my own life I do not want to fight the battle that way. I would rather fight the IRS legally, by purchasing the assets.

For example, you buy a $200,000 fourplex. That building, hopefully, is growing in value because you bought it as a good investment, and, hopefully, you got it under market value. (If you don't know how to do that, you ought to be getting my Real Estate Cash Flow System, so you learn how to buy things at substantial discount.)

The point is that you get the property at a bargain, or it's growing in value, or you create some immediate value. If it's not producing a positive cash flow for you right now, it will probably do so in the future. Regardless, it's producing tax write offs that you can not only use against your income from that property but also use against other income that you're making. So, one property can produce a positive cash flow and yet have enough paper losses that would offset that income, and move over to other income and offset that, too. You see the point? Those people that are getting wealthy are getting wealthy a lot of the time with tax shelter type investments. That's a good way to go.

Along with my philosophy I'm going to paraphrase Ronald Reagan. He basically said that if we wanted to be patriotic, we should quit sending all of our money to Washington, D. C. We should keep it at home, building up neighborhoods, creating jobs, et cetera. Our representatives in Washington, D. C. just waste our money.

We can keep it at home beautifying neighborhoods and fixing up houses, buying investments and helping companies start that are creating jobs. We could do so much more with our money. I think that if we want to be patriotic, we need to learn every legal way that we can minimize our tax liabilities. That is what this is all about.

This topic is not going to be earth shaking to a lot of people. As a matter of fact, it may be a little depressing to some of you. There are three ways of taxing people or items: by the activity, by an identity, or by ownership. Let's go through these again.

82

How We Are Taxed

One way of taxing people is by an activity, for example a sales tax. With sales tax, people are taxed according to the services or products they use.

Another way is by identity. This is why everyone has to have a Social Security number. Everyone is going to be attached to a number, and every number will be taxed.

One of the things the government does not like to have happen is for people to form contracts with each other. For example, trust arrangements, Living Trusts, and things like that, are not entities established by the state or by the government. They are established by a contractual arrangement between people; two numbers that are currently taxed by identity. The government cannot regulate those contractual arrangements, therefore, they don't like them.

They want to make sure that everybody is an entity that has an ID number that can be taxed and tracked. So you can do a lot of things outside the normal system if you do not have one of these numbers attached to you. I'm not saying here that you should be in the black market or doing anything illegal, just that you can have all kinds of relationships between people that are not going to be taxed. If you do set up an entity, like a corporation, then you need to get a federal ID number, and that corporation then becomes an entity and, therefore, an identity. It has profits and losses and has to pay taxes.

The third way of taxing you is on what you own. For example, you pay property taxes on your house and other properties that you have.

These are the three basic ways of taxing. As we go through this, I'm going to show you several different ways of minimizing that.

I remember a cartoon I saw awhile ago that looked like a congressional debate, and there was a man standing up there and he said, "Gentlemen, let me tax your memories." He was obviously referring to something that happened in the past. One of the other congressmen looked at another one of his friends and said, "Wow, tax your memories. Why didn't I ever think of that?"

It's like any time that Congress or any state legislatures can figure out a way to tax people, they do so. If we're going to avoid taxes, we need to make sure that we don't cut back on our income to lower our tax liability. I see too many people saying, "Well, if I go work overtime with my company, I'm going to make too much money. I'm going to pay so much in taxes." I think we need to get out of that whole mentality. Instead, we need to establish legal entities or write offs to lower our taxes.

Talking about different identities, up until 1986 there was a major move all across in this country. Financial planners and advisors were telling people how to use their children. For example, instead of buying stock in your own name, you open up an account for your children and buy stock in their name.

83

Using Your Children

If you were in a 28, 30 or 40% tax bracket, and your kids were at a 15% or, better yet, a 0% tax bracket, then any profits made from dividends, interest, whatever are going to be taxed at a lower tax bracket. This was the big rave. Everybody was using children. Grandparents were giving gifts to children, and the children were making money, and that money was taxed at a lot lower rate than the parents.

But as of 1986 everything changed. The IRS changed the law. From then on, children were to be taxed at the same tax bracket as the parents. Everybody said, "Well, there goes that idea." All the CPAs, financial planners, and tax attorneys said, "That was sure wonderful while it lasted." Everybody just gave up on this whole idea about using children. Well, not me.

I'm in the real world. I'm working with people. You don't give up on good ideas. You keep looking at the law. You keep staring at the paragraph until something happens. Listen to the law again. From now on, children are taxed in the same tax bracket as the parents. Well, it seems to me that one of the things we've got to do then is get the parents in a lower tax bracket. Also, we need to make sure that if the children are over 14 they are making money in their own names, because that will definitely be taxed in a different tax bracket.

Don't get me wrong, now. If Mom and Dad have three kids—a 10 year old, a 12 year old, and a 16 year old—the 10 and 12 year olds' money will be taxed with the parents. They'll be aggregated as one whole. If the parents are making money and the children are making money, they can't escape paying taxes on the whole thing as if it was made as one. If you have children over the age of 14, then this becomes really exciting.

If they're teenagers and/or if they're older, then you can do a lot of fun things. Let's go back and talk about the limited partnership, for example. I'm going to give you several things from a tax point of view besides the tax brackets for the children. One of the things that we've got to do is to pay Social Security (FICA) taxes.

Now, if you work for a company, you know that they withhold Social Security taxes of 7.65% (1997) from your paycheck and then your employer matches that amount. Part of the withholding tax is for Medicare (1.45% if you are an employee, matched by your employer, and 2.90% if self employed) with an additional percentage of 6.20 for other things. FICA ends at $62,700 (1997) and the Medicare tax has no limit. But if you are self-employed that 15.3% (7.65% employee and 7.65% employer) has to be paid by you. After you pay Social Security taxes on the first $62,700 of your income, then you still have that 2.9% that goes on up to infinity.

That's a bad deal. I mean, let's just talk about a simple little company making $50,000 a year. This is net profit. It's a little mom and pop operation making $50,000 a year. They owe the IRS $9,000 out of that $50,000, and they're going to have to pay 15.3% of the $50,000 toward Social Security. It's going to go on their Schedule SE , their self employment taxes, and they're going to owe about another $7,500. That's one of the most pitiful things around. Any studies that you read right now say that you're never going to get back out of Social Security what you put into it.

Right now we have tons of younger people feeding the Social Security system to support the older people who are currently living on Social Security. If you could take your money that's going into Social Security and stick it into any kind of investment at 4, 5, or 6%, you're going to do better on that and have more, and I mean a lot more, money upon retirement than you're ever going to get out of Social Security. I think a lot of people realize that Social Security is a bad investment.

Now everybody says, "Well, but, there's going to be the Social Security safety net. I'll at least have something coming in." No, no, no. That money could earn so much more, than you're ever going to get out of Social Security if it was just put into some simple investments.

So, from a philosophical and a financial point of view, Social Security just doesn't work. Even if we just did away with it and people started taking care of each other and churches and younger people got involved with taking care of their parents, there would be so much more happiness. If you could take the money that you're paying into Social Security right now and use it to support your mom and dad, or whatever, why not? That's the way it should be. People taking care of people, not people relying on the government.

I heard on a radio program how the government is going to pick up the tab for this—the federal government will pay this. Instead those news reporters should say, "The money for this project is going to be paid for by you. You're going to have to pay taxes on that, and the federal government is going to take your money away from you and then give it to these other people over here." We don't hear that.

Well, let's go back to this limited partnership and I'll show you how to kill two birds with one stone. Limited partnerships are taxed at the partners' level. At the end of the year a limited partnership fills out a Form 1065, which is an information return, and issues K-1s for all the different owners. So, if you have a limited partnership owned 5% by Mom and 5% by Dad—maybe they are the general partners, or their Nevada Corporation is a general partner—that is another way of moving money around into different tax brackets. Then you have some of the units in the partnership owned by your children, maybe 15% each to your three kids—that's

45%. Then you have maybe 10 or 20% of the units owned by your parents and maybe your nieces and nephews or somebody else that you choose. Now, remember, the partnership is not taxed; the shareholders—the unit holders— are taxed.

You go on down the road, and your little company makes $100,000. Toward the end of the year you have to pay taxes on it. So, the money does not have to be pulled out, but you pay taxes on it as if you had pulled it out. The losses and the profits are taxed down at the unit holders level.

At the end of the year the partnership has a net profit of basically $100,000; it pays no taxes. Mom and Dad each own 5% of the units, so they have to claim 5% of the income, or $5,000 each, that's $10,000 total. They have two children under the age of 14 owning 15%, so that's $30,000 to them, $15,000 each, and they have a child over the age of 14 owning 15%, or $15,000. They also have their mom, dad, and others who own the balance of the units.

Remember, again, that none of the money has to be actually pulled out, but the people are going to be taxed on it. You may have to gift your mom, dad and the others enough money to pay the taxes on the money that should have come out, but didn't, which is held by the partnership.

So the partnership, or the mom and dad, keeps the $100,000. The people running the partnership take all the money home, stick it in their account, pay their bills with it, pay their house payment with it, whatever. The money does not have to be paid to the partners, it can be paid to whomever: you may want to pay some of the partners, such as the grandparents. Now, just follow this thing through.

You have 5% that has to be claimed by the parents, 15% by the kids, but you've now kept all the people under 14, and the parents, under around $30,000 to $40,000. Most of that money is going to be taxed at 15%. The child who is over the age of 14 is going to be taxed on her $15,000, and up to $24,650 of income (1997) for single people, they're taxed at 15%. Grandma and Grandpa are getting $10,000 each and they're taxed at 15%. You see the point? You do this instead of having $100,000, wherein you would have some of it taxed at 15%, some at 28%, and some even at 31% for Mom and Dad, if they took home everything. They still get to take home everything, or almost everything, but the whole $100,000 is taxed at 15%.

When the law changed and everyone abandoned it, you know me, I just stuck with it. When I'm on the case, we're going to stick with this deal and we're going to figure it out. So, now you have a little company that you really work hard at making $100,000, and every bit of it is taxed at 15%. I just saved you 13%, and sometimes even more, on all of that money; and we're not done. It even gets better.

The money coming out of a partnership, if it comes out as earned income, let's say Mom and Dad draw a fee out of $10,000 or $20,000. It is earned income, and they're going to have to pay Social Security taxes on that money. But all the money that is paid to the unit holders at the end of the year is unearned income, and, watch carefully now, there are no Social Security taxes on unearned income.

So, you have a little business held as a limited partnership. (By the way, the S Corporation could be treated the same way.) This company, held as a limited partnership, is easy to set up, easy to operate, and easy to set up your bank accounts for. The business makes $100,000. We got all of it taxed at 15%, with no Social Security taxes being paid at all. Not only can you use your children, but you can use your children in conjunction with these entities to really give you a double whammy and double savings on these taxes.

84

New Depreciation Rules

This strategy deals with the new depreciation rules. Briefly let me tell you what they've been in the past. If you have a house, a duplex or two, and they create write offs, depreciation expense, other kinds of losses, whether they are real or on paper, you may only take $25,000 of those losses against your active income—that's the law. That's the way it is today. Once you hit $100,000, for every dollar over $100,000 that you make, you lose 50¢ of this $25,000. It kind of fades away, so by the time you go from $100,000 to $150,000, you've lost your ability to write off anything.

Now, you can move that right or ability to the future. You can put it off and use it some time when you sell the property and have passive capital gains down the road. Then you could use these passive capital losses that you haven't been able to use against your income. That's the way the depreciation rules are today.

By the way, they have not changed. That's the way the laws are, but there is another variation on this. If you're in the real estate business, you develop properties, you build properties, you buy, fix up, and sell properties, you rent them, et cetera. If you're in the real estate business, and one-half of your time is spent—a minimum of 750 hours a year which you have to keep track of—conducting your business, pay attention to the following paragraph.

Let's say the husband in the family is making $80,000 a year, and the wife basically handles the rental properties, collects rents, does this and that, whatever it takes to run the business. Let's say that they have a number of rental properties and they create $60,000 a year in losses. If they meet this new criteria, the 750 hours, they may now take all of the $60,000 in losses against the $80,000 in income. That puts them in a lower tax bracket, and with personal exemptions, donations, they may get out of paying taxes altogether. You can zero out once again.

This is the point: you can zero out. You don't have to pay taxes. The problem is that you have to buy enough rental real estate, which most people are not willing to do. A lot of people have tried rentals in the past and they haven't cut it. They haven't been all that they are cracked up to be. But, if you're willing to play the game, you may now offset all your income; even create other losses that could offset other years.

Also, if either of the spouses—if you're married—goes out and spends half of their time, or a minimum of 750 hours a year, the losses created by the rental real estate activities could be used against both of their incomes. You don't need both spouses to qualify. Just one spouse can qualify and wipe out both of their incomes. These are the new depreciation rules.

If you're in business or thinking about being in business, even a part-time business, you will be buying computers, copy machines, telephones, cars, and other kinds of equipment to use.

85

Asset Expensing

This does not involve real property, but with equipment, you may now take the first $17,500 of all the equipment purchases in any given year and write it off that year using section 179 of the IRS Code. You don't have to depreciate over five, seven, or 10 years the first $17,500 worth of depreciation. If you have a little business and you make $67,500, not only do you have income tax to pay on those profits, but you also have Social Security tax to pay as well. You could take the $17,500 of losses right now instead of deducting $2,000 or $3,000 this year and depreciating the rest over a period of time. You now have a $50,000 net income. You not only saved money on Federal Income taxes you saved money on Social Security taxes.

A lot of the states recognize Section 179, too. If you have a state income tax and your state recognizes Section 179, you can use it to save on taxes to your state on that same $17,500. This is a nice deal, but it's not going to make or break anybody. If you have a $17,500 write off and you're in a 28% tax bracket—let's round it to 30%—30% of $17,000 is a little over $5,000. Taking the write off now will put that cash in your pocket; you do not have to send it to the IRS.

With this knowledge of Section 179, when you walk in and talk to your CPA say, "I bought all this equipment for my business and I want to Section 179 it." They'll say, "Okay," and fill out the proper forms. If you don't tell them, few CPAs out there—like one in a hundred—will actually do Section 179 for you. The other 99 will just depreciate all the equipment over the five to seven years, so that they have a job calculating your taxes instead of taking it all right now. You ought to get to know Section 179, because it is a nice savings every year.

86

Deduct The Intangibles

This strategy is about being able to deduct the intangibles when selling a business or buying a business. As you know, the tax law right now is really strange. Whether you buy a business for $2 million (and a lot of big companies are buying businesses in the hundreds of millions of dollars) or if you buy a business for $200,000 or $2 million, you have to determine the value of the equipment and the inventory. You can deduct the inventory, and now you can also spread out claiming the equipment over seven or 10 years.

Now, let's say you buy this $2 million business and $500,000 of it is land and equipment, you get to depreciate it. What about the other $1.5 million? Why are you paying $2 million? Well, you're paying that for employees in place. You're paying that extra money to buy an existing business that has a location, a customer base, a mailing list, possibly some intangible type copyrights or rights to other things. You're buying the business for $2 million because it makes money and it's worth $2 million to you. But you only get to deduct $500,000, and that's unfair.

Under the new tax law, almost all of those intangibles are now deductible over a 10 year—some of them 15 year— period of time. So, not only do you get to deduct the $500,000 of your $2 million purchase on different schedules, you now can deduct the goodwill or blue sky business part of it, the other $1.5 million. Let me tell you where this is important.

If you're trying to sell a business, you can sell a business for a higher price, because the person buying the business can possibly pay you some of the money they're not going to pay over a period of time due to tax savings. If you're trying to purchase a business, you can purchase even a bigger one than you planned, because you get these extra tax write offs that give you extra money in your pocket every year. You can afford to pay more for the business and/or save more or keep more of your profits because you get extra tax write offs.

Section 42 of the Internal Revenue Code involves low income housing credits. Please don't get turned off by the phrase "low income." Low income means 60% or less of the median family income in any particular area. Now, if the median family income in your area is $34,000 a year, you take 60% of that, or around $20,000. Now here's the way it works. If you

87

Low Income Housing Credits

have tenants in a house, a duplex, a fourplex or a twentyplex that qualify as low income people, you can apply for IRS or federal tax credits.

A tax credit is a dollar for dollar write off against the tax liability that you owe. So, for example, if you're making $140,000 a year, your taxes on that are $36,000. Now if you had a $10,000 tax deduction that would go against the $140,000, you'd now be making $130,000 and you'd save about $3,000 in income taxes. If instead of having a $10,000 tax deduction you could actually go out and get a $10,000 tax credit, that credit would go right against, dollar for dollar, the $36,000 tax liability that you owe. So, instead of owing $36,000 you would now owe $26,000, and there would be, obviously, a $10,000 savings. There are energy credits, research and development credits, some historical credits, and now low income housing credits.

When this program started in the mid 1980s, it was really popular. Watch what happens here. If you get a building qualified, and the IRS contracts with an agency in this state to handle the distribution of these credits, each state gets $1.25 in credits each year for every resident that they have. So, if your state has 20 million people, it's going to get about $25 million in tax credits—that's just the way it works. Now, there has to be a state agency distributing these credits, and you have to go down and fill out a million pages of forms to get these. In just a minute I'll show you how not to do that. But the credits are so phenomenal you may want to go jump through all the hoops to get one of these deals put together.

Let's say you buy a nineplex, and this nineplex costs $500,000. You get a tax credit if it's considered new, which means that it's never been lived in or you've done substantial remodeling to each of the units. You now receive a 70% tax credit on the full $500,000. Oh yes, yes, you still get to depreciate it, too. You take out land with a value of $100,000 and you still get to depreciate the $400,000, which will give you $14,000 or so a year in tax deductions. We're not talking tax deductions here, we're talking tax credits. You get a 70% tax credit on the full $500,000, or $350,000 in tax credits. The way it works is you divide that by 10 years, you spread it out over 10 years, which gives you $35,000 a year in tax credits. There is a $25,000 limitation that you can take. You can only wipe out $25,000 in taxes with these types of tax credits.

You're all smart; think this one through. Own 15% of this building as a corporation and the corporation is going to get 15% of these tax credits. Own an additional 15% in another corporation and that corporation is also going to get some of these tax credits. By the way, in corporations it's unlimited; you can take as many of these tax credits as you want and wipe out all the taxes you owe. So, even if you have a company making $1 million a year, and you owe, say, $300,000 in taxes, you could buy enough of these tax credit type investments to wipe out all of your $300,000 and pay no taxes at all on your corporation. But as an individual, you're limited to $25,000.

If the property is old—a lot of people will not go to new properties—then you get a 30% tax credit. So, 30% of the $500,000 is $150,000 a year. Divide that again by 10, spread that out over 10 years, and you get $15,000 a year. You could buy a couple of properties and get them qualified for the tax credits.

Think about having a property. Hopefully, it's producing cash flow, making money for you and growing in value. It's also giving you tax depreciation, so you're wiping out some of your income and having a lesser tax liability. Whatever tax liability you have, you now get this tax credit to wipe it out. A lot of you will not go through all the necessary paperwork and jump through all the hoops necessary to put one of these deals together on an active basis, but you can do this on a passive basis. There are a lot of big companies around that have put these together in the past, and as this law becomes more uniform, there's going to be a lot more people getting involved. A lot more big companies are getting involved like they were in the past.

You can get involved as a passive investor. Put up $15,000 or $20,000 as a passive investment. I've seen some in the past where you put up $20,000 and get back almost $5,000 a year in tax credits for the 10 years, plus you get some of the cash flow, some of the growth, and all that as one of the limited partners in a partnership. So, go looking for these tax shelter type of investments. They're called low income housing credits.

There are a lot more details, obviously, that I haven't covered in this book, but it's worth looking into. Section 42, low income housing credits, are phenomenal because you can zero out again. You can use the other strategy I talked about back in point number 84 regarding the use of rental properties, and that will help you zero out, but you've got to buy a lot of them. Do you understand? With this one property—one $500,000, $300,000, or $400,000 property—you can wipe out all the taxes that you owe.

88

Claiming Your Income

This one is about claiming income when you want to claim it as income. If you allow the IRS to tell you when you're going to have to claim income as income, they're always going to tell you that you have to claim it at the worst possible time for you. You can control that though. Let me give you a couple of ways. One way is when you set up your corporation, have an off year end, say January 31st. The company goes out and starts making money on February 1st or in May, in October, whenever, and make your first corporate year end January 31$^{st.}$ The point is that you get the year end past December 31st.

Start off in February, March, April, May, the spring, the summer, the fall, et cetera, and you take some of your money clear into the winter of the next year, you get it past December 31st. If you pull out a big chunk of money in December, say for Christmas, you're going to have to pay heavy duty taxes on that. Just leave some of that money in there and pull it out in January. Get it past December 31st.

Now, you received the money in January and you may want to give it to two or three people, like wives, kids, et cetera, so you can avoid the estimated quarterly taxes. Just get your money out of this entity right before January 31st. On January 31st, when that corporation does its year end tax returns, it could zero out. It could have paid you all the money in January and pay no taxes at all. But you received the money in January, you and several other people, and you don't have to pay taxes on that money now until perhaps April 15th of the next year, 15 months from right now.

This is when all the big corporations have their year end, January 31st, March 31st, et cetera. By the way, I like March 31st, too, even though I may have lost a couple months of earning power before December 31st comes around, but it's on a calendar quarter. If you choose January 31st it's better, but it's worse from a bookkeeping point of view, so your CPA will like it more if you're on a March 31st year end. You want to get it as close to the end of the year as you can, but on a calendar quarter basis.

January 31st year ends have been used by big corporations for years. Big corporations all have their sales at Christmas time, and they have passed out their store manager bonuses and all the regional managers bonuses right before their corporate year ends. They don't particularly care when the people get the money. They just want to get all their expenses out before the year end, so they can lessen their tax liability.

Another way of getting control of when you claim income as income is to borrow the money from your corporation. Literally, create what is called a forgivable loan. Now, it has to be done at a fair interest rate, but if your corporation is making a mediocre amount of money and you're making really good money, you may want to pull out another $50,000 from the corporation. If you do, you'll get killed on taxes, so you say, "Let me just borrow the money." So, you borrow the money on a one, two, three, four, or five year demand note.

Let's say four years from right now the situation changes. You've got other tax write offs, you've got some of these tax credits now available, you're still making pretty good money, and the corporation is having a great year. In the year that you did this, the year that you loaned yourself the money, you didn't have to claim it as income, but the corporation also doesn't get to deduct it, so the corporation has to pay taxes on it. That was okay, though, because the corporation was in a low tax bracket that year.

Now the situation has reversed. The corporation's in a big tax year, I mean big tax bracket, but you are having a mediocre year. Well, the corporation just forgives the debt. In the year that the corporation forgives the debt, the corporation can now deduct it. It needs to deduct that $50,000, because it's in a high tax bracket and needs the write offs. But you, however, you have to claim it now.

It's debt relief, in effect. You don't pay the money back, the corporation forgives the debt. You have to claim all or part of that $50,000, depending on how much you forgave, so let's say you have to do the whole $50,000. Why is that okay this year for you? Because you've got other tax write offs and things to do. This is called a forgivable loan. If you go into your CPA, he can handle it for you. This is very, very common; big companies do it all the time.

Another way to have the benefits of assets and not have to claim them as income is to have the corporation pay for them for you. It would pay for things that you can pay for yourself but you cannot deduct them and the corporation can. For example, an S Corporation can only deduct part of medical insurance, and sole proprietorships are limited, but a regular ordinary C Corporation, which I like the best anyway, can write off all the money for medical insurance, and some life insurance. It can buy a car or truck for you. It can have a company get-together. It can pay for trips. It can do all kinds of things that you can pay for but you cannot deduct. These are several ways that will help you get a handle on reducing your personal taxable income.

If you really want to make a lot of money and live a little bit richer than normal, you need to quit acting like an employee. This means that you quit taking home money, paying taxes on that, and then whatever is left over goes into your different activities. For example, how many of you right now think that it would be in the best interest of your corporation, your fam-

89

Quit Acting Like An Employee

ily corporation, for your customers and clients to have two season tickets to the Lakers or the Boston Celtics, or to whatever football or basketball or baseball team? You see, if you go down to a baseball field or a football field, you'll notice on all the box seats that a lot of those boxes are purchased by CPAs and law firms. Instead of you spending your money—$20 or $30—to go to a game, why not have the corporation pay for those tickets for you? How many of you, by the way, also think that your corporation, in the best interest of your employees and your customers and clients, should buy a boat or a yacht for sailing in the bay? You use it for taking out your customers and clients. The corporation starts acting like the big corporations in purchasing these different kinds of things that will really save you a lot of money.

As we wrap up this tax section, I hope I've given you enough to get you going and start saving money on taxes. I've only covered the tip of the iceberg here with all the different strategies that you can use. I'm just going to say one thing in conclusion—you need an effective bookkeeping system.

90

Effective Bookkeeping System

The irony of this whole thing is that the very nature of somebody who is really good at making money, really good at being aggressive and going out and making a lot of money, is usually the same kind of person who is not very good at keeping receipts and keeping track of all that they are doing. So, let me give you several things to do.

Obviously, you need to keep receipts. I don't want to belabor the point, if you don't get a receipt the cost of a tank of gas goes up 30%, depending on your tax bracket. You need to get receipts. I use debit cards all the time to keep track of my expenses, because I'm not very good at keeping receipts and writing things down.

Another thing you could do for effective bookkeeping is to realize the form that your items have to end up on. Everybody wants to set up a bookkeeping system, but really the most effective ones are the ones that are going to end up on the IRS forms that you have to fill out. For example, if the IRS calls maintenance "maintenance" then you call it maintenance instead of repairs or whatever.

Look at the form, for example a Schedule C or an 1120, and you realize all the different items you can list there. Make sure that your bookkeeping system conforms, so as you're keeping track of all that information. It'll not only give you the proper information that you need, but from a tax point of view, it will be applicable to the exact form that you have to use.

Also, if I can just say one more thing about effective bookkeeping: you get what you inspect. I think all of us in business thrive on information. We need information not only about where our bank account stands, but about what's working from an advertising point of view. If we know and we can monitor what we're doing, then we can get a lot further ahead because, what's the alternative? If you don't know where your bank account stands, if you don't know where you're heading, if you don't know what your profits are going to be, if you don't know what to set aside for tax liability, then it's just tough. So why not stay a step ahead in this format by knowing exactly what you want all your tax information to do for you.

Let me just summarize a few things here. You can, once again, zero out. There are many ways of doing that—depreciation, low income housing credit, or other energy credits. I'm now purchasing some stock that has energy credits and depletion allowances with the stock in the company. You can go looking for tax credits. You can go looking for deductions.

In short, those same things that are going to help you get wealthy in terms of cash flow and in growth, hopefully, will be the same type of investments that are producing tax write offs. Then, you can not only wipe out the income from that particular investment, but use those write offs, depreciation expenses or credits against income. With the 1996 tax law revisions you can even go back two years and go forward twenty. So, one year's enterprise, one year's situation can effect 23 different tax years—two in the past, this year, and twenty in the future if you create NOLs (Net Operating Loss).

Now, if you follow my advice on real estate, though, you're going to make a lot of money and you're not going to have a lot of NOLs. What we're talking about here are paper losses. So we need to create the paper losses to go along with the actual profits. We need to make sure that we're keeping our chips on our side of the table, working for us, doing the best job for us that they can, and to keep us growing so that we'll have more cash flow in the future, more growth.

Then that growth, again, will produce more cash flow. We get in a cycle where we're always running short, always behind, always trying to catch up and always cutting back because we're not making enough. The cycle we want to get into is one of prosperity. Read on and I'll show you how you can be an integral part of it.

SECTION EIGHT

Welcome to the last section of the book. For some of you this is going to be really exciting and others may say, "I've heard this kind of stuff before." I don't believe anyone's heard this before because my angles on motivation are totally different. This is not designed to be a motivational book, but good solid information that you could take and implement. Information you can take to the bank.

I don't think people need motivation from a financial seminar. They need hard hitting, industrial strength financial information. If you have a chance to learn to make money or learn to change your personality, what would you rather learn how to do? Well, I'd rather make money. If you learn how to make money you can change your personality later.

You, Inc.

When you get up in the morning and you look in the mirror you are looking at You, Inc. You're the president, the vice president, the secretary and treasurer, you're the board of directors, you're everyone. Because you are on the board of directors and you're controlling this little corporation—You, Inc.—it's very important that you understand just a few things about business.

If another company were taking over your company, when the new directors and officers show up on Monday morning they look at the balance sheets, the assets, the liabilities, they look at everything about the company. They've got to make some decisions about what they're going to keep, what they're going to help grow, what they're going to throw money into, and what they're going to try to pay off. They're going to look at your assets. They don't care when you bought something or even why you bought something. They want to know, "What is this asset producing for us? What is it making? And if we wanted to have it making more money how much more money will it take?"

Right now, you have a portfolio of stocks and bonds. You have real estate. No matter what you have, what I'd like you to do is to pretend you're doing a merger and another board of directors shows up. They look at your asset sheet and they say, "What is there about these holdings, investments, and assets that I would get rid of and what would I keep?" This is really tough to do, by the way, because you need to look at yourself from an outside person's point of view.

Get rid of all the emotional stuff and say, "What is producing me money and how much is it producing?" By the way, you can do this from a personal point of view, too. You can say, "I'm too sarcastic. Well, hey, that serves no purpose whatsoever. I need to get rid of that." You can get rid of some of the baggage. You can get rid of some of those things now. It's really tough to do, but you can do it if you decide to.

On the road to wealth we have to change a lot of things and the only motivational thing I'll say is that you're never going to change your bottom line until you change your head—what's in there and your attitude. It's not a complicated process.

When you see a rocket taking off, do you see that great, big tank on the back? What is that? It's fuel and it's only designed to get it a few thousand feet off the ground. Once it's out in space it takes very little fuel to run.

Remember what I said before about rockets? To get something up off the ground, let's compare it to a hot air balloon if you will. I lived in Arizona for many years. Can I share something with you that I learned about hot air balloons? I was out there watching these hot air balloons and I noticed that they only went up in Arizona in the winter time because it's so hot in the summer time. I thought at first that it must be a lot of work to launch and people don't want to work in the heat. But that's not the answer. The answer is that the hot air balloons do not go up in the summer because they need the cool air on the outside for them to rise. They need opposition. I think we're all kind of like that. We're going to have opposition. We're going to have things that we need to overcome, things that we need to do.

Life is a journey. I was retired at an early age and after being retired for seven months I realized that I really didn't like it. So, I went back out and started doing a lot more deals. There's more fun to me in the chase than in the catch.

Even now, I'm in my late 40s, and I've retired a couple of times. I could retire again, but I love teaching and I love working with people. I love structuring people. I love teaching my Wall Street Workshop and Wealth Academy. That's what I enjoy doing. So while we're trying to overcome all these things, it's good to realize that probably a lot of us have things in our portfolio, things in our asset liability sheet that do not need to be there.

What debts can we clear up? What things can we get rid of that are holding us back? What investments do we have that we need to buy more of or get them making even more money? What can we do to improve them? So remember, regarding You, Inc. doing this pretend merger is a great exercise and I do it a couple of times a year. A couple times a year I look at everything that I have and make some decisions on some of the investments I have that are just not panning out and get rid of them. I cut my losses and get on to other things that really make a lot of money.

Being more, doing more. I learned this from a friend of mine, who was also a seminar speaker. He was really big into rental type real estate and solving problems with rentals by taking on partners and by getting the tenants in the property to act more like owners of the property. He has a sentence in his seminar that I think is

92

Being More, Doing More

really powerful. He said, "Grow out of your problems." If you have a cash flow problem, buy more, create more to solve that cash flow problem. Don't cut back. If you have a tax problem, don't cut back growth. Purchase more things that will help you solve that problem.

Now a lot of us have been behind the eight ball before. We sometimes get in trouble with our businesses. They're not doing the right things, they're not making us the kind of money we want. If we really think it through and if the business is worth saving, a lot of times as we go through bad times, we come out on the other side of the eight ball a lot better off than we were before.

If you look at those kinds of things, we have to possibly let some people go or scale back on different projects—kind of regroup if you will. But when we come fighting back out, we can usually be a lot bigger and better than we were before. So grow and do more.

93

Having More Fun

This one is about doing what excites you and having more fun. One of the things that I really tried to do at my seminars is to get people to have more fun with making money. Now you go to a seminar and you get all excited. You're going to go out and buy this house and you're all excited about the potential of rental real estate and what it's going to produce for you. Or you hear about mutual funds and you want to become a really top notch stock market investor—you get really excited about that. But when you go home you're all alone. You're sitting there staring at the walls and you're saying, "Oh no, now what do I do?"

I suggest, everyone, that you get so excited about your business that you can hardly wait to get out of bed in the morning. By the way, it's pretty easy to do that in real estate. When I was doing my Money Machine I could buy a house in the morning for $86,000 and sell it by that afternoon for $94,000. I knew I was going to make $8,000 before I went to bed that night. That's exciting and it's easy to get out of bed in the morning. I love being excited about things and I love being excited about the little things in life.

People keep asking me what it is that drives me. I used to say caffeine but I gave that up awhile ago. What I enjoy is teaching; I love teaching. I define a lot of who I am by my ability to teach. I really enjoy doing adult education and I want to deliver and give them a lot of information. I love the teaching process and I think you can feel my enthusiasm for that. I love teaching, so I teach my staff. We work on training to make sure that they're doing a good job for people in structuring their entities. I'm living my ideal retirement because I'm doing what I love.

Another thing about having fun, about traveling. One of the bonus packages that we have with the Financial Fortress is information on travel. Because I travel so much, I wanted to save some money so I thought about becoming a travel agent.

I'm going to suggest to you right now that you also should become an outside travel agent. If you're going to travel, why not travel and save a lot of money? And, if you could travel and save a lot of money, how many of you would travel a lot more? Let me just share this with you about becoming a travel agent because it's fun. For your information, I've said this before and I've said it many times, if you purchase a seminar that's an investment type seminar, it's probably not tax deductible. But if you purchase a seminar for business purposes, for starting a business, for running a business, then those seminars are tax deductible.

For example, I do seminars in Hawaii a couple of times a year. Anytime you want to go to Hawaii, call my office, find out when we're doing a seminar in Hawaii, and go over there as a business seminar. All or part of that trip could be tax deductible because you're attending a business seminar in Hawaii.

Let's get back to travel. We've made arrangements with a company out of Orlando, Florida—Ideal Travel—to take people on as outside travel agents. An outside agent is not somebody sitting there with a computer all day long book-ing tickets and such. You operate out of your bedroom, out of your home, out of your business and you become an outside agent. You call an 800 number if you want to book tickets.

The cost is around $500 to do this, depending on whether it's a couple or just one person. For $500 to $600 you can become an outside agent. They send you training manuals and other information. Let me tell you why you should consider doing this.

First of all, you get incredible savings. Hotels and other travel companies in the industry will offer you certain courtesies to extend their business and to make sure that you're well taken care of because you're in the business. You can book tickets for other people. I stay at hotels that sometimes cost $250 night for $80 and $90 a night. I stay at $120 hotels for $40 or $50. I save about 50% on all my hotel bills almost all the time, sometimes even 70%. I used to rent cars for $40 or $50 a day now I'm renting them for $12 to $18 a day and getting upgrades from a $12 car to a Cadillac for $16.99 a day.

We have special arrangements at major theme parks. They usually allow travel agents in for free with parties of up to four people. You show your travel agent ID card and boom, you're in.

You can also save money on airline tickets. Because Ideal Travel is associated with several consolidators, they can shop for and get the very, very best tickets they can. This is not being on some travel agent's ARC (Airline Reporting Corporation) list where you get 75% off the coach fair. It has nothing to do with that. We get a standard ordinary ticket. When you show up to the airline and you get on the plane, you get your frequent flier miles and you're paying for a ticket just like anybody else. You save money only because they'll shop for you and find the very best that they can.

Number three is that you can earn commissions—in the industry typically it is a 10% commission. So, if you have an $800 flight the commission on that would be $80 and you get half of that. You get 50% of the 10% or about $40 in this example. You're not going to get rich off of this and you'll get a 1099 form at the end of the year, but you'll get checks every few months on all the commissions that you've earned up till that point in time.

Another reason for being a travel agent is upgrades. Almost 80% of the time I fly, I buy a coach ticket and I get upgraded to first class because I'm a travel agent.

Upgrades: sometimes I come into a hotel and I've got a $35 a night a room, which is normally $120, but then they go ahead and put me in the presidential suite which is a $300 or $400 a night room for $35 or $45. I've stayed all over the place in really nice hotels and gotten upgrades. Upgrades to first class, upgrades to better cars, I mean, they really try to take care of people in the travel agent industry.

Another thing are the FAM packages. FAM stands for familiarization—technically, it's familiarization and educational packages. These companies, hotels, and airlines put together whole trips for travel agents. Some that I've been on in the past include a four day and four night trip to a brand new Radisson Hotel in Acapulco for free, a ski trip to Vail, Colorado, airfare in and out, bus tickets to Vail from Denver, four nights lodging, the whole thing for $150. And this is like a $1,500 trip that you get for $150 as a FAM package for travel agents.

My wife and I went to London. Whole trip to London, a whole week long trip to London for $459. Eight days, eight nights, airfare, everything. All we do is bring money for food. I highly recommend that you look into Ideal Travel's outside agent program.

94

Become An Expert

You should become an expert at something. I read a book many years ago by a man who did research on millionaires and why they made it. I used to ask this, by the way, at my seminars. I'd say, "How many of you have made money in real estate?" Now, if there was an audience of 200 people there and people were millionaires, most of them were from real estate. A few from other kinds of investments, but most of them were from real estate.

According to my research, and the man that wrote this book, they found out that most people that got to be worth $1 million did not do so by any form of investment, they did so by getting to be an expert in their own field.

For example, one man who was making $40,000 a year went back to college, got a masters degree and got a better job making $60,000. He then went out and got a PhD and was making $90,000 a year. When he finally got up to $120,000 a year he was still living on about $30,000 to $40,000 and he was able to put aside $60,000 to $70,000 a year into his different savings and investments.

They did research on this and found out that most of the people that were millionaires, did so by getting to be an expert in their field. They were not good at investing. Their average rate of return on their investments was 5 or 6%. Now, any one of you can just buy a better mutual fund and get 12% and 18% return. These people were not investors, they were experts in their field.

My contention is that if you could get to be an expert in a field that has a really high rate of return, for example real estate investing or some of my ideas in the stock market; if you could just narrow down the things we've done here in this book, you can go home, continue studying and get to be an expert in that field.

I don't want to get mushy on you here, but I have found in my own life that the times that I'm the happiest, the times that I grow the most and excel the most is when I'm doing the most for other people. I don't know what there is about this, but it's like one of those old kung fu movies. You throw the rock in the pond and the ripple goes out and it always comes back. The ripples always come back.

95

Giving And Serving

When I found myself getting selfish sometimes or concentrating on making money from my own point of view, nothing ever worked. When I went for myself, doing everything I can to make sure that I'm secure, hardly anything ever worked. But, when I just kind of let it all hang out, when I just kept doing my investments, created a little bit of chaos and made sure that a lot of things happened, then at those points in time I grow the most.

Ironically, almost every time that I give away something or help somebody through different charities the more I've gotten back. You could help to buy houses, give gifts to the needy, the more that you can do anonymously, the better. It's the old sack of groceries to a poor family at Christmas time where you anonymously leave it on their porch. Don't let them know that you're doing it. Almost every time I do that it seems like something good happens.

It's almost as though I can never give away anything. Every time I do something nice, it comes back. I don't know if you want to apply that to religious principles or whatever in your life, but there is something to giving and serving. The ultimate source of happiness is in doing things for other people. I don't think anything as far as being selfish helps, either from a financial point of view or from a personal point of view. Giving good honest service, giving love unfeigned and taking care of people is really what it's all about.

96

Creating Your Own Reward System

This has to do with rewards and possibly creating your own reward system. I have all kinds of games that I play and I think you should, too. When I was buying and selling my houses I had a game called "Friday." It only had one rule: don't ever buy anything unless you can get it sold by Friday. Now if you're talking to a real estate agent and you ask, "How much can I make on this property by Friday?"

They say, "Oh, no, no, no. This is a great investment. You'll love this one for your retirement."

"No, how much can I make by Friday?"

"This is a tax write off; you'll love this. Every April 15th you'll love this property."

"No, how much can I make by Friday?"

Later on you go for the tax write offs and all that, but right now a lot of you reading this need to build up your cash flow. So, when you look at a stock or a mutual fund you ask how much can I make by Friday? Most of the time you're not going to make very much, so you don't even get involved. When you look at a piece of real estate and ask, "How much can I make by Friday?" I don't even buy a property unless I can get it sold. If it takes me two or three Fridays to get it sold, so be it. But the point is that I'm concentrating on making sure that I get results now, not some time in the future. So, my game called Friday is really good.

Right now I have a thing that I do that is just another reward system for me. Every time I teach a seminar, when I get home I go down and buy a one ounce gold coin. It's usually a one ounce American Eagle, like I talked about before. I've hardly ever noticed that $300, $400, or $500 going out, so I do that two or three times a month. Now I have something to show for my time and energy. I would venture to say that had I not done that, all that money would have gotten spent anyway. Instead, now that I have these gold coins, I basically have my hedge against inflation. That's my reward system.

We do a lot of things in our company with sales programs. If one of our sales associates or entity structuring people gets 15 or 20 Nevada Corporation sales in one month, we give them a $5,000 zero coupon United States Treasury Bond. Instead of giving them $500 or $1,000 as a bonus, we give them a bond; they get $5,000 more. We're helping them be more. A lot of them keep them; they haven't sold them and we're always giving them more.

I used to believe that we didn't need the little pats on the back. When I would see basketball teams slapping each others' hands and all that, I'd say, "Hold it. Don't slap each others' hands after you win the game." Now I realize that along the way, a lot of people need that encouragement, they need that pat on the back, and some people need a kick in the rear end. I do a lot myself and I do a lot with my family on creating a reward system.

I used to do it with my renters and people giving me payments on my houses. If I was going to charge $600 in rent for an apartment, I would charge $640, or whatever, and I'd say, "If your payments are made on time or early, then you get $40 off." We also had penalties if they didn't make it on time, but instead of having a penalty in place we'd have a reward system. So if they made their rents early they got a reward, and we would create this whole situation where people get rewarded for good behavior, with good results.

97

Think Big In Bite Size Pieces

Think big in bite size pieces. I'm going to paraphrase this story. I've heard it said so many times, by so many different people, I don't even know what the truth is anymore. Back in the mid 50s Ray Crock was going to take over McDonald's. I can just imagine him going home and saying to his wife, "Honey, I'm going to buy this hamburger stand and I'm going to open up a chain of them all over the country," and his wife says, "Honey, Americans won't eat hamburgers. They won't eat that many hamburgers." Well that was the early 50s, and now it's a lot later and look at what's happened to McDonald's and all the other hamburger chains out there.

I see a lot of people getting bogged down by thinking that they have to make killings on big deals. For example, a lot of people have come to my real estate seminars in the past and they're not even going to buy a property unless they're going to make $80,000, $90,000, or $100,000. Well, that's not my style. The absolute bottom line key to wealth is duplication and repetition—McDonald's succeeded because a hamburger in Tampa Bay tastes like a hamburger in San Francisco Bay. They found a way to make burgers people wanted and they duplicated it.

From a financial point of view I don't think you should ever do anything unless it can be duplicated. If it can't be duplicated, why do it? When I started doing real estate, even though every property was a little bit different, they were a lot more similar than they were different. I started creating clones of each one. And, by the way, I started using the profits from one property to springboard me into the other properties. So, every time I would buy and sell a property, the new down payment that I received would become the down payment for the next property, and it just got repetitious.

It got so I could train people and have a lot of people doing certain things for me. I would think big. I made thousands of dollars and I did it in bite-size pieces. I think that you should do so, too.

You need to latch on to something in your company. And once again, you're not going to get rich if you have an air conditioning business and you're out all day long just fixing people's air conditioning units. You can't get rich that way. But if you can invent something for an air conditioning unit, or you can create a system where air conditioning units are fixed by different people, then you can think big in bite size pieces and eventually create wealth by, again, employing the principles of duplication and repetition.

We should all be pursuing excellence. I don't want to go back to some of the books that you've read on quality control, but there are several things that I would like to share with you here. I learned a long time ago that if you're not going to go for the gusto yourself, then you ought to latch on to somebody who is going to go for the gusto. If you know of a company

98

The Pursuit Of Excellence

that is dedicated to research and development, dedicated to coming up with new products, then great. Try to get in on the entrepreneurial phase of the company; that's the best time to invest in it.

When I find myself wanting to invest in a pharmaceutical company or a computer chip company, I want to latch on to the person, not the company, but the person who's going to make all of that happen. I want to find people who have, as their underlying goal, the pursuit of excellence and making things better. So let me give you four things that we can do in regard to that.

First, always go for quality. I noticed people that are in the pursuit of excellence are always after quality. They create a lot of chaos in their life in this pursuit, especially at the very beginning, but they are always interested in quality. Recently, my nephew had saved up his money to buy some boots for horseback riding; the ones that he wanted were $50. When he went to buy them he realized that they weren't good quality after he put them on. Then he decided to get the ones for $70 because they were of a lot higher quality. He came out and he told me about his decision, and I said, "You've learned a lesson."

I've been the other way. I've tried to get by with the cheaper version. If you can't fix something, get another board and stick it over it. Get a bigger hammer. But I've since realized that you need to hire quality people and use quality material.

I like tinkering with my car, but I've not even touched my car for the last 15 years because I'd rather hire a professional mechanic—the best that I can find. It's the same thing. Go for the best and the best will always pay off. I mean, I know that you know this—if you buy a shirt for $20 it will last about half as long, perhaps not even that, as a shirt for $60. The shirt for $80 or $100 lasts a lot longer and looks better. You always go for quality.

Second is that you need a commitment to learn new things. I don't know how to stress this enough—always expanding the envelope, always expanding the edge. Even in financial architecture and financial structuring we're always looking for new products, new entities, and new applications of those entities.

Third is to surround yourself with good, high quality people. Usually you cannot rise above the people that you're hanging around, and they really control a lot of the direction you go.

Fourth is to be an idea centered person. You'll notice that when good people or good companies get together they talk about ideas. They don't talk about people. You need to be an idea centered person. I don't even like getting out of the shower in the morning unless I've thought of a $5,000 or $10,000 idea. It's ideas that make the world go around.

If you don't know how to do that, maybe you could take a creativity course, which is a conundrum in and of itself. You need something that's going to help you get up and get going. I don't know what that's going to be for you. For example, people used to come to some of my real estate training and they'd say, "Wade, if you could just give me a list of everything I need to say on the phone when I call somebody about buying their house. If I had that list and could just go down through a questionnaire." (I know a lot of other people, by the way, that have since left the seminar business who would go ahead and make up that list; they would create a script. Here, follow this and you'll get rich. Well, I don't agree.)

If you need a list, if you can't call up somebody on the phone and say, "Hi. I saw your ad in the paper and I want to know how much your house is going for and what's the financing like? Can I assume the existing loans? Tell me about it." If you can't say that, and gather up enough information to help you make a decision, then you probably should not be doing real estate deals. If somebody has to make a list up for you on how to be successful, you're not going to be successful.

A lot of people think the things necessary to becoming successful come from the outside. If I could just do this. If I could just get my life in order. If I can just have this day planner then I'll be organized and I'll be better and I'll make a lot of money. They don't realize that real true wealth comes from the inside.

99

Health And Wealth

I really believe that there is a high correspondence between health and wealth. If a person is unhealthy they can go out and create a lot of wealth, but it's not usually the case. I encourage you to do whatever you can to keep your mind keen and alert. I know that you've all heard this before: you are what you eat, especially when it comes to our brain power. A lot of what we do is based on the food, the energy, the fuel source that we take into our body. As we get older we need all the help we can get.

But let me tell you what I'm really into from a financial point of view. It's walking. If you look at the history of mankind, virtually every major contributor, every major philosopher walked a lot. If you go out and walk, there's just something about it, about the movement of your backbone, your sacroiliac. Your brain gets active and you start thinking about all kinds of things besides burning up calories and all that. Just walk and walk, and when you're tired of walking, walk some more. If you haven't thought of a good idea, keep walking some more and that will help you.

There is a high correspondence between health and wealth. I think that if you have a choice of getting healthy or wealthy, obviously, you take the health because you can get the wealth later. We need to create an atmosphere wherein our money, our finances, our family are all integrated. The best way to do that is to be healthy, so that we can take care of business.

I've hinted at this so many times—to whom are you listening? I've mentioned this before, but one of the questions I always ask in my seminars is, "How many of you want to make over $100,000 a year?" Hands shoot up all over the room. And I say, "Now look, if you really want to make $100,000 a year, why are you talking to anybody about making money who's making under $100,000?"

100

To Whom Are You Listening?

You've got a hot business idea and you want to go talk to your attorney. Well, the average attorney in this country makes $58,000 a year. The average CPA makes $38,000. The average real estate agent makes $19,600 a year. What the heck are we talking to those people for? If they knew how to make money, they'd be out making money. They don't know how to make money.

Why are we talking to them about making money? When people come through my training, they come and they just get blown away by all of the dynamic information. They have to go home and be at the whim or mercy of their CPA, who is going to shoot down every good idea I've tried to give them. I guess that's just nature. Others will try to shoot down any idea you have.

It won't work here. Can't do that here. Can't do that now. Did you know somebody becomes a millionaire every 37 minutes in this country? When is it your turn? Go talk to people and they just don't know how to make money. I know how, and I tell them how. Then it's up to them.

Recently, I was on a plane and I sat next to a man who, the year before, had made $2 million, and that year had made $3 million. This guy took home just under $200,000 a month. At that point in time I'd never made that much money. Now, if I wanted to make that kind of money, to whom should

I be listening? Where should I be going for advice? Not the guy's CPA, but him, to the guy. This guy went through four families on his way to making that kind of money. I would not trade my family for all the money in the world. But, if I wanted to make that kind of money, I should be hanging around with the kind of person that makes what I want to. I recommend that you be very, very careful of whom you're hanging around with.

If you want to do things from a financial point of view, we invite you to come out and be part of our different seminars. You can take me with you in your car if you purchase my home study courses, and you can get to be an expert at whatever you choose.

101

Knowledge Unlocks The Doors Of Opportunity

"Stay a step ahead by knowing what your education will do for you." I saw this when I was back in junior college. I got really excited about it because I saw people getting educated just for the sake of getting educated—which may be good in and of itself. I like knowledge for the pure sake of knowledge, and I like learning anything as long as it's interesting to me. But, from a financial point of view, the right knowledge really does unlock the doors of opportunity. It unlocks doors of opportunity that people don't even know exist.

For example, how many of you, before you read this, even knew that you could roll stock within a certain range? Or that you could buy real estate, sell it right away, receive a monthly check and make a profit over the next 20 to 30 years?

Derrick Bock was the Dean of Harvard Law School when he said, "If you think education is expensive, try ignorance." Again, you need to get to be an expert on these different things. Now, if I may, let me use that as a way of telling you just a little bit about the Financial Fortress, Cook University, and the various other products and services we have available to you.

People enroll in Cook University for a variety of reasons. Usually they are a little discontented with where they are—their job is not working, their business is not producing the kind of income they want, or they definitely see that they need more income to prepare for a better retirement. That's where Cook University comes in. As you try to live the American dream, in the life-style you want, we stand ready to assist you to make the dream your reality.

The backbone of the program is the Money Machine concept—as applied to your business, stock investments, or real estate. Although there are many, many other forms of investing in real estate, there are really only three that work: the Money Machine method, buying second mortgages, and lease options. Of these three, the Money Machine stands head and shoulders above the rest. In the stock market, systems other than the Money Machine may give you growth, but only the Money Machine gives you cash flow.

It is difficult to explain Cook University in only a few words. It is so unique, innovative and creative that it literally stands alone. But then, what would you expect from Wade Cook? Something common and ordinary? Never! My staff and I always go out of our way to provide you with useful, tried and true strategies that create real wealth.

We are embarking on an unprecedented voyage, and we want you to come along. Success takes commitment. Yes, it takes drive. Add to this the help you'll receive from our hand-trained experts, and you will enhance your asset base and increase your bottom line.

We want to encourage a lot of people to get in the program right away. You could save thousands of dollars if you don't delay. Class sizes are limited so that students get personal attention, but this means they fill up fast

Perpetual monthly income is waiting. We'll teach you how to achieve it. We'll show you how to make it. We'll watch over you while you're making it happen. Thank you for your consideration. We hope to see you in the program right away.

AVAILABLE
RESOURCES

Because I enjoy providing my students, and you, the reader, with as much knowledge as possible, I am using this section to furnish you with information regarding resource materials available to you for continuing education. The following can help you with your real estate and stock market investments. These books, videos, and audiocassettes have been reviewed by myself and the Wade Cook Seminars, Inc. staff and are being suggested to you to aid you in your quest for knowledge.

Available Resources

Stock Market materials I've produced include: **Income Formulas**. This is a free cassette. You will learn the 11 cash flow formulas taught in the Wall Street Workshop. Learn to double some of your money in 2½ to 4 months.

Stock Market

My book, **Wall Street Money Machine**, appearing on the *New York Times* Business Best Sellers list for over one year, contains the best strategies for wealth enhancement and cash flow creation you'll find anywhere for generating cash flow through the stock market.

Read **Stock Market Miracles** next, and you'll find that it improves on the strategies from **Wall Street Money Machine**, as well as introducing new and valuable twists on our old favorites.

Bear Market Baloney is a timely book! Some of my predictions came true while the book was at press! Look into what makes bull and bear markets and how to make exponential returns in any market.

The **Dynamic Dollars Video** is the 90 minute introduction to the basics of my Wall Street formulas and strategies. Designed especially for video, in it I explain the meter drop philosophy, Rolling Stock, basics of Proxy Investing, and Writing Covered Calls.

A powerful audio workshop, **Zero To Zillions** will help you in understanding the stock market game, playing it successfully, and retiring rich. Learn eleven powerful investment strategies to avoid pitfalls and losses, catch "Day-Trippers" and "Bottom Fish," write Covered Calls, double your money (from time to time) in one week on options on stock split companies, and so much more. I will teach you how I make fantastic annual returns in my accounts, so that you can do likewise.

The **Wall Street Workshop** video series will help you get a head start if you can't make it to the Wall Street Workshop. Ten albums containing eleven hours of intense instruction on Rolling Stock, Options on Stock Split companies, Writing Covered Calls, and eight other tested and proven strategies designed to help you earn *18% per month* on your investments. By learning, reviewing, and implementing the strategies taught here, you will gain the knowledge and the confidence to take control of your investments, and double their value in $2^1/_2$ to 4 months.

The Next Step video series is presented by me and my Team Wall Street instructors, and is the advanced version of the Wall Street Workshop. Full of my power-packed strategies, this is not a duplicate of the Wall Street Workshop, but a very important partner. The methods will supercharge the strategies taught in the Wall Street Workshop, and you'll learn how to find the stocks to fit the formulas through technical analysis, fundamentals, home trading tools, and more.

Wealth Information Network (WIN) is our subscription internet service which provides you with the latest financial formulas and updated entity structuring strategies. New, timely information is entered several times a day. If you are just getting started in the stock market, this is a great way to follow people who are proven successes. If you are experienced already, it's the best way to confirm your feelings and research with others who are generating wealth through the stock market.

Subscribing to **WIN+** will ensure that Team Wall Street will email you with timely updates and information that you can't afford to miss. This is a must for anyone who cannot spend all day searching the web for time-sensitive information. Go to www.wadecook.com.

IQ Pager is a paging system which beeps you as events happen and announcements are made on Wall Street. The key to the stock market is timing. Especially when you're trading in options, you need up-to-the-minute (or second) information. However, most investors cannot afford to sit at a computer all day looking for news. We recognized this need and came up with an incredible and innovative solution—**IQ Pager.** You'll receive information such as major stock split announcements, earnings surprises, or any other news that will impact the market.

This new product is selling like crazy. Just imagine sitting in a meeting during the day and having the pager go off! Within minutes, sometimes before it hits the news wire you could know about a stock split. Two hundred characters of information can show up on the pager, so it gives you enough to get you involved in a timely manner. We don't make any claims that we get every stock split or every piece of good news announced out there, but we sure get a lot of them. Right now the pagers are going off between five and 15 times a day, so I believe they are very much appreciated. If you want to get on board, you need to call your representative at 1-800-872-7411 and talk to them about getting the **IQ Pager.**

Have you ever considered entity integration? I recorded *Power Of Nevada Corporations*, a free audio cassette, where you'll learn that Nevada Corporations have secrecy, privacy, minimal taxes, no reciprocity with the IRS, and protection for shareholders, officers, and directors. This is a powerful seminar.

Entity Integration

My *Brilliant Deductions* manual is coming out again, now in book form and even better than before! Do you want to make the most of the money you earn? If you want to have solid tax havens and ways to reduce the taxes you pay, this book is for you! I will teach you how to get rich in spite of the new tax laws. Read about new tax credits, year-end maneuvers, and methods for transferring and controlling your entities. Learn to structure yourself and your family for tax savings and liability protection. Available in bookstores or call our toll fee number.

I created **The Incorporation Handbook** so you can make incorporation easy! This handbook tells you who, why, and, most importantly, how to incorporate. Included are samples of the forms you will use when you incorporate, as well as a step-by-step guide from the experts.

The **Financial Fortress Home Study Course** is an eight-part series on entity structuring. It goes far beyond mere financial planning or estate planning, it helps you structure your business and your affairs so that you can avoid the majority of taxes, retire rich, protect yourself against lawsuits, bequeath your assets to your heirs without government interference, and, in short, bombproof your entire estate. There are six audio cassette seminars on tape, an entity structuring video, and a full kit of documents.

Are you interested in operating your own real estate money machine? My free cassette, **Income Streams**, will instruct you on how to buy and sell

Real Estate

real estate the Wade Cook way. This informative cassette will instruct you on building and operating your own real estate money machine.

My first bestselling book, **Real Estate Money Machine**, reveals the secrets of my own system—the system I earned my first million from. This book teaches you how to make money regardless of the state of the economy. My innovative concepts for investing in real estate not only avoid high interest rates, but avoid banks altogether.

Do you want to become an expert money maker in real estate? I wrote **How To Pick Up Foreclosures** to show you how to buy real estate at 60¢ or less on the dollar. You'll learn to find the house before the auction and purchase it with no bank financing—the easy way to millions in real estate. The market for foreclosures is a tremendous place to learn and prosper! **How To Pick Up Foreclosures** takes my methods from **Real Estate Money Machine** and super charges them by applying the fantastic principles to already-discounted properties.

Owner Financing is a short, but invaluable, pamphlet I wrote for you to give to sellers who hesitate to sell you their property using the owner financing method. Let this pamphlet convince both you and them. The special report, "*Why Sellers Should Take Monthly Payments*," is included for free!

Real Estate For Real People is a priceless, comprehensive overview of real estate investing. This book teaches you how to buy the right property for the right price, at the right time. I explain all of the strategies you'll need, and give you twenty reasons why you should start investing in real estate today. Learn how to retire rich with real estate, and have fun doing it!

Do you want to personally achieve success after success in real estate like I did? **101 Ways to Buy Real Estate Without Cash** fills the gap left by other authors who have given all the ingredients but not the whole recipe for real estate investing. This is the book for the investor who wants innovative and practical methods for buying real estate with little or no money down.

Paper Tigers is my personal introduction to the art of buying and selling second mortgages. In this set of six cassettes, I share my inside secrets to establishing a cash flow business with real estate investments. You will learn how to find discounted second mortgages, how to find second mortgage notes and make them better, as well as how to receive six times your money back, while structuring your business to attract investors and give you the income you desire. Also included is a manual filled with sample forms, letters, and agreements. When you buy **Paper Tigers**, you'll also receive **Paper Chase** for free. **Paper Chase** holds the most important tools you need to make deals happen. I created these powerful tapes as a handout tool you can lend to potential investors or home owners to help educate them about how this amazing cash flow system works for them. Your cash flow asset base will profit as you use this incredible tool over and over again.

Legal Forms is a set of pertinent forms I have collected, containing numerous legal forms used in real estate transactions. These forms were selected by experienced investors, but are not intended to replace the advice of an attorney. However, they will provide essential forms for you to follow in your personal investing.

Record Keeping System is my complete tracking system for organizing all of the information on each of your properties. This system keeps track of everything from insurance policies to equity growth. You will know at a glance exactly where you stand with your investment properties, and you will sleep better at night.

Money Machine I & II is an audiocassette series with my system for creating and maintaining a real estate money machine. It will teach you the step-by-step cash flow formulas that made me and thousands like me millions of dollars. Call us and learn the benefits of buying, and more importantly, selling real estate.

Now that I have offered my Wall Street, entity planning, and real estate strategies to you, I will also make available to you some assorted financial wisdom in the form of a free cassette. This one, **Money Mysteries of the Millionaires**, will teach you how to make money and keep it. This fan-

Assorted Financial Wisdom

tastic seminar shows you how to use Nevada Corporations, Living Trusts, Pension Plans, Business Trusts, Charitable Remainder Trusts, and Family Limited Partnerships to protect your assets.

Inspired by the Creator, the Bible truly is the authority for running the business of life. Throughout my book, **Business Buy The Bible**, I provide you, the reader, with practical advice that helps you apply God's word to your life. My goal is to teach people everywhere how to become wealthy so that they can lead their lives in service to God, their families, and others.

BE-ing! Prioritize and get into action. It is important to be moving in the right direction. My book, **Don't Set Goals (The Old Way)**, tells you how taking action and "paying the price" is more important than simply making the decision to do something. Don't set the goals. Go out and simply get where you want to go!

Some of my top Wall Street Workshop instructors and I—Debbie Losse, Joel Black, Dan Wagner, Tim Semingson, Rich Simmons, Gregory Witt, JJ Childers, Keven Hart, Dave Wagner, and Steve Wirrick—have joined together to create **Blueprints For Success**, a compilation of chapters on building wealth through your business and making your business function successfully. The chapters cover education and information gathering, choosing the best business for you from all the different types of businesses, and a variety of other skills necessary for becoming successful. Your business can't afford to miss out on these powerful insights!

Your business cannot succeed without you. This course, **High Performance Business Strategies,** will help *you* become successful so your company can succeed. It is a combination of two previous courses, formerly entitled Turbo-Charge Your Business and High-Octane Business Strategies. For years, my staff and I have listened to people's questions and concerns. Because we know that problems are best solved by people who already know the ropes, my staff wanted to help. They categorized the questions and came up with about 60 major areas of concern. I then went into the recording studio and dealt head on with these questions. What resulted is a comprehensive collection of knowledge to get you started quickly.

Turn your car into a "university on wheels" and listen to my **Unlimited Wealth** audio set. This is the "University of Money-Making Ideas" home study course that helps you improve your money's personality. The heart and soul of this seminar is to make more money, pay fewer taxes, and keep more for your retirement and family. This cassette series contains the great ideas from **Wealth 101** on tape, so you can listen to them whenever you want.

Is your IRA idle? Take that IRA money now sitting idle and invest it in ways that generate bigger, better, and quicker returns. **Retirement Prosperity** is a four audiotape set that walks you through a system of using a self directed IRA to create phenomenal profits, virtually tax free! This is one of the most complete systems for IRA investing ever created.

My good friend, John Childers' and my **Travel Agent Information** package is the only sensible solution for the frequent traveler. This kit includes all of the information and training you need to be an outside travel agent for a stable company. There are no hassles, no requirements, no forms or restriction, just all the benefits of traveling for substantially less *every time*.

The workshops I currently have to offer you are held all over the United States, including Hawaii and Alaska. **Wall Street Workshop** is presented by me and by my hand trained instructors, Team Wall Street. The **Wall Street Workshop** teaches you how to make incredible money in all markets—tried-and-true strategies that have made hundreds of people wealthy.

Classes Offered

Our *Next Step Workshop,* also presented by me and Team Wall Street, is an Advanced Wall Street Workshop designed to help those ready to take their trading to the next level and treat it as a business. This seminar is open only to graduates of the Wall Street Workshop.

We believe the best financial gift parents can give their children is the desire and knowledge to be self-sufficient, a team player, passionate, and willing to do "what it takes" to support themselves and their families. Whether he or she is starting from scratch or maintaining the family dynasty, *The Youth Wall Street Workshop* will give your children the tools they need to get ahead.

The time has come. This three day seminar, designed for twelve to eighteen year olds, will cover basic and advanced investment strategies, vocabulary, business, entrepreneurship, options, attitudes, altruism, economics, communication, and more. In fact, it is many seminars rolled into one. This seminar is designed for teenagers, but if you know younger, capable students who could benefit from attending, they will not be turned away. And while we recognize that all of our adult students would love to attend, this workshop is just for teens. Give your children the gift of knowledge—financial knowledge that will enable them to change their lives.

Come to our *Business and Entity Skills Training (BEST),* presented by me and the Team Wall Street instructors. You will learn about the six powerful entities you can use to protect your wealth and your family. Learn the secrets of asset protection, eliminate your fear of litigation, and minimize your taxes.

Our *Executive Retreat* (with the same instructors as above) is created especially for the individuals already owning or planning to establish Nevada Corporations. The Executive Retreat is a unique opportunity for corporate executives to participate in workshops geared toward streamlining operations and maximizing efficiency and impact.

The new ***Real Estate Workshop*** is a two day "hitting the streets," finding, evaluating, buying, and selling properties, experiential workshop that will make Real Estate investing come alive for you! Learn what to look for, what to offer, and how to make $5,000 by Friday without using one cent of your own money. Learn the strategies of "cooking" properties that can let you retire independent, with a large monthly cash flow. I made my first fortune in real estate, and my methods have revolutionized the real estate industry. Now you can learn them from the master, and from Team Main Street, a few handpicked students and instructors who have even outdone the master! This Real Estate Event is not to be missed.

Call one of our representatives at Wade Cook Seminars, Inc. today and sign up for these workshops. The toll free number is 1-800-872-7411. See you there!

If you really want more help, then I encourage you to get more information. I hope I have provided you with enough information to help you make some decisions right now on the road that you are presently taking, or the one you are going to take.

I realize there's a good chance that you are at a fork in the road right now, undecided as to which road to take—if you say "yes" to more knowledge and information, what results will that bring you? Or if you say "No," what results will that obtain for you? All I can do is tell you and continue educating you on what I've done over the last decade and a half in the seminar field, and in the educational field, to help people like you get your businesses up and running. I will continue to help you make more money, and keep more of what you are making. Join me on the road to living your version of the American Dream.

If you'll do for a few years what most people won't do, you'll be able to do for the rest of your life what most people can't do!

To order a copy of our current catalog, please write or call us at:

Wade Cook Seminars, Inc.
14675 Interurban Avenue South
Seattle, Washington 98168-4664
1–800–872–7411

I mentioned my web site earlier. The internet address is **http://www.wadecook.com**, and Lighthouse Publishing Group, Inc., the publishing company who published this book, has an address at **http://www.lighthousebooks.com**.

I would love to hear your comments on our products and services, as well as your testimonials on how these products have benefited you. I look forward to hearing from you!

Get to be an expert in something.

APPENDIX

Suggested Reading

Some of the magazines and newsletters I read and use to gather information from are listed here for your convenience.

Bottom Line   **1-800-274-5611**
Box 58446
Boulder, Colorado 80322
The "most fun" of the batch. The second page usually has a lot of tax information

Comstock's   **(916) 924-9815**
1770 Tribute Road, Suite 205
Sacramento, California 95815

Creative Real Estate   **(619) 756-1441**
Drawer L
Rancho Santa Fe, California 92067
A must for everyone—whether you buy real estate or not. Mention me and they might give you a deal.

Dick Davis Digest   **1-800-654-1514**
P.O. box 350630
Ft. Lauderdale, FL 33335-0630
I really like this newsletter.

Financial World
1328 Broadway
New York, NY 10001-2116

1-800-829-5916

Forbes
Box 10048
Des Moines, Iowa 50309
*I like it. From a money point of view
the back sections are really good.*

1-800-888-9896

Individual Investor
Subscription Fulfillment
P.O. Box 37289
Boone, IA 50037-0289

1-888-616-7677

Mutual Fund Forecaster
3471 North Federal
Fort Lauderdale, Florida 33306
If you're into Funds this is a must.

1-800-422-9000

National Review
150 East 35th Street
New York, New York 10016
*My favorite. Mostly political. The
section "Random Wealth" has good
insights.*

(815) 734-1232

Reason
Box 526
Mount Morris, Illinois 61054
*More political than economic but
still really good.*

1-800-998-8989

Tax Update Newsletter
81 Montgomery Street
Scarsdale, New York 10583
*A must if you're serious about stay-
ing informed and cutting taxes.*

The Economist   **1-800-456-6086**
Box 58524
Boulder, Colorado 80322
*Written from an international slant.
I love this magazine.*

The Wall Street Journal   **1-800-221-1940**
200 Burnett Road
Chicopee, Massachusetts 01021
*Obviously a must for every serious
investor and business owner. I particularly like the editorial section.*

Worth   **1-800-777-1851**
P.O. Box 55420
Boulder, CO 80322